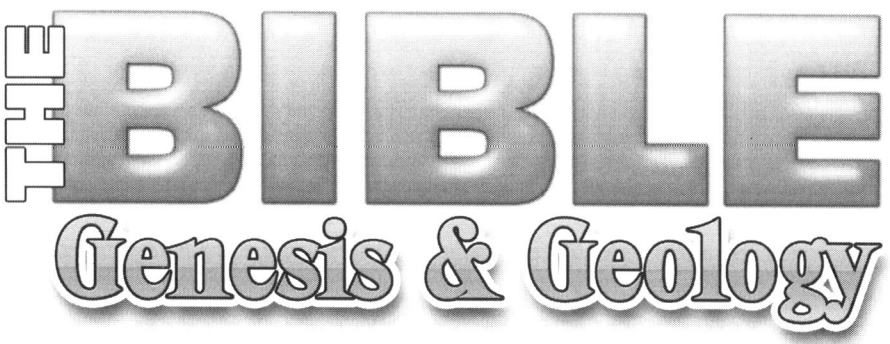

Gaines R. Johnson

Copyright © 2010 by Gaines R. Johnson

All rights reserved. Except for brief quotations in critical reviews or articles, written permission must be secured from the publisher to use or reproduce any part of this book.

Gaines R. Johnson website: www.kjvbible.org

Unless otherwise noted, Scripture quotations are from The Holy Bible, King James Version, which is in the public domain, and images used in this publication are from clipartconnection.com and used with permission, ©2007 JUPITERIMAGES, and its licensors (all rights reserved).

All Woodcuts used herein are in the Public Domain and free of copyright.

All Figure illustrations used in this book were created by the author and are protected under copyright laws, © 2010.

Unless otherwise noted, cover design and interior Illustrations: Fred DeRuvo
Editing: Marti Rieske

Library of Congress Cataloging-in-Publication Data

Johnson, Gaines R., 1950 –

ISBN 1451549326
EAN-13 9781451549324

1. Religion - Religion and Science

Contents

Foreword:	....	5
Chapter 1:	Beyond the Gap Theory of Genesis	7
Chapter 2:	Worlds and the Earth	31
Chapter 3:	Geology and Genesis	38
Chapter 4:	Contrasting Major Creation Models	60
Chapter 5:	Fossils Produced by Noah's Flood? NOT!	65
Chapter 6:	Global Dust Spikes and Paleoclimate Indicators	71
Chapter 7:	Fountains of the Deep	83
Chapter 8:	Windows of Heaven	97
Chapter 9:	Days of Peleg and Sea Level Changes	106
Chapter 10:	Relationship of Flesh and Spirit	117
Chapter 11:	Pre-Adamite World	123
Chapter 12:	The Firmament	141
Chapter 13:	The Fourth Day of Genesis: A Paradox?	154
Chapter 14:	Geologic Evidence and Death of the Ancient World	159
Chapter 15:	Life Forms During Ice Age, After Seven Days of Genesis	167
Chapter 16:	Sevens of the Bible in Time and Nature	180
Chapter 17:	Kingdom of Heaven and the Kingdom of God: Doctrinal Differences	188
Chapter 18:	Exact English KJV Wording: Is It Important?	197
Chapter 19:	Geology and Prophecy: The Dead Sea Rift	214
Chapter 20:	Lost Rivers of the Garden of Eden	224
Chapter 21:	The Book of Daniel is Unsealing	240

Every half-truth is more damaging than an outright lie. There are at least three sides to every argument. This book is dedicated to every intellectually honest man or woman who not only has the willingness to seek out the truth, but the courage to embrace the truth when it finds them. – Gaines R. Johnson

FOREWORD

I have no idea how I came across Gaines Johnson's web page, though I am very glad I did. I recall that I was in the middle of researching for my latest book, *Nephilim Nightmare*, when I found myself on Johnson's page, which is a unique combination of presenting the truth of God's Word by marrying His truth with the facts of science, specifically geology.

After I read a few of the articles, I printed out the remainder and devoured them. In the course of my reading, I sent Gaines an email and asked why he had not published these articles in book form. After numerous email exchanges, Gaines finally agreed that it might be a good idea to do so, though he was unsure of the best way to accomplish it.

I soon realized that the Lord had directed me to Gaines' site for two reasons; (1) to learn what I did not know, and (2) to help Gaines put that information into book format. What a privilege it has been for me to be able to do just that.

The book you hold in your hands is the result of Gaines' careful study during years of research. My part was nothing compared to his. If you are blessed by the insights he presents, may I humbly request that you tell others about it?

This book is for *everyone*. It is for young Christians, old Christians, and Christians in between. Moreover, due to its scientific basis, it is also for atheists and agnostics. Rarely does a book cover that much ground, especially one in which the main subject is the Bible.

I am very glad you are reading this book. I pray that the Lord will bless you mightily. If you are already His child, I pray that you will grow beyond measure because of the truth found within these pages.

If you are not yet His, I pray that during the reading of this book, the Lord will grant you the knowledge required so your faith in Him and in the substitutionary atonement of God the Son, Jesus Christ, would be yours in good measure.

In any case, you may find it difficult to disagree with Gaines' premises in this book. While you may not agree with all of his conclusions, his presentation of the facts is extremely difficult to ignore.

I seriously doubt that you will be able to put this book down until you have closed the back cover after reading the final page. If you are a person of science, know that you will be reading the words of a man who is also seriously scientific. If you are not a person of science, the fact that Gaines' writing style is easily comprehended does not go beyond notice.

Fred DeRuvo, April 2010

Chapter 1
Beyond the Gap Theory of Genesis

"For this they willingly are ignorant of, that by the word of God the heavens were of old, and the earth standing out of the water and in the water: Whereby the world that then was, being overflowed with water, perished: But the heavens and the earth, which are now, by the same word are kept in store, reserved unto fire against the day of judgment and perdition of ungodly men." (2 Pet 3:5-7)

What Peter states in 2 Peter 3:5-7 is not a reference to Noah's flood. There are only two places in the entire Bible where the Earth is flooded by water. One, of course, is at the time of Noah's flood (Genesis 7). The other is at Genesis 1:2, where it speaks about the condition of the Earth at the time just before God said, "Let there be light." If 2 Peter 3:5-7 is not a cross-reference to Noah's flood, then it MUST be a cross-reference to Genesis 1:2.

The Gap Theory or Ruin-Reconstruction

"In the beginning God created the heaven and the earth." Genesis 1:1	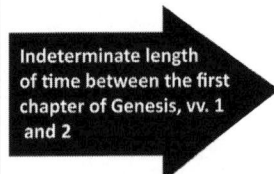 Indeterminate length of time between the first chapter of Genesis, vv. 1 and 2	"And the earth was without form, and void; and darkness was upon the face of the deep. And the Spirit of God moved upon the face of the waters.." Genesis 1:2

Once God began the *re-creation* process beginning with Genesis 1:3, all elements of creation are <u>literal</u>. There is <u>nothing</u> that should be taken allegorically, as there is no reason to do so. Each 24-hour period ("the evening and morning") for instance, is exactly that: *an actual 24-hour period*. The entire re-creation took 6 literal days, with God resting on the 7th literal day.

(There is no other alternative - simple logic.) And if 2 Peter 3:5-7 is a cross-reference to Genesis 1:2, then the Holy Spirit is calling your attention to something very significant that millions of Young Earth Creationists are blindly overlooking; specifically, that a glorious ancient world that God created in the distant past (Genesis 1:1) had long since been utterly destroyed, plunged into deep darkness, and overflowed by a raging flood of great waters on a universal scale at the time of Genesis 1:2. The seven days of Genesis which follow chronicle God's methodology of restoring the heavens and Earth and repopulating the world with living creatures, including modern man. There is a time gap between the first two verses of the Bible. It is a time gap that is obscurely declared but not greatly detailed in the book of Genesis. It is the very first *mystery* found in the Bible. Knowing that there is a time gap between Genesis 1:1 and Genesis 1:2 and WHY, will allow a more perfect understanding of what the Creation narrative is actually saying and begin to cut a clear path through the confusion of conflicting theories and interpretations that have occupied the Creation/Science debate.

More on that shortly. For now, it is very important that we first show you the Biblical clues that tell us why 2 Peter 3:5-7 is not a reference to Noah's flood.

Clue #1:

Compare the phrase "the heavens and earth, which are now" to the phrase the "heavens were of old."

What does that mean? Ask yourself these questions: When Noah's flood occurred, did it change anything in the upper heavens? Would a flood on the Earth have any effect on the sun, moon, or stars? The obvious answer is NO. The heavens of Noah's days were the same heavens as in Adam's day; same sun, same moon, same stars, same planet Mars.

FACT: Noah's flood had no effect on the upper heavens. All of Noah's flood's effects were confined to the Earth's surface and atmosphere. Although the Bible speaks about the windows of heaven being opened and water coming down (Genesis 7:11), the context of that reference is the first heaven of the Earth's atmosphere. That is where rain comes from. (Keep in mind that the Bible says there are three heavens. See 2 Corinthians 12:2.) This is explained in great detail later.

Again, note the contrasting comparison between the phrases "the heavens were of old" (before the waters of 2 Peter 3:5-7) and "the heavens and earth, which are now" (after the waters of 2 Peter 3:5-7). If Noah's flood did not alter the upper heavens, this verse must be speaking about an event other than Noah's flood, and Genesis 1:2 is our only other Biblical candidate.

Clue #2:

Notice also in the passage that the Earth is said to be standing out of the water and in the water. In our English language, these terms suggest that these particular waters were not confined to the surface of the planet. The Bible says that part of the planet was standing out from these waters (that is, the sphere of the planet was partially overflowed), and the location of the bulk of the waters was external

"Earth Without Form and Void"

to the Earth itself. The Bible says the planet was in the water of this particular flood. (Think about a round fishing floater bobbing in a flowing stream.) In other words, part of the Earth is protruding from the waters and not simply just covered by waters on the surface. The literal English wording of this passage does not describe a flood event confined to the Earth's surface. This passage describes a deluge that raged across the solar system and beyond. (Our solar system and outer space are the second heaven of the three heavens.)

Try to draw this mental picture. Think of a dark and ruined solar system with water strewn throughout it like one big, messy galactic spill. That is what Genesis 1:2 is speaking about. Imagine the planet Earth drifting awash in this roaring and rolling formless mess. Where would those waters have come from? It is an established scientific observation that dying stars create and give off lots of water. (You will find the references to that fact elsewhere in this study.) Certainly there must have been lots and lots of stars in the heavens that were "of old," and if the cosmos had gone dark and the stars had died, there would have been excessive water everywhere throughout space. If that was indeed the case, all those extinguished stars would have needed to be reignited to be seen in the present heavens. That is exactly what was done on the 4th day.

However, before any reconstruction of the heavens and Earth could begin, God had to do something with all that water scattered across space (Genesis 1:2). That is why the Bible says the waters were <u>divided</u> (Genesis 1:6-7). It was the first order of business after the Lord God turned on the work lights (Genesis 1:3) and began to clear up the mess:

"And God made the firmament, and <u>divided the waters</u> which were under the firmament from the waters which were above the firmament: and it was so." (Genesis 1:7)

The bottom line interpretation of the Genesis narrative is this: Those seven days of Genesis were indeed seven literal 24-hour days, but they are not a description of the original creation of all things (Genesis 1:1). Rather, they are a Divine special regeneration of the cosmos from what was here before the present world of Man. In other words, there are two creation events in Genesis. The first is described in a one-sentence statement at Genesis 1:1, and the second was accomplished in 7 days and very detailed, beginning at Genesis 1:3. This is why the Bible at Genesis 2:4 says:

"These are the generations [plural] of the heavens and of the earth when they were created, in the day that the LORD God made the earth and the heavens," (Genesis 2:4)

Again, the Creation account contains the story of two creative events. Only the latter event, the seven days, is outlined in great detail. The first one requires study and searching out and, most importantly, requires FAITH in the infallibility of God's written Word.

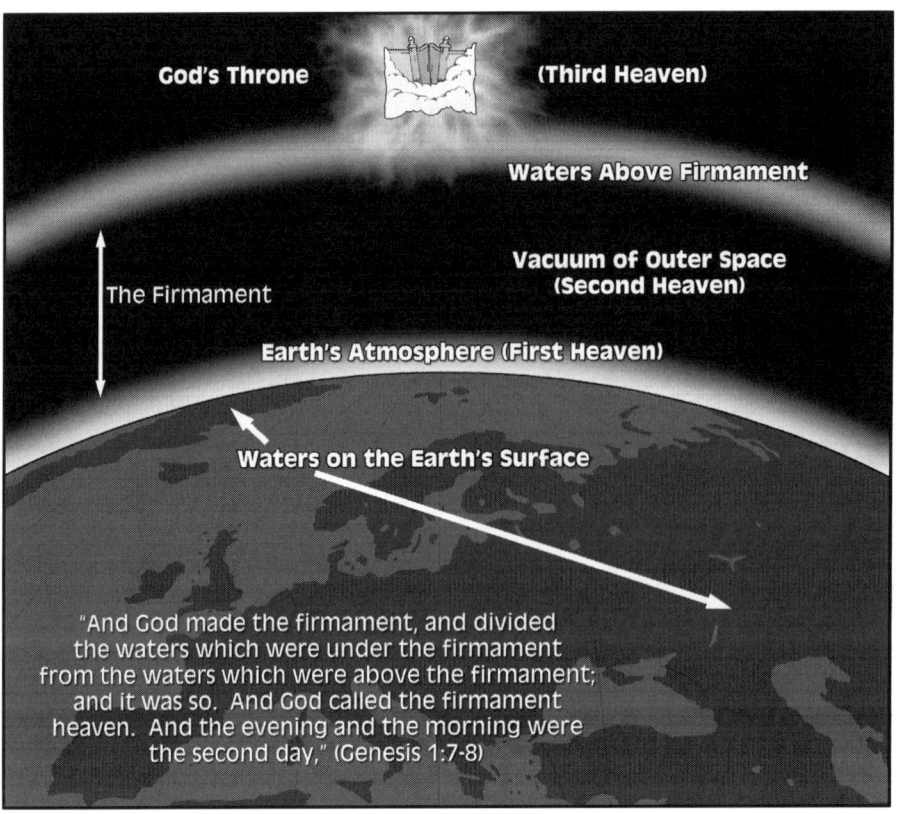

"And God made the firmament, and divided the waters which were under the firmament from the waters which were above the firmament; and it was so. And God called the firmament heaven. And the evening and the morning were the second day," (Genesis 1:7-8)

This Ruin-Reconstruction interpretation of Genesis (better known as the Gap Theory) was the bread and butter Creation doctrine of the Fundamentalist movement in the early part of the 20th century. The interpretation has mainly been credited to the Scottish theologian, Thomas Chalmers, who began to preach it back in the early 19th century. There is, however, documented evidence that there were theologians who also held this view long before Chalmers' day. Contrary to Young Earth Creationist allegations, Chalmers did not invent the Gap Theory as a compromise of the Word of God to accommodate science. That gap has always been in the Scriptures since the day Moses penned the book of Genesis. However, only in post New Testament times, and only after man's knowledge about Earth's natural history increased greatly, has the Spirit opened people's eyes to its existence. The reader can only start to comprehend the doctrinal significance by rightly dividing and gaining true knowledge through the Lord Jesus Christ.

Keep in mind that from the days of the Apostles, through the Dark Ages, and until just a few centuries ago, a 6,000-year age for the heavens and Earth was accepted dogma in the institutions of both the Church and academia. Until that time, the real age of the Earth was not a burning issue. However, after the Bible was published for the masses and afterwards, as the scientific case evidence for an old Earth grew, so did the breech between the establishment Church and establishment science.

To his credit, Thomas Chalmers refused to accept that the Scriptures had been broken by the growing body of geological truth of his time. He did not lose his faith in the accuracy of the Holy Bible, nor did he go into denial of the forensic geologic facts. As a Protestant theologian honest enough to realize the truth of those emerging observations while remaining steadfast, faithful, and committed to defending the Scriptures, Chalmers (and others) were inspired to observe the time gap between Genesis 1:1 and 1:2 in the Creation narrative. And he did so many years before Darwin had published his Theory of Evolution! In other words, an Old Age for the Earth had already become an accepted fact long before the Theory of Evolution came on the scene. Therefore, the argument that acceptance of an Old Earth is a compromise to Evolutionary Theory is simply not true and has no foundation in historical fact.

What we have in the case of Thomas Chalmers and the Post-Reformation times is an example of Progressive Revelation from the Holy Scriptures. That is, when the proper time came, the Word of God had once again proved itself timely and relevant to the level of scientific and Spiritual understanding of the day. That Bible is still just as timely and relevant today and can still provide true and faithful answers to scientific discoveries that appear to challenge the fundamentals of the Christian Faith. The problem today is that for the most part, people have abandoned faith in the infallibility of the Holy Scriptures.

As the world moved into the Industrial Revolution, and since about the middle of the 20th Century, there have been copious publications of new English Bible translations, each claiming (1) to be an improvement on the one before it and (2) to be better than the common King James Bible. This is the Bible that Chalmers and the main body of Protestant Fundamentalism used over the years to bring so many people to a saving knowledge of the Lord Jesus Christ.

Although an in-depth study of this phenomenon is beyond the immediate scope of this study, it is important to point out that this departure from the old Authorized text has had a profound effect on the spirituality of the Fundamental Church. Since that time, the Ruin-Reconstruction (Gap Theory) interpretation of Genesis has also been systematically relegated to the Fundamental Doghouse and displaced on the center stage of Creationism by the Neo-Creationists - the Young Earth Advocates.

Looking objectively at the Fundamental Church in historical retrospect, it is observed that as the juggernaut of Evolutionary Theory became a growing mainstay in academia across the latter half of the 20th Century, the Fundamental Church has increasingly retreated into a shell of denial and self-preservation. Having thrown aside its best source of Scriptural Authority and defense (the King James Bible), and with declining numbers who were scientifically educated and intellectually honest enough to deal with the geological arguments, the Fundamental Church has consequently lost the ability to effectively address the overwhelming body of evidence for an Old Earth from a true Biblical perspective. Consequently, it has also lost the ability to effectively minister the Gospel of the Lord Jesus Christ to the educated masses when it comes to the accuracy of the book of Genesis.

This falling away has precipitated the rise to power within Fundamental Christianity of today's Neo-Creationist power brokers. These are the militant Young Earth Creation Scientists like Hovind, Brown, Ham, and Gish et al, who have beguiled the flock through emotional appeals to archaic traditionalism presented in the new and improved wrapper of *Creation Science*. The faithful are exhorted to put logic and reason aside and stand firm in the proscribed Party Line of Young Earth Creationism, all in the name of Jesus and defending the faith against the evil evolutionists and the scientific conspirators.

While their motivations and intentions are, without doubt, completely honorable and worthy in their own minds, they have embraced a fanaticism and collective group-think that has degenerated into a less-than-intellectually-honest religious and political juggernaut in its own right. Full of pride and arrogance and stopping their ears to any justification for and Old Age of the Earth (even Biblical), they proudly claim to be defenders of the Bible. But when confronted with rightly-divided Scripture on this matter, they will not hesitate for a moment to criticize the old King James Bible, or any variant of Scriptures for that matter, that contradicts their dogmatic paradigm of reasoning. This is unfortunate but true.

Consequently, most Christians of today, regardless of denominational persuasion, can only agree on what the first verse of Genesis states - *"In the beginning God created the heaven(s) and the earth."* (Genesis 1:1) Beyond that first verse, all agreement quickly disintegrates, and the battle for hearts, minds, and souls (and money) begins.

Concerning that first verse, there are those who hold that the KJV Bible has translated the verse inaccurately (missing an "s" on the word *heaven*). Criticism of the accuracy of the KJV Bible is not restricted to the Young Earthers. Some of the traditional Gap Theorists claim that the second verse of Genesis was also badly translated in the KJV. *"And the earth was (had become) without form, and void; and darkness was upon the face of the deep. And the Spirit of God moved upon the face of the waters."* (Genesis 1:2)

In this case, there are those who claim that the word *was* should have been translated *had become* in the KJV. Of course, in both cases, the criticism of the KJV text by the respective proponents was in defense of their own paradigm of interpretation. This was unwise. Notice that it is almost ALWAYS the KJV Bible translation that is challenged by anyone trying to prove a pet doctrinal point.

Neither is it wise to dismiss the literal wording of Genesis in an attempt to reconcile it to Evolutionary Theory. The school of Creationists known as Theistic Evolutionists generally holds that the Earth is very old, and life evolved as it was intelligently designed to do by the Creator. Their position on the interpretation of the seven days of Genesis is that each day represents an indeterminate period of geologic time that closely matches the progression of the Earth's theoretical evolutionary development over the millennia. But a literal interpretation of the KJV Bible's wording does not support this notion.

The key crux of resolving the Genesis narrative requires the reconciliation of these apparent contradictions: (1). How can the Earth be only 6,000 years old (according to the Bible chronology) when the forensic evidence of Geology and the fossil record reveal that the Earth is very ancient? (2). How could death have started with the fall of man about 6,000 years ago (according to the Bible), when evidence for death is found throughout the geologic ages? (3). How could man have been on the Earth for only about 6,000 years (according to the Bible), when there is evidence of manlike creatures inhabiting the Earth for hundreds of thousands of years? Any interpretation of the Genesis narrative that cannot answer these three key facts is insufficient. Are we really listening to what the

Spirit is saying? Not if you have lost faith in the infallibility of the KJV Bible.

Since the days of Thomas Chalmers, the body of scientific knowledge about natural history and an old Earth has accumulated exponentially. It is equally true that faith in the infallibility of the King James Bible has declined exponentially, while the production of new Bible versions and commentaries has been explosive. Many will disagree with this statement, but you are not going to learn anything new outside of heeding and correctly parsing the literal wording of the old Reformation Age Bible. Throughout this book, we will demonstrate that fact.

In this chapter, we will show that Thomas Chalmers (and others of his day and even before his day) were correct in their initial interpretation of the Genesis Gap. Unfortunately, because they had insufficient knowledge of Natural Science and Geology relative to what we know today, they could not even begin to reconcile many doctrinal issues of the faith with the emerging geological evidence. Today, if you can still place your faith in the infallibility of the Holy Bible's words, you will find that the Bible can still answer the tough questions that continue to elude men of carnal reasoning, be they scientists or Bible scholars. You will not be disappointed.

Thus we now begin this in-depth study by a thoughtful, logical, and critical examination of the most hotly debated passage in the book of Genesis. "*And the earth was without form [תהו], and void; and darkness was upon the face of the deep. And the Spirit of God moved upon the face of the waters.*" (Genesis 1:2)

Most people gloss over this verse almost like it is not even there. Ask a random sampling of people on the street what the first thing was that God created, and over 90% of the time, the answer will be, "Light!"

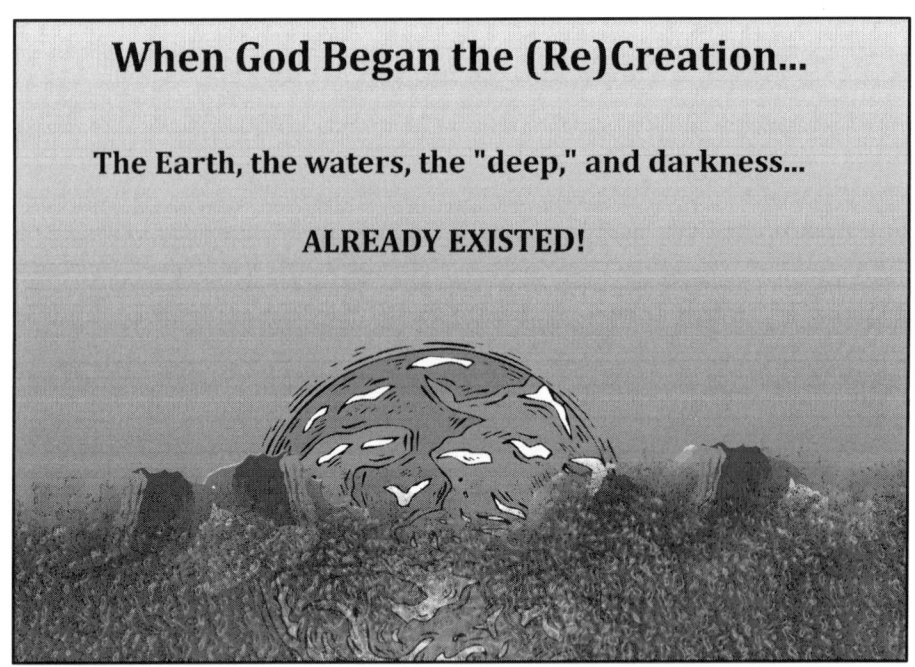

"And God said, Let there be light: and there was light. And God saw the light, that it was good: and God divided the light from the darkness. And God called the light Day, and the darkness he called Night. And the evening and the morning were the first day." (Genesis 1:3-5)

According to the Bible, those 90% who answered "Light" are wrong. Here is why. Applying some English grammar, common sense, and basic science to the issue, we look back at Genesis 1:2 and find that on the very first of the Genesis days, *before* God says, "Let there be light," several things are already there, most notably (1) the Earth, (2) waters, (3) the deep, and (4) darkness. These four things already existed on the first day, so light was not the first thing God created. The first thing God created was the heaven and the earth (Genesis 1:1). Genesis 1:2 describes the *condition* of the Earth at a point in time *after* the heaven and earth were first created. Genesis 1:3 is the beginning of a seven-day restoration process. More precisely, it was the Divine work of making a new *generation* of the heavens and Earth.

"These are the generations [תּוֹלְדָה] of the heavens and of the earth when they were created, in the day that the LORD God made the earth and the heavens," (Genesis 2:4)

Technical point: Where the wording of Genesis 1:3 says, "Let there be light," that in no way implies the initial creation of light; it implies turning on the light or calling for light to shine. In fact, the physics for light were already in place back in verse 1:2 because time, matter, and space are already established, and light is an integral part of the space-time fabric. The darkness of Genesis 1:2 merely indicates an absence of light in time and space.

In response to this line of reasoning, Young Earth Creationists will then argue that God created the Earth without form and void, (and we must assume also the waters, the space called the deep, and the concept of time) at the very beginning of the first day. But the Holy Spirit has a counter-argument to that objection. Compare these two verses and the Hebrew word definitions:

"For thus saith the LORD that created the heavens; God himself that formed the earth and made it; he hath established it, he created it not in vain [תֹּהוּ], he formed it to be inhabited: I am the LORD; and there is none else." (Isaiah 45:18)

"And the earth was without form [תֹּהוּ], and void; and darkness was upon the face of the deep. And the Spirit of God moved upon the face of the waters." (Genesis 1:2)

Isaiah 45:18 tells us that the Lord God did not originally create the Earth in such a desolate condition. The word *vain* in Isaiah 45:18 and the term *without form* in Genesis 1:2 are from the same Hebrew word (*tohuw*). These verses by themselves, when rightly divided in either language, destroy the core premise of Young Earth Creationism. When Genesis 1:2 is compared with Isaiah 45:18, it rules out God initially making the Earth as a formless mud ball, turning on the work lights, and starting the decorating process.

The verse clearly states that the Earth is already there. Although it is without form and void on the surface of the planet and covered in waters, it is most certainly already the formed planet Earth. It even has a name...it's called THE EARTH. The presence of water, in either liquid form or ice (or both), tells us that this planet already has some form of an atmosphere.

Since nowhere else in the Genesis narrative does the Spirit tell us about God establishing the Earth's geologic structure, we can safely assume that the planet's crust, mantle, and core structure are already fully differentiated. There is already nuclear decay in the mantle, producing the heat that drives the Earth's tectonic and volcanic processes.

The dynamo at the Earth's core was already generating the magnetic field which protects the Earth's surface from lethal radiation from outer space. Oh yes, outer space is already there too because the Earth is in space rotating on its axis on a 24-hour clock (the evening and the morning).

After seeing that all these things are already present, can we realistically be expected to accept the Young Earth Creationists' argument? Are we to believe that God went "poof" and made the planet Earth, outer space, time, and lots of water, all at the very beginning of the very first day without a single sentence outlining this complex work, - especially since God then only says, "Let there be light" and calls it a day? That seems somewhat out of character in light of the fact that God then spends another five full working days on just the surface features, which the Bible documents in great detail. Did Moses sleep through that part of the lecture? I don't think so.

The only common sense, logical, and truly Biblical conclusion that these things collectively tell us is that the seven days of Genesis were a reconstruction from the ruins of what was already there. It was a new generation of all things. The Word makes a statement of fact on the Earth's ruined condition and then proceeds to tell us how God regenerated all things. That is the simplicity and truth of the narrative. Man has been guilty of reading his own understanding into the meaning of Genesis instead of just taking God at His word.

The Earth's preserved geological history (which God also authored) tells us that this planet is very old. Therefore, there MUST be a Biblical explanation that confirms this observation and provides a Biblical reason why these things are so. The Ruin-Reconstruction interpretation does exactly that. The Bible gives no specific time when God first created the heaven and the Earth (Genesis 1:1), but it does give the time when the Earth is found in this desolate condition and for the start of the seven literal 24-hour days. Geologically, that time was indeed very recent. In this respect only are the Young Earth Creationists fully correct. This is the context for the gap on which Ruin-Reconstruction doctrine is based. Exactly how long that time gap represents no one can say for sure. It most certainly could accommodate hundreds of millions of years or less, but a gap is most certainly there.

It is here that the diehard Young Earth Creationists still refuse to consider the Scriptural facts just presented, brush reason aside, and pontificate that the doctrine of this gap is nothing more than a compromise of the Scriptures to accommodate the long periods of time required by the Evolutionary model. This is their answer to anything Biblical or Scientific that allows for an old age for the Earth. Is this a valid argument? Not really!

The Earth is without form and void at Genesis 1:2 and in darkness. There is no indication of anything being alive on the surface of the Earth at this time, and that time is roughly 6,000 years ago. Common sense and reasoning tell you that if nothing was alive at that point of time, there could be nothing (man or beast, fish or fowl, tree or bush) that survived from any previous old world from which this world's life forms could have evolved. The literal wording of Genesis 1:2 rules out the possibility that anything (or anyone) living today evolved from anything that existed before the seven days. Every living thing today was made/created during the days of Genesis. This is why the specific phrasing "after his kind" or "after their kind" is used by the Spirit to describe the Lord's regenerative work. There is no room for Evolution. The implication is that creatures living on the Earth today were modeled after the same pattern as living things that were alive on the Earth in the world before this one. There was a clean break in the genetic lines of descent. Since there is not an unbroken genetic line of ancestry, there is no evolution from the previous world to this one.

Remember the fact that when Thomas Chalmers began to preach about the gap in Genesis (in the early 19th Century), it was well *before* Charles Darwin even published. Chalmers' motivation never was to accommodate the Theory of Evolution because it had not even been proposed at that time. (Gee, I wonder why YECs don't bring up that fact.)

That answer has not fully addressed one important question. If the Gap Theory is not a compromise to evolutionary theory as our Young Earth Creationist friends fraudulently claim, what is the Biblical purpose in allowing for an old age for the Earth and an old world order before the seven days of Genesis? The truth is that it points the way to understanding what happened in the Earth's ancient history shortly after the beginning (Genesis 1:1) of all things and reveals the origins and background of Satan, mankind's mortal and spiritual adversary. He has been around for a long, long time, and the Earth's geological and fossil record of catastrophes and mass extinctions is the legacy of his original fall in the distant past. This knowledge

leads directly to the core of understanding who we are, why we were placed here afterward, and why we need salvation through the Lord Jesus Christ. It is a sobering body of Biblical information that the god of this world fights hard to suppress.

Have you never wondered why there is darkness present at Genesis 1:2, when the Scriptures say that God is light and in Him there is no darkness (1 John 1:5)? Where did Satan come from, and when did he turn against God? In the Garden of Eden, he was already an enemy of God before Adam and Eve transgressed. So why is there no mention of that creature's creation or fall anywhere in the Genesis narrative? (Actually, it is found in the books of Isaiah and Ezekiel and will be discussed in detail later.) When were the Angels created? If man was made a little lower than the angels (Psalms 8:5), what are they, and when were they made? What are the devils in the Gospels, and where did they come from? These are the mysteries that the Gap Theory interpretation of Genesis unlocks with prayerfully considered observations of the rest of the Bible and many things in the geologic record. This is all covered in greater detail later in the study.

The reader should keep firmly in mind that state-of-the-art of scientific knowledge is constantly changing and completely disregards any input from the Holy Bible. To assume that the scientific theories of today are the end of all true knowledge is foolishness. Conversely, to shun and deny sound scientific evidence under the banner of defending the faith against evil evolutionists is equally unwise and foolish - a discredit to the Faith that claims to be the fountain of all truth. As Christians dedicated to finding and defending the truth, we should make every effort to understand what the literal Biblical text is actually saying by its own Scripturally-defined terms before attempting to harmonize it with our current scientific understanding or traditional belief system.

God is the Divine Author of both the Scriptures and the Earth's Geologic record. Both are from His hand. Both witness to historical and spiritual Truth. He established the principles and physics by which we can search out the answers to things preserved within the Earth's geology. His Scriptures provide us with a definitive source of Authority and a faithful guide to verify the validity of those answers. Therefore, it is our firm belief that there cannot possibly be any real contradiction in facts between Geology and Genesis. Any such contradictions only arise within the paradigm of our understanding, be it scientific or Scriptural.

Let's be honest. Creationism will never find fair and equal standing and acceptance with the non-believing world's accepted paradigm of origins. The Truth of the Bible must be accepted by faith as the Word of God. The world has placed its faith in the Theory of Evolution and carnal reasoning. The supernatural intervention or acts of an invisible Divine Sovereign can neither be proved nor disproved by the scientific method. Regrettably, a large segment of Fundamental

Christianity has placed its faith in an interpretation of Genesis which denies not only the historical facts contained within the Earth itself but, in some cases, the concise wording of the Holy Bible as well. A rightly-divided exegesis of the Genesis account, however, reveals the full truth when the geologic evidence is examined in the light of a truly literal Scriptural context.

Without the original Hebrew and Greek Bible manuscripts (the originals no longer exist - only variants of copies), one must either put his trust in the opinions of modern scholars or in a reliable Bible translation he can trust as a final authority in all matters. Without apology, we have taken a stand for the King James Authorized Version of the Bible as that Scriptural authority in the English language. This translation (and it is a translation) once command wide respect within the Fundamental Church. It still does in some faithful congregations.

In the course of their work, the translators of the King James Bible were led to leave two subtle textual indicators within their 1611 English translation of the book of Genesis to call the readers' attention to the doctrine of a time gap between Genesis 1:1 and 1:2 in the creation narrative. This was done almost 400 years ago, long before Darwin or the founding of the modern geological sciences. These indicators are not found in more recent English translations because contemporary scholars say they were mistranslations of the Hebrew words. But were they really?

The first of these so-called mistranslations involves these two verses: *"In the beginning God created the heaven and the earth."* (Genesis 1:1)

" Thus the heavens and the earth were finished, and all the host of them." (Genesis 2:1)

The word *heaven* (singular) in Genesis 1:1 and the word *heavens* (plural) at Genesis 2:1 are both from the same Hebrew word [שָׁמַיִם] *(sh'mayim)*. Modern scholars insist that the word heaven in Genesis 1:1 should also be rendered plural; thus all new versions say *heavens* in Genesis 1:1. Technically, that is not quite correct. The tense in the Hebrew is the dual. It is easily confused with the plural, inasmuch as Hebrew words take on an *im* ending when made plural. *Ha'shamayim* looks like a plural word. However, the *ayim* ending is a special dual case ' It always describes exactly two (unlike the strict plural), but the two are considered as one. We have a similar case in English. For example, when we speak of a pair of pants or a pair of glasses, we never think of these items as more than one despite the "s" ending on the nouns (normally a plural indicator). The AV1611 translators obviously knew this. As you study the materials on this site, you will begin to understand their choice of English rendering.

In respect to Gap Theory doctrine, the implication is that there was a structural difference in the heavens of the old world (when the heaven and Earth were originally created) as contrasted with the three-heavens structure God established in the new world after the seven days of regeneration. That is discussed in greater detail later in this book and will give insight into the ambiguous phrase, "no more sea," found at Revelation 21:1 after the Final Judgment. (It references back to the dividing of the waters on the second day.)

The second mistranslation concerns these two verses: *"And God blessed them, and God said unto them, Be fruitful, and multiply, and replenish the earth, and subdue it: and have dominion over the fish of the sea, and over the fowl of the air, and over every living thing that moveth upon the earth."* (Genesis 1:28)

"And God blessed Noah and his sons, and said unto them, Be fruitful, and multiply, and replenish the earth." (Genesis 9:1)

The fur really flies over the KJV Bible translators' choice of English words in these two verses, but especially so in Genesis 1:28 of the creation narrative. Modern scholars (and most Young Earth Creationists) insist that the Hebrew word [מלא] (*male*) should be translated as *fill* (which certainly is one meaning of the Hebrew word) and *is* rendered as fill in most new translations. In the case of Genesis 9:1, where Noah and his family are instructed to RE-populate an Earth that has been wiped out by the flood, the word *replenish*, as translated in the old KJV Bible, renders a more accurate English meaning than does the word fill. Because the KJV translators used the word replenish in both Genesis 9:1 and Genesis 1:28, on the surface this seems to indicate that the translators were pointing to a similarity in circumstances between Adam and Noah in their respective Divine commissions. If the word replenish stands in Genesis 1:28, then both Adam and Noah are told to repopulate a desolate Earth after a major destructive event, specifically a flood. (Note: Remember, the Earth was flooded at Genesis 1:2 before the seven days of Genesis.):

"And the earth was without form, and void; and darkness was upon the face of the deep. And the Spirit of God moved upon the face of the waters." (Genesis 1:2)

Since the flood of Noah's day was a judgment upon the world of that time, a flood before Adam's creation would imply a previous judgment upon an old world order before the seven days of the creation narrative. To insist that the word fill is the best rendering implies that the King James Bible translators did not understand the true meaning of the Hebrew word and mistranslated male in both those verses. But did they really? Just five verses before rendering male as replenish in Genesis 1:28, the same translators rendered male as fill in Genesis 1:22. *"And God blessed them, saying, Be fruitful, and multiply, and fill the waters in the seas, and let fowl multiply in the earth."* (Genesis 1:22)

This fact shows that those translators most certainly knew the subtle differences in meanings of the Hebrew word male and were well aware of the interpretive implications of using the English word replenish in Genesis 1:28 and 9:1 in the King James translation.

If these were the only places in the Scriptures that gave support to the Gap Theory interpretation, it would be very skimpy evidence indeed upon which to base sound doctrine. But, as we have already pointed out, there are other literal wording considerations within the Holy Bible that raise valid interpretative issues. For example, there is the issue of the Biblical word Generations.

Like mankind, the Bible says that the Earth and the heavens also have generations in their histories. *"These are the generations of the heavens and of the earth when they were created, in the day that the LORD God made the earth and the heavens,"* (Genesis 2:4)

"This is the book of the generations of Adam. In the day that God created man, in the likeness of God made he him;" (Genesis 5:1)

"These are the generations of Noah: Noah was a just man and perfect in his generations, and Noah walked with God." (Genesis 6:9)

In all three of the verses above, the word *generations* [תולדה] is defined as a line of descent, a family history from one generation to the next, and the Hebrew word for generations is plural. If God only made the heavens and Earth once, as Young Earth Creationists would have you believe, then the term generations should have been in the singular, which it is NOT in either Hebrew or the KJV English translation.

The Holy Scriptures are clearly saying that the seven days' work was a new generation of the heavens and the Earth when God made the world of Man following the desolation found at the time of Genesis 1:2. Something similar will be done in the future. The Bible says there will be yet another generation of the heavens and Earth at the second coming of the Lord Jesus Christ. *"And Jesus said unto them, Verily I say unto you, That ye which have followed me, in the regeneration when the Son of man shall sit in the throne of his glory, ye also shall sit upon twelve thrones, judging the twelve tribes of Israel."* (Matthew 19:28)

"Nevertheless we, according to his promise, look for new heavens and a new earth, wherein dwelleth righteousness." (2 Peter 3:13)

"For, behold, I create new heavens and a new earth: and the former shall not be remembered, nor come into mind." (Isaiah 65:17)

The geologic and fossil records are the surviving evidence that God preserved for us to testify to the truth that the Earth is very old and was inhabited for a long period before the seven days of Genesis chapter one. Those records, written in stone, also provide evidence of a long reign of death upon the old Earth and the end of the old world order by a universal destructive event.

One of the greatest remaining mysteries of modern geology is an episode of mass destruction and extinction which occurred in the recent geological age called the Pleistocene, the age just before the Holocene, also called the age of Man. This extinction event appears to be closely linked to the Ice Age. Part of the evidence of this global catastrophe consists of vast animal cemeteries found in many places around the world, which seem to show a catastrophic and sudden destruction of life all across the planet only a few thousand years ago. This evidence was documented by many back in the 19th century but is mostly ignored by the leading scientists of our day because it does not fit into the prevailing Evolutionary paradigm. The Young Earth Creationists, however, have seized upon these reports as their proof of Noah's flood. We will show that this evidence is actually the proof of a global extinction event and flood which happened before Noah's flood (indeed before the time of Genesis 1:2) and was only a component of a universal catastrophic event which saw the end of all life on the surface of the Earth before the seven days of Genesis. At various places throughout this book, we will present this evidence and discuss its relevance within the context of the Biblical time line. That time line is discussed in the next chapter.

If we believe the literal wording of the Bible, there was indeed a universal creative event during the seven days of Genesis, about 6,000 literal years ago, but the literal wording of the Bible and the Earth's geology reveal that there is more to the story. It was not the original creation of all things. Understanding the time gap in Genesis opens a vast knowledge gap. You just can't rely on your own understanding or the traditions of man to obtain this knowledge. You have to TRUST THE BOOK.

"For my thoughts [are] not your thoughts, neither [are] your ways my ways, saith the LORD. For [as] the heavens are higher than the earth, so are my ways higher than your ways, and my thoughts than your thoughts." (Isaiah 55:8-9)

We stressed previously that in order to understand what the literal Biblical text is actually saying, it must be interpreted by its own Scripturally-defined terms. We will discuss two of these very important terms and the differences in conceptual meanings they convey. It is essential that students of God's Word comprehend these terms and differences in order to discern truth from traditional assumptions. These words are Earth and World, and they are not same.

Chapter 2
Worlds and the Earth

THE EARTH – ONE PLANET

THE WORLD – EARTH, STARS, EVERYTHING ON THE EARTH AND THE PRESENT EVIL SYSTEM

The King James Authorized Version of the Holy Bible has its own internal set of words and definitions, which are self-interpreting in their specific meaning and context. From Genesis to Revelation, translated from Hebrew, Aramaic, and Greek manuscripts, the KJV Bible's English translation is an integrated whole throughout the sixty-six books.

The English words world and earth are different words and have distinct, separate conceptual meanings in the Holy Bible and the

English language. These meanings are defined by the Scriptures when used in context. Understanding that difference in distinction is CRUCIAL to rightly dividing the word of truth, for therein is found one of the keys to unlocking the paradox of the creation account of Genesis chapter one and the geologic evidence of an ancient Earth.

In the book of Hebrews, the Lord Jesus Christ is said to be the maker of the worlds (plural). *"Hath in these last days spoken unto us by [his] Son, whom he hath appointed heir of all things, by whom also he made the worlds;"* (Hebrews 1:2)

"Through faith we understand that the worlds were framed by the word of God, so that things which are seen were not made of things which do appear." (Hebrews 11:3)

The Greek word in these two verses for *worlds* is 'Αιωα' (as in eon), which is an age or perpetuity of specific prevailing conditions in time upon the face of the Earth. Therefore, the word world as doctrinally defined in our Bible does not refer to other planets in outer space, but rather to defined ages and prevailing conditions during those ages - past, present, and future.

The Earth is a planet. It is a spherical-shaped mass of matter in time and space. The world is the specific set of conditions prevailing upon the face of the planet Earth at a specific point in Biblical time. The Earth is a part of our present world, past worlds, and the future world to come (Matt 12:32; Mark 10:30; Hebrews 2:5), but the Earth itself is not the whole world. Our present world also consists of the stars in the sky, the trees of the field, the people, the cities of the nations, and the present evil world system on the face of the Earth.

"And it shall come to pass after the end of seventy years, that the LORD will visit Tyre, and she shall turn to her hire, and shall commit fornication with all the kingdoms of the world upon the face of the earth." (Isaiah 23:17)

"Who gave himself for our sins, that he might deliver us from this present evil world, according to the will of God and our Father:" (Galatians 1:4)

The Earth itself is not evil, but it is cursed (Gen 3:17-19). When Adam sinned, death entered the world of Adam, who had just been created on the sixth day and placed by God upon the face of the regenerated Earth in that new world...the world of MAN, made in the image of God.

"Wherefore, as by one man sin entered into the world, and death by sin; and so death passed upon all men, for that all have sinned:" (Romans 5:12)

Adam's newly created world was pristine on the surface. But under Adam's feet, entombed and hidden in the sedimentary rocks of the planet, was the buried fossil record - God's material testimony to the truth of the existence of a previous world on the face of the Earth and a long reign of death across ancient ages past, long before the new world of Adam. This material evidence (there all along but only scientifically examined and understood by man over the past two to three centuries) now speaks to us today about the existence of that previously-created world (Genesis 1:1), which came under subjection to death, was eventually destroyed (Genesis 1:2), and was Divinely replaced by the present world (Genesis 1:3-2:1). That ancient, pristine world was under the stewardship of the covering cherub, Lucifer. Through Lucifer's sin of rebellion against God, that old world under Lucifer's stewardship was first subjected to death and, through time, eventually died. At the end of its time, when the stars of the old universe (including Earth's sun) perished, their remaining hydrogen oxidized into waters, and physical and spiritual darkness took their final toll upon the ancient Creation. *"And the earth was without form [תֹהוּ], and void [בֹהוּ]; and darkness [חֹשֶׁךְ] was upon the face of the deep*

[תְהוֹם]. And the Spirit of God moved upon the face of the waters." (Genesis 1:2)

"For this they willingly are ignorant of, that by the word of God the heavens were of old [εκπαλαι], and the earth standing [συνιστάω] <u>out</u> of the water and <u>in</u> the water: Whereby the <u>world that then was</u>, being overflowed [κατακλύζω] with water, perished [απολλυμι]: But the <u>heavens and the earth, which are now</u>, by the same word are kept in store, reserved unto fire against the day of judgment and perdition of ungodly men." (2 Peter 3:5-7)

The old world was the first generation of the heavens and the Earth (Genesis 1:1). It perished in a flood of waters. The passage of 2 Peter 3:5-7 is NOT a reference to Noah's flood because who today is ignorant of Noah's flood? But many are willingly are ignorant of this previous flood because it speaks of things which happened before the events of the six days of Genesis, and that upsets some theological apple carts.

The heavens and Earth which are now are the second generation of the heavens and the Earth, the creation of which began when God said, "Let there be light."(Gen 1:3) and was accomplished in six literal 24-hour days, with God resting on the seventh day. God regenerated our present Earth and heavens from the physical remains of the old world. This is why the Bible says,

"These are the generations [תּוֹלְדָה] of the heavens and of the earth when they were created, in the day that the LORD God made the earth and the heavens," (Genesis 2:4)

Our present world (the whole universe) is a regeneration of the original creation of God. That is a Scriptural reality which fits the geologic evidence but not the secular theories of uniformitarian geology and Evolution. Neither does it fit the doctrines of the contemporary Young Earth Creationist movement.

Young Earth Creationists demand that the universe and all things were first made only 6,000 years ago and that there was no death on the Earth until Adam and Eve sinned. Romans 5:12 and Exodus 20:11 are the proof texts cited as the defining doctrines of the faith. Therefore, by their simplistic interpretation of those two verses, they claim that there is no Scriptural proof of death before Adam and therefore no Pre-Adamite world. Since they deny a Pre-Adamite world, all of the fossil record and the Ice Age must (according to their reasoning) be the result of Noah's flood. This is nothing less than classical Archaic Creationism presented in the new and improved wrapper of Creation Science and peddled on the claim of strict adherence to the literal wording of the Bible. However, as we have already started to document, that claim is not exactly the full truth.

The Bible is the word of God, and God cannot lie! Spiritual principles are universal throughout all 66 books. Romans 5:12 and Exodus 20:11 are absolutely true, but only within the context of the full truth as defined within the Scriptures and by the Scriptures as a doctrinal whole. We will demonstrate this.

Exodus 20:11 states, *"For in six days the LORD made heaven and earth, the sea, and all that in them is, and rested the seventh day: wherefore the LORD blessed the sabbath day, and hallowed it."*

Notice that the sea is set apart from the Earth in this verse as something separate. This is the contextual qualifier of the verse because the Sea spoken of here is the waters (or sea) above the firmament, placed there at the time of Genesis 1:6-8 but which is no longer there after the final judgment. *"And I saw a new heaven and a new earth: for the first heaven and the first earth were passed away; and there was no more sea."* (Revelation 21:1)

Thus, Exodus 20:11 is absolutely true. This present heaven and Earth and that Sea above the firmament were indeed made in six days just as the book of Genesis states. Exodus 20:11 is not a reference to the first-time creation of all things. Genesis 1:1 does NOT read, "*In the beginning God created the heaven and the earth, and the sea.*"

Romans 5:12 states: "*Wherefore, as by one man sin entered into the world, and death by sin; and so death passed upon all men, for that all have sinned:*" (Romans 5:12)

Young Earth Creationists adamantly claim that a literal reading of Romans 5:12 proves there was no death or previous world before Adam, yet they ignore the phrase "world that then was" in the previously-mentioned verse in the book of 2 Peter. "*For this they willingly are ignorant of, that by the word of God the heavens were of old [εκπαλαι], and the earth standing [συνισταω] out of the water and in the water: Whereby the world that then was, being overflowed [κατακλυζω] with water, perished [απooλλυμι] : But the heavens and the earth, which are now, by the same word are kept in store, reserved unto fire against the day of judgment and perdition of ungodly men.*" (2 Peter 3:5-7)

In Romans 5:12 and 2 Peter 3:5-7, the term world in BOTH verses is from the Greek word *kosmos,* and that is the Scriptural nugget of wisdom that puts Romans 5:12 into its proper context of interpretation. The universe *kosmos* was not destroyed by Noah's flood. (The Earth was only flooded.) Therefore, 2 Peter cannot be speaking of Noah's flood. It is telling about the destruction of a previous world or order of all things - The Cosmos. Adam did not live in that previous world. He lived (and sinned) in this one.

Adam's sin brought death into his and our world. The fact that the Earth's geology shows a long and ancient track record of death on this planet long before Adam does not contradict the Bible. Using the spiritual principle that death comes by sin, as the Scriptures clearly state in Romans 5:12, we will show you from the Scriptures that there was a sinner before Adam, in an ancient world that was here before Adam - Lucifer, a.k.a. Satan, the Dragon, the Serpent. Death came upon his ancient world when he fell - long, long before this present world, and the Earth's fossil record is the evidence of this truth, preserved by God (as a physical witness to truth) in the ancient rocks of our planet.

On the pages which follow, we will show that this is not heresy, but Scriptural fact supported by both the Bible and geologic evidence. We will also show that Noah's flood was a real and global event, which could not possibly have been the source for the sediments and fossil record found in the Earth today. This is followed by a discussion of indirect scientific evidence in the geological and archaeological records which supports the Biblical account of the flood AND the Ruin-Reconstruction interpretation of Genesis.

Chapter 3
Geology and Genesis

This study of Old Earth Creationism, the Gap Theory, and Noah's flood deals with a variety of dispensational Bible doctrines and scientific concepts. The material covers topics and observations from multiple fields of study including geology, physics, chemistry, paleontology, meteorology and, of course, the Holy Bible. Considerable effort has been made to present this material in a format that is comprehensible to the widest possible audience.

In addition to topics from various disciplines of science, this study also deals with various subjects of the Bible including literal history; Premillennial Eschatology; the doctrines of Salvation and eternal security of the believer; the origins of angels and devils; the structure of the Temple; the divisions of the body, soul, and spirit; the structure of the three heavens; and the biblical systems of sevens (and other numbers). We also focus on the role of geology, the history of the lost rivers of the Garden of Eden, and the future role of geology in prophecy. Consequently, this chapter is an overview of all the important topics covered in this book. It is our sincere hope that you will find this presentation both interesting and enlightening in your personal study of the Holy Bible.

The Necessary Dividing Lines Between Science and Faith and the Vanity of the Ongoing Creation vs. Evolution Debate
The physical world we live in is governed by specific laws of nature that are understood from experimentation and observation. Those laws and principles were established by the Lord God Himself, and He said that they were very good (Gen 1:31). Understanding how these laws govern the order and workings of the physical universe is the pursuit of good science.

Readers should keep firmly in mind that the Lord God, who established the observed physical laws of nature, is not Himself in subjection to those laws. The Bible is replete with instances in which the Lord God has supernaturally intervened against the laws of physics and nature. Examples are the parting of the Red Sea (Exodus 14:21); the turning back of the shadow of the sundial (2 Kings 20:9); the stopping of the Earth's rotation for about 24 hours (Joshua 10:12-14); the virgin birth of the God-Man, the Lord Jesus Christ; and all the miracles performed by Him when He was on the Earth. With God, nothing is impossible. The creative work of the seven days of Genesis is the first example of such Divine intervention in the Bible.

On the other hand, God sometimes uses the established natural laws and physical things of this world to accomplish His Divine purposes. Noah's flood is just one example.

"And God said unto Noah, The end of all flesh is come before me; for the earth is filled with violence through them; and, behold, I will destroy them with the earth." (Genesis 6:13)

Understanding these natural laws and principles can tell us how Noah's flood happened, what changes were precipitated in the order of all things on the Earth afterward, and why direct physical evidence for the flood has not been found. The geophysics of Noah's flood will be discussed shortly as a part of this overall study.

The Creationism vs. Evolution Debate
It is necessary to state up front that the ongoing controversy of Creation vs. Evolution will never be resolved to the satisfaction of the secular scientific community. It cannot be resolved in a secular context regardless of the well-intended efforts of many on either side of the debate because the current focus of the argument is emotionally and factually misdirected.

Armed with only the observations of current and historical geologic processes and other empirical data, and assuming natural history has been a continuum across billions of years, the present secular paradigms of geological and evolutionary theory are about the best belief system that the educated carnal mind of man could be expected to conceive and accept from the available physical evidence. Without the input of Biblical Authority, current theories are incomplete, and many questions and mysteries remain unresolved, especially in relation to the origins of mankind.

Secular scientists are confident to point out scientific inaccuracies of the Bible because they have been led to view the Bible through the distorted lens of traditional Biblical interpretation. What these scientists have successfully contradicted is traditionally-held Biblical interpretation; specifically, that all things were created out of nothing only about 6,000 ago, as espoused by Young Earth Creationists. However, when you get down to the solid core of what the Bible actually and truly says, Scripture compared to Scripture, there is no scientific evidence in existence today to refute what it actually says. All life, indeed an entire ancient world order, had already perished from the face of the Earth long before the seven days of Genesis. The rightly-divided Scriptures reveal that the seven days of Genesis are a *regeneration* of the heavens and Earth, and that life on this planet has not been an actual continuum. Both the Bible and scientific data are most certainly in agreement on one very key point. This planet Earth is very, very old, and if God authored both the Word and Earth's geologic record, no real contradiction can possibly exist. The fault *must* be interpretive on both sides.

Noah's flood and Divine creative intervention by a Holy God are not factored into the world's accepted origins model because God can't

be observed or quantified in a physical system or seen under a microscope, although the results of His work can be observed and quantified. For these reasons, there is an unbridgeable gap between secular Empirical Science and the Christian faith in respect to both Creation and Noah's flood. Empirical Science is the pursuit of quantifiable facts and repeatable observations and is limited to the physical sphere of reality. From this purely physical perspective, the geological evidence appears to indicate that this planet and the life on it are the result of natural processes over time, and that the existence of all life forms and extinction must be credited to a natural process of random mutations and selection by nature itself. In such a paradigm of interpretation, the researcher's faith is in a theory or synthesis of theories which seems to best fit the observations.

On the other hand, Christians must also deal with spiritual things, just as real as physical things, but which can only be seen through the agency of faith by the illumination of the Word of God. Honest born-again Christians (who are also scientists) cannot be fully objective in an empirical perspective in dealing with the question of origins. The acceptance of God's Words on matters of original sin and supernatural agency holds us accountable to a higher interpretive system, a system which has no place of welcome in the institutional physical sciences of the world. No amount of compromise will be acceptable to either the Naturalist or Creationist extremes of each respective school. Please do not misunderstand. A lot of good knowledge emerges from the practice of good science and the scientific method, and there are a lot of good Christians who are scientists. But when it comes to matters of origins and the things of God, natural science without God is as much out of its depth in providing the full truth as the Young Earth Creationists who ignore solid scientific data.

***"Science without religion is lame; religion without science is blind."* - Albert Einstein.**

Behind the scenes, however, the real driving issue between Naturalists and Creationists is not the existence of God. The real issue is whether all things were created by the Hebrew God of the Holy Bible and according to a designed purpose and specific time scale. The authority of the Bible and the moral issue of personal accountability to God are the hidden roots of all contention in that debate.

Leaving behind the vanity and politics of the Creation/Evolution debate, those who have a well-grounded faith in the Scriptures and a good knowledge of the geological evidence (not theories) are in the better position to attain to a more perfect understanding of how all the pieces of the puzzle fit together. It is only when we accept God and His Words as the final authority in all matters that we are able to perceive the complete picture and resolve the "6,000 years problem" at the heart of the controversy. It is our goal to provide you some of those answers.

The Bible will always have an answer, although we may not immediately see it. For example, it was not until a few centuries ago that the Geological sciences had progressed to the point where the previously-accepted 6,000-year age of the Earth, which was dogma in both the institutions of Church and science, began to be questioned by what was observed in the geological record. Some theologians of the day who were honest enough to realize the truth of those emerging observations and were steadfast, faithful, and committed to defending the Scriptures, were inspired to observe the possibility of a time gap between Genesis 1:1 and 1:2 in the Creation narrative. That gap had always been there - ever since the day Moses penned the book - but not many eyes were open to seeing or understanding it until the times were right. It was already there when the Scottish theologian, Thomas Chalmers, first noticed and began to preach it in the early 19th century. Until that time, the real age of the Earth had not been a burning issue. But when the proper time came, the Word of God once again proved itself timely and relevant to the level of scientific understanding of the day.

This is Progressive Revelation, and it continues even in our present age. Here is another example of Progressive Revelation in the book of Revelation: *"And they of the people and kindreds and tongues and nations shall see their dead bodies three days and an half, and shall not suffer their dead bodies to be put in graves."* (Revelation 11:9)

The question is posed as to how these people all over the world, in different nations and places, could all see these dead bodies on a street in Jerusalem at the same time. Certainly, from the time John wrote it in about 90 AD, until about the middle of the 20th century, nobody could understand how that would be possible. But today, with global satellite Television and Internet Web Cams, anyone can understand how it is possible. The point is this: It was a truth that was not revealed to mankind until it was time, even though that literal truth had always been there. The same holds true for the Genesis narrative. When it was time for man to learn about geology and Earth's natural history, as well as the full truth about origins, the qualifying verses and explanations were already there in the Genesis narratives and elsewhere in the Bible. It was time for those truths to unseal. It is now time for the Fundamental Christian Church to accept this paradigm shift.

This line of thinking is completely lost on the Young Earth Creation Scientists of today, who preach that the original creation of all things occurred only 6,000 years ago. They also use Noah's flood as the catchall solution to explaining the Earth's sedimentary rocks. They claim that all the Earth's hydrocarbons (coal and oil) were made by Noah's flood. Some claim that most of the Earth's mountains were uplifted during Noah's flood. Some even claim that the Ice Age was precipitated by Noah's flood. Because their theology demands that all of the Earth's natural history be jammed into a narrow 6,000-year period, they are required to have the dinosaurs roaming the Earth before the flood, side by side with mankind, and a few even have dinosaurs listed as part of the animals on Noah's Ark. The *science* (1 Timothy 6:20) for support of this belief system is based mainly on appeals to anomalies, "what if" arguments, water canopies which defy the laws of physics, and a peculiar collection of urban legends. It is neither good science nor good Biblical interpretation.

I do not dispute that Noah's flood was real because the Bible tells us that Noah's flood was real. We will propose a flood model that addresses the real-world Scriptural and scientific requirements. The major point which must first be clearly understood is that both the Earth's geology and the Scriptures tell us that Noah's flood could not have been responsible for the Earth's extensive sedimentary, metamorphic, and igneous petrology. Freshman-level knowledge of the Law of Superposition and field observations of Angular Unconformities in folded mountain sediments say otherwise. More importantly, the Bible itself witnesses against these false claims. This is discussed more in depth in the chapter titled *Fossils Produced by Noah's Flood? NOT!*

The notions of alleged major tectonic and/or volcanic activity at work during Noah's flood are conclusively shown to be false by the low levels of SO_4 ions (acid) in the ice layers of the Greenland Ice Sheet, which can be correlated to the time of the flood. That same Ice Sheet contains a wealth of Paleoclimate data, which show that all of Earth's geologic history cannot be compacted into a 6,000-year time frame, especially when its layer history can be dated and traced back over a period in excess of 100,000 years and cross verified with assorted proxy dating methods. The bottom line is this: We should not lightly dismiss the claims of Young Earth Creationists - we should violently discard them. Noah's flood is not a credible scapegoat to evade the tough technical and Scriptural issues.

For a faithful Bible believer, the full truth about Creation and Noah's flood must fit all the observations and verses, not just some of them.

The full truth is only revealed by a prayerful examination of the exact wording of the Scriptures through the Spirit of Truth and faith in those words combined with some common sense and reasoning (Isaiah 1:18). It also takes courage and trust in the Lord's Words and His wisdom, not yours, to see how it all fits together, as well as the ability to stand against the majority position in such matters when necessary. You cannot disregard the full truth revealed by Genesis 1:2 and remain in denial, hiding your head in the sands of traditional interpretation.

Remember, in order to effectively witness to the lost, we must be able to demonstrate to the unsaved scientist or intellectual that one does not have to give up his/her brain to believe in Jesus and the Bible. We must tell them that God published so that they would not perish. (Let the reader understand the play on the metaphor.) If you can deal with the facts on their turf and show them you know what you are talking about, you are better able to convince them of their need for Jesus. An honest interpretation of the Scriptures and unprejudiced consideration of the geologic data will enable the Bible Believer to effectively witness.

Before getting down to the Scriptural and Scientific support for the Gap Theory and a focus on the key truths revealed in Genesis 1:2, we need to falsify some of the Creation Science of the Young Earth Creationists by clearly showing what Noah's flood was and was not responsible for in respect to the Earth's geologic record.

Noah's Flood: Water 101

In addition to showing why Noah's flood could not have formed the Earth's petrology, we will also demonstrate how such a global event occurred according to a literal translation of the Holy Bible. The flood model presented will explain both the dynamics of the geophysics involved and the so-called lack of evidence of such a flood event in the historic record. Before proceeding to those chapters, it is necessary to examine the complex range of behavior of this world's most simple and basic substance - WATER!

Most of the basic properties of water are quite commonly known; others are not. For example, your body is composed of about 2/3 water. Water turns into a solid (ice) at 32 F and expands about 9% in volume. Water turns into a gas (steam) at 212 F under normal atmospheric pressure. Water is a molecule composed of two atoms of hydrogen and one atom of oxygen. Individual atoms of these common elements come in a variety of electronic configurations called *ions*, which can combine to form 18 different and rare variations of the H_2O molecule. With one particular but extremely rare variation, you could drink gallons of it and still die of thirst. But for now, let's stick with the practical aspects and set aside the theoretical.

Water is a substance born of fire. It is formed when hydrogen and oxygen combust to produce heat energy. Water is the resultant product of the reaction. Water under great pressure can remain in a liquid form at temperatures much, much higher than 212 F (water's boiling point at sea level atmospheric pressure). The common kitchen pressure cooker works on this principle. If the pressure is suddenly released, the water will flash into steam, and you'll have a mess on the kitchen ceiling.

Water deep underground beneath the Earth's crust is a few hundred degrees hotter than 212 F and is in the liquid state because of the great pressures at those depths. Deep hydrothermal vents are a real-world example. Water has been observed to come out of volcanoes in large quantities. Water has been detected as a gas on the surface of the Sun and around stars (especially dying ones) and planets elsewhere in the universe. Under low atmospheric pressures, sunlight can break apart the water molecule into Hydrogen and Oxygen gas. The same thing can be done under normal pressure by passing an electric current through salt water.

Water, the most common substance in nature, plays the central role in several spiritual themes in the Bible and is also central to the interpretation of many scientific matters in respect to the Bible. The knowledge of how water behaves under heat, pressure, and light energy finds application in understanding the dynamics of Noah's flood. The chapters titled *Fountains of the Deep* and *Windows of Heaven,* deal with the beginning and end of the flood and the reason behind the changes in the life span of man afterward. In the chapter titled *Days of Peleg and Sea Level Changes,* we will answer questions about post-flood migrations. In the chapter titled *Global Dust Spikes & Paleoclimate Indicators*, we will discuss the indirect forensic evidence for dating Noah's flood.

Essential Doctrinal Knowledge for Correctly Interpreting the Genesis Creation Account

Throughout the centuries, countless theologians and laymen have sought to reconcile the words of the Genesis Creation account with the reality on the ground. Their quests have resulted in numerous and sundry interpretations to explain the meaning of the seven days of Genesis.

In our chapter titled *Contrasting Major Creation Models*, we will show diversity of opinions and beliefs on the matter and the justifications behind those interpretations as well as the logical faults and strengths.

Most interpretations of the Genesis account arise from trying to read something into the Bible that is just not there and dealing with only the things of the physical realm. Taking the literal words of the Holy Bible at face value is the more prudent route, and doing so requires consideration of both the things that can be seen and the invisible things of God. The truth that those words reveal is not hard to understand, but a great many find them very hard to believe.

In order to grasp the full truth, it is crucial to have an understanding of how physical things and spiritual things are actually very closely interrelated.

Flesh and Spirit: Biblical Metaphysics 204
The world into which we have been born consists of physical things which can be seen, touched, tasted, tested, and comprehended by the mind of man. That is the physical aspect of reality; it is observable and quantifiable. On the other hand, the Bible reveals to mankind that there is a spiritual component of reality that requires the Spirit of God to observe and fully comprehend (Romans 8:7.). Although the physical and spiritual realms seem to be two different things, this is not exactly so. The forces of the spiritual realm directly determine the behavior and function of the things in the physical realm.
"Wherein in time past ye walked according to the course of this world, according to the prince of the power of the air, the spirit that now worketh in the children of disobedience:" (Ephesians 2:2)

The substance known as air is a physical thing composed of various gases (mostly nitrogen and oxygen). Satan, the Devil, is the prince of the power of the air. He is a spiritual being of very ancient origin that currently has control over the physical things of this present world (under God's permissive will, of course).

Men and women are a synergy of flesh and spirit. Air is necessary for the life of the flesh, and the life of the flesh is in the blood. The flesh is composed of various physical elements from the Earth and functions through physical electrochemical processes. The spirit of man directs the workings of his flesh (mind over matter).According to the Scriptures, mankind's flesh is under the influence of the spiritual power of death.

"For I know that in me (that is, in my flesh,) dwelleth no good thing: for to will is present with me; but [how] to perform that which is good I find not." (Romans 7:18)

Both the spirit and the mind of the unsaved are under that malignant control. (I'm not going to *mind God*, so it does not *matter)* If they are saved, their Flesh and Spirit are in constant conflict and will be until the day they die (unless the Lord returns before they die). We cover this topic in detail in the chapter titled *Relationship of Flesh and Spirit.*

This corruption in nature is not limited to either people or the Earth. The Bible tells us it permeates the entire physical universe.

"Behold even to the moon, and it shineth not; yea, the stars are not pure in his sight." (Job 25:5)

"Behold, he putteth no trust in his saints; yea, the heavens are not clean in his sight." (Job 15:15)

If these things are true, the bottom line is that all present physical life forms in the universe are generated by a process driven by death because all nature feeds on death. You kill and eat dead things in order to live and procreate other life forms; then things kill and eat you. Mankind is not at the top of the proverbial food chain; worms, viruses, and bacteria are. The physical life cycle of this present world is a violent and insatiable downward spiral toward total corruption and entropy. It is not evolving, but *devolving* into more and more corruption. To be one with nature so to speak, is to be one with the spirit of death, not holiness. As can be seen from these verses, there is much more to understanding the Biblical meaning of death than is apparent on the surface.

"Dead [things] are formed from under the waters, and the inhabitants thereof." (Job 26:5)

"Like sheep they are laid in the grave; death shall feed on them; and the upright shall have dominion over them in the morning; and their beauty shall consume in the grave from their dwelling." (Psalms 49:14)

Death has both a physical and spiritual component. Understanding why this is so is crucial to understanding many things in the Scriptures, especially the Genesis Creation narrative.

Since the entire course of physical nature is affected and influenced by spiritual forces, we must therefore conclude that the correct interpretation of the Genesis account is revealed in the dualistic context of both the physical and spiritual realms, not just the realm of matter. That is the fundamental flaw in the myriad past and present interpretations of the seven days of Genesis and what has been missing from most previous presentations of the Gap Theory of Genesis.

Creationism cannot be defended in a purely physical context. It is only when this dualistic precept is understood and accepted that it becomes possible to begin to more perfectly understand and interpret what the Spirit is saying in the Genesis narrative. (See Genesis 1:1-2:1 to review the verses.) In order to fully comprehend exactly what is being stated in the Genesis Creation narrative and why, we must look back in time through the Scriptures to the very beginning; to the time of Genesis 1:1, when the sons of God rejoiced over the initial creation of the heaven and the Earth:

"Where wast thou when I laid the foundations of the earth? declare, if thou hast understanding. Who hath laid the measures thereof, if thou knowest? or who hath stretched the line upon it? Whereupon are the foundations thereof fastened? or who laid the corner stone thereof; When the morning stars sang together, and all the sons of God shouted for joy?" (Job 38:4-7)

Where did Satan and the Angels come from? Who are these sons of God spoken of here and in Genesis 6:1-2? They certainly were not men, as they were here before the Earth was created. Who are the devils spoken of in the Gospels? The perceptive student will immediately see from the wording of the above verse that these angelic beings were also created creatures, created BEFORE the Lord God began the work of the original creation of the heavens and Earth. How these created beings fit into the overall story is only revealed by the Spirit through the Scriptures. Many of those answers are found in the chapter titled *Pre-Adamite World,* in which we discuss the origin of Satan, the nature of the world which existed at his beginning, his rebellion, and the unleashing of death across the original Creation in the ancient past as a result of his rebellion against God.

Returning to matters of natural geologic history, the Bible does not give a specific number of years for the age of the planet Earth as it does for the age of this present world on the face of the planet, approximately 6,000 years. Neither does it provide much direct knowledge about what transpired on the Earth from the time it was originally created in the ancient past (Gen 1:1) until it is seen again in darkness and ruin (Gen 1:2) prior to the six-day regeneration by the direct intervention of the Spirit of God (Gen 1:3-2:1). God has chosen to preserve for us the geologic record and His Words to assist us in our search for those answers. The Bible only tells us why it became without form and void and provides much insight into the sequence of past events leading up to it. It is only a matter of knowing where to find it in the Bible. Fortunately, much of what happened at the very end of the Pre-Adamite world can be observed in the geology of the Pleistocene. In the chapter titled *Geologic Evidence and Death of the Ancient World,* we talk about some reported observations that provide a glance into what was happening on the face of the Earth at the end of that world.

After the ending of days for the old Earth and heaven of the Pre-Adamite world, and as part of the Lord's preparations for the new regenerated world of Man, a cosmological structure of three heavens was established on the second creative day. It is instructive to note that God does not say that it was good after ending the work of the second day. (See Genesis 1:8.) That omission speaks volumes. The

Apostle Paul related his vision and knowledge of the Third Heaven in 2 Corinthians 12:2 of his Epistles. The chapter titled *The Firmament* will provide some additional insight into the Creation account and other Biblical doctrines.

Additional knowledge can be gained by closely examining what was alive on the Earth at the end of the old world and what was different about the creatures God placed here at the beginning of the new world. This topic is covered in the chapter titled *Life Forms During Ice Age, After the Seven Days of Genesis.*

Based on the materials you will read in those chapters, and as you learn more about what is revealed in the Bible and what is found in the fossil record, the following thought will deserve serious consideration. Could the Pre-Adamite race of hominids that was on this Earth before Adam, and whose physical structure was so similar to modern man, actually have been the physical remains of the fallen sons of God who took on flesh and bone to dwell in the world of the old physical creation? The Bible tells us that they did something similar both before and after the days of Noah.

"There were giants in the earth in those days; and also after that, when the sons of God came in unto the daughters of men, and they bare [children] to them, the same [became] mighty men which [were] of old, men of renown." (Genesis 6:4)

If this is true, it would go a long way in explaining the real truth about the ancient remains of Neanderthal and other ancient hominids, which the Evolutionists claim are the ancestors of modern man. Without the knowledge or acceptance of the Biblical Gap Theory, the logical assumption would be that they were ancestors. However, as we will discuss in the chapter titled *Life Forms During Ice Age, After the Seven Days of Genesis*, there is NO DNA biological connection between those remains and modern living humans. The missing link is still missing. Those creatures, which had a physical likeness similar to man, were not the ancestors of man. They may have been fallen angels or the mutated offspring of angels breeding with biologics. This makes perfect sense because everywhere in the Bible where angels appear in our present world, they appear as men. Consider the following:

"And he measured the wall thereof, an hundred [and] forty [and] four cubits, [according to] the measure of a man, that is, of the angel." (Revelation 21:17)

"Yea, whiles I [was] speaking in prayer, even the man Gabriel, whom I had seen in the vision at the beginning, being caused to fly swiftly, touched me about the time of the evening oblation." (Daniel 9:21)

If the good angels appear as men, does it not make sense that the bad ones would also? We therefore conclude that when God told Adam and Eve to replenish the Earth (Genesis 1:28), that which Adam and Eve (true man, made in God's image) replaced was the fleshly race called sons of God who inhabited the face of the old world and perished along with everything else by the time of Genesis 1:2, where the Earth is found to be without form and void.

CONCLUSION: Putting All Things Into Their Proper Biblical and Scientific Perspectives

Taking the literal wording of the King James Bible and the face value of the available scientific observations to be presented, the only possible interpretation which meets BOTH the literal wording of the Scriptures and the scientific data is the Ruin - Reconstruction (Gap Theory) scenario, as fantastic as it may seem.

The fictional detective, Sherlock Holmes, is credited with this nugget of deductive reasoning:

"When you eliminate the impossible, whatever remains, however improbable, must be the truth"

Although the originator of the principle was fictional, the principle itself is a very sound one in the search for truth.

We realize, of course, that the material presented here does not meet the acceptable standards of scientific empirical evidence because in our interpretation of the available scientific evidence, we have elevated the Word of God to a position equal to, yea more than equal to, the prevailing body of scientific thought and opinion on matters of origins. As Christians, we place our faith in the authority of the God of the Holy Bible over the wisdom of men in all matters, be they scientific or religious. We also realize that the material presented here does not meet the acceptable standards of many within the Christian community because we have elevated the King James Version and Premillennial eschatology to positions of authority higher than all other English language translations and schools of prophetic interpretation. We make no apology for this, but we do hope the reader will objectively and without prejudice consider the worth of the material presented, using that which is found to be of value to enrich his own pursuit of sound doctrine.

There are many fundamental Christians who espouse the Young Earth Creationist position and are quick to dismiss this work as a compromise to the Evolutionists. That is an emotional and irrational defensive mechanism and part of human nature. All men fear what they do not understand. Anyone who objectively reads this material and comprehends the argument will see that this is most certainly not the case. As we will show throughout this book, acceptance of an old age for the Earth is not an acceptance of Evolution. On the other hand, we make no apology for accepting the validity of sound geologic evidence (not theory) when that evidence is in harmony with what the Bible actually says.

As Christians, as Creationists, and as Bible Believers, we are in agreement with the doctrine that the Lord God made the present world, complete with the heavens and Earth, in six literal 24-hour days about 6,000 years ago, just as the Bible states in Exodus 20:11. (See also Heb.1:2.) But that fundamental doctrine of the faith, in itself, is not the end of all Biblical truth. Neither Exodus 20:11 nor Romans 5:12 contradicts or invalidates the empirical geologic data that reveal that this planet Earth is also very ancient (on the order of hundreds of millions of years) and has a definite fossil history of existence and habitation prior to the creative events that begin at Genesis 1:3.

Why such a statement is not a contradiction of the doctrine of Romans 5:12 is a difficult concept for many of our Brethren to grasp because they have wrongly vilified all science in their zeal to stand for the defense of the Bible against Evolution. Unfortunately, many do so because of insufficient instruction in the Holy Scriptures and the sciences, which would empower them to make well-reasoned determinations by themselves. The result is seen in the current Creation Science movement, in which misdirected loyalty to defending traditional Fundamentalist positions has had the exact opposite effect. This has actually led to abandonment of sound doctrine and the embracing of corrupt translations to defend their position on this matter. Once you begin to question the literal wording of the KJV Bible in order to make a doctrinal point, you have already lost the argument.

Instead of wasting time arguing about better translations and holding up geological anomalies as proof against scientific realities of fact, spend more time learning about some very important Christian doctrines and Spiritual truths, which are vanishing from today's pulpits because of the sin of unbelief.

Study and understand the full truth about the Sea that God placed above the physical universe (Gen 1:6-10, Rev 4:6, Rev 21:1), what it is, and why it is presently there. (See the chapter titled *The Firmament.*) Understanding the Spiritual importance of such things is interrelated to a comprehensive knowledge of other equally important Scriptural doctrines and precepts. Study and learn about the dispensations (different times) as revealed in the Holy Bible. Get a firm understanding of the Chronology of the Worlds past, present, and future as revealed by your Bible. Learn the extremely important doctrinal differences between the terms *Kingdom of Heaven* (Matthew 11:12) and *Kingdom of God* (Luke 17:21) as presented in the Scriptures. (See the chapter titled *Kingdom of Heaven and Kingdom of God: Doctrinal Differences.*)

From the very beginning of time until the end of time, control of the Kingdom is the central theme of struggle behind the whole Biblical story. If you don't get this down solid, you won't be able to get the full truth from the book of Genesis.

Learn all the truth about the 1,000-year literal reign of the Lord Jesus Christ and the regenerated heavens and Earth (a new world) when He returns (Matt 19:28, Isaiah 65:17-25, Revelation 20). Understand the continued existence of death for surviving mankind (not resurrected saved Saints), who gets the victory over the Beast, lives through the Great Tribulation, and obtains entrance into that regenerated world (Isaiah 65:20) called the Kingdom of Heaven. Learn why the Kingdom is here on the Earth during that period of time yet to come, a period that correlates in prophetic type to the Seventh Day of Genesis (2 Peter 3:8). Once you grasp these truths, you will more perfectly understand the full import of the final abolishment of death after the 1,000-year Kingdom of Heaven on the Earth (Rev 20:14) and the change of structure and dimensions of the new heaven and Earth, which will be created after the final judgment (Rev 21:1). Then the disappearance of the Sea in Revelation 21:1, which was between the second and third heavens and first established at the beginning of the days of true man (Genesis 1:6-10) will make sense, and you will better understand the reasons for the gap between Genesis verses 1 and 2. Confused? That is why you need to study and rightly divide the words of truth.

Within the pages of the King James Authorized Version of the Holy Scriptures, you will find the EXACT English language wording that can still faithfully and effectively reveal the truth and full import of these matters today. Full truth can only be found when the Scriptures are taken as a whole and interpreted as such. You will learn how important this is in the chapter titled *Exact English KJV wording: Is it Important?*

You also must be a born-again child of God to understand and accept some of these doctrines because they are spiritually discerned (1 Cor. 2:14; 1 John 2:20). Even for many saved people, some of this material is difficult at first; but as you learn these doctrines, more and more of your Bible will begin to open to you.

"Trust in the LORD with all thine heart; and lean not unto thine own understanding." (Proverbs 3:5)

"For my thoughts [are] not your thoughts, neither [are] your ways my ways, saith the LORD. For [as] the heavens are higher than the earth, so are my ways higher than your ways, and my thoughts than your thoughts." (Isaiah 55:8-9)

All learning takes place on the periphery of what we have previously learned. The more you study the Scriptures, the more you learn; and as you learn and accept, more will be revealed to you. *"Whom shall he teach knowledge? and whom shall he make to understand doctrine? [them that are] weaned from the milk, [and] drawn from the breasts. For precept [must be] upon precept, precept upon precept; line upon line, line upon line; here a little, [and] there a little:"* (Isaiah 28:9-10)

Claim these spiritual promises by faith in full assurance that your King James Bible is still a sure Authority. Don't let some over-educated scholar or preacher convince you that the KJV Bible is inaccurate or out of date. That Bible is an inexhaustible source of true knowledge and wisdom. A firm grounding in some of the basics of science and logic will complement a prayerful study of the Scriptures and enhance your understanding, and God's Spirit will reveal those which are true and show which things are not. God is the author and creator of all things, both physical and spiritual. His Scriptures are the Final Authority in all matters, including the science of natural history. What we learn from the geological evidence beneath our feet provides important details to the whole story. That is why it is there. The rocks and fossils, as well as the other things in this world, testify of His workings, glory, and judgment across time and space (Psalm 19).

Chapter 4
Contrasting Major Creation Models

Beginning on the next page, we have included the major Creation Models for comparison purposes. Note that each strength and/or weakness is included with the information.

Of course, we believe that the only model that fits the criteria of an old Earth with a literal seven-day creation period is the Ruin-Reconstruction, or Gap Theory model.

DAY-AGE

- Description:
    - This model is structured on the premise that each of the days in the Genesis narrative represents a period of 1000 years.
- Justification:
    - *"But, beloved, be not ignorant of this one thing, that one day is with the Lord as a thousand years, and a thousand years as one day."* (2 Peter 3:8)
- Logical Faults:
    - If each day was 1000 years long, the plant life made on the 3rd Day would have been in the dark for 1000 years until there was sunshine made on 4th day. 7000 years inadequate time for geologic processes.
- Strengths:
    - None

YOUNG-EARTH

- Description:
    - The young-Earth model proposes (1) that the universe did not come into existence until about 6000 years ago, (2) that the days are literal 24 - hour days, and (3) that the Earth's sediments and oil deposits were produced by Noah's flood.

- Justification:
    - *"For in six days the LORD made heaven and earth, the sea, and all that in them is, and rested the seventh day: wherefore the LORD blessed the sabbath day, and hallowed it."* (Exodus 20:11)

- Logical Faults:
    - The Young-Earth model cannot explain the antiquity of the Earth's Geology as determined by Radio Dating and fossil record.

- Strengths:
    - Adheres to the literal years count of Patriarchs from Adam onward. Allows for literal 7 days Creation.

OLD-EARTH/THEISTIC EVOLUTION

- Description:
    - Blending secular opinion and the Bible, as well as promoting Natural Selection and evolution, this theory states that God was the initiator and guide in the process. Also called Process Creation, Progressive Creation, Intelligent Design. Promotes idea that the Bible's 7 days closely correspond with natural history.

- Justification:
    - Scientifically-proven antiquity of the Earth's natural history based on observations.

- Logical Faults:
    - Cannot account for a literal Adam and Eve. Idea that Bible days correspond with natural history falsified by the fact that evolution holds that sea life came before plant life on land, while Bible's 7 days actually state just the opposite.

- Strengths:

    o Meets the demands of Radio Dating and current scientific theory.

ORGANIC EVOLUTION THEORY

- Description:

    o The basic theory as advocated by Darwin in his book, *Origin of the Species*, and championed by Thomas Huxley, that all present life forms are the end result of a natural process which originally emanated from a microorganism.

- Justification:

    o Accepted scientific theory based on observations without appeals to Divine creation.

- Logical Faults:

    o Completely rejects the notion of Biblical Creation.

- Strengths:

    o Meets demands of Secular Science and all non believers.

OLD-EARTH CREATION RUIN-RECONSTRUCTION (GAP THEORY)

- Description:

    o This model is a refinement of the so-called Gap Theory, and proposes that God created the universe in the ancient past, that it was tainted with death by the rebellion of Lucifer early in its history, and was eventually ruined. God then regenerated the heavens and Earth in six literal 24 - hour days, about 6000 years ago.

- Justification:
    - The Earth was already present before the start of the 7 days (Genesis 1:2).
    - Bible declares previous world was here before the present one (2 Peter 3:5-7).

- Logical Faults:
    - None. As documented in this book and on *www.kjvbible.org* website.

- Strengths:
    - Meets the requirements for both an old-Earth (according to Geology) and a literal 7 - day creative event, including literal Adam.

Chapter 5
Fossils Produced by Noah's Flood? NOT!

Proponents of Young Earth Creationism, who hold to the belief that the planet Earth is only about 6000 years old, preach that the vast sedimentary deposits of the Earth's crust were deposited during Noah's flood, and that all the fossils found within that strata are the result of creatures that died during that flood. The Scriptures, the Earth's geology, and a little reasoning show the fallacy of that belief system.

The Bible says that the Earth's mountains are very, very old. "*And for the chief things of the ancient mountains, and for the precious things of the lasting hills,*" (Deuteronomy 33:15)

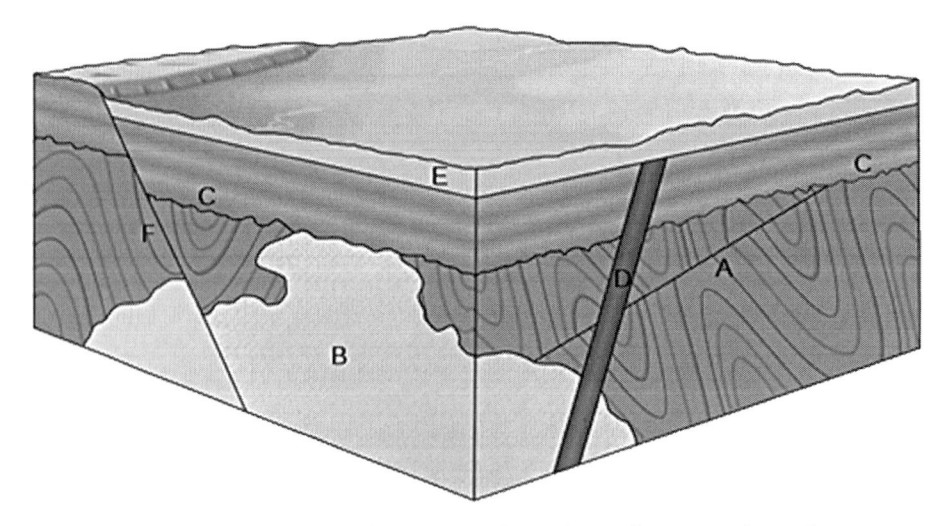

Diagram illustrating cross-cutting relations in geology. These relations can be used to give structures a relative age. Explanations: A - folded rock strata cut by a thrust fault; B - large intrusion (cutting through A); C - erosional angular unconformity (cutting off A & B) on which rock strata were deposited; D - volcanic dyke (cutting through A, B & C); E - even younger rock strata (overlying C & D); F - normal fault (cutting through A, B, C & E).

When Noah's flood occurred, the Scriptures say the waters of the flood covered the tops of the mountains, so the present-day mountains already existed. *"And the waters prevailed, and were increased greatly upon the earth; and the ark went upon the face of the waters. And the waters prevailed exceedingly upon the earth; and all the high hills, that [were] under the whole heaven, were covered. Fifteen cubits upward did the waters prevail; and the mountains were covered."* (Genesis 7:18-20)

Geologic Fact: Portions of most of the Earth's mountain ranges are composed of sedimentary strata or metamorphosed sediments, which contain fossils (the evidence of living creatures long since dead and buried). Three examples are the Appalachian mountain range of the eastern United States (one of the older ones), the Alps of Europe, and the Himalayas. (one of the younger ones).

The sedimentary layers that were uplifted to form these great mountain ranges are many thousands of feet thick in places and well above sea level today. In many places, especially in the older Appalachian range, angular unconformities abound, showing where ancient sediments have been tilted and partially eroded with newer, more horizontal sediments being deposited atop the tilted erosion contact surface.

If these mountains existed before Noah's flood (which the Bible says they did), and these mountains were formed from uplifted sediments containing fossils (go climb a mountain and see them with your own eyes), then the creatures that these fossils came from all died sometime long before the great flood.

In the Appalachian mountain range, you can drive down Interstate Highway 64 from the West Virginia/Kentucky border eastward into Virginia and see deep road cuts exposing repeating sequences of coal, sandstone, siltstone, shale, coal again, shale, etc. The presence of neat, multiple seams of coal in the sequence indicates periods of time

Source: http://www3.uakron.edu/geology/Foos/Energy/pcoal2.html

when the surface of the land was above sea level, allowing vegetation to flourish, die, and accumulate. The sequences of sandstone, shale, siltstone, and the like indicate submerged or delta-associated deposits.

Because it takes vegetation time to grow, die, and accumulate, you can be sure that these kinds of alternating coal/rock sequences, which contain coal seams ranging from inches to several feet thick, required many, many years to form. (Coal is formed from the remains of trees and ferns.)

According to the Bible, Noah's flood only lasted one year; therefore, it is impossible for these seams to have been formed by the single global flood event. These formations are orderly and well differentiated, which is uncharacteristic of deposits left by rapid flooding. In many locations, these sequences, which originally formed in a horizontal position, are now tilted at various angles; some are now vertical, and others have been found to be turned upside down. The tectonic processes to accomplish this require millions of years. You can be sure it occurred long before Noah's days, not during a one-year flood.

Further, if you take the time and effort calculate the amount of carbon in the coal that has already been mined and couple that with the total known deposits that have yet to be mined, there is no possible way that the amount of vegetation required to make that much coal could have been growing on the face of the Earth during any single year.

It takes great pressures and long periods of time for sediments to compact and cement into rock. There was insufficient time in a one-year flood period to produce the massive sedimentary deposits of the Appalachians, to say nothing of the differentiation of all the sedimentary layers. Here is another show-stopper: Whatever materials and debris may have been left on the land after the waters of Noah's flood receded would have been quickly eroded by rains in a few brief years following the flood. That is why there is no remaining widespread physical evidence of a worldwide flood today. When you read our chapters on Noah's flood and the dynamics involved, you will learn that there would have been very little sediment load in the floodwaters outside of what washed down from the mountains of the land areas during the 40 days and nights of torrential rains.

Petroleum (oil) is a complex mixture of hydrocarbons, which occurs in many places in the upper strata (sedimentary rock layers) of the Earth's crust. In some instances, petroleum seeps to the surface.

The La Brea Tar Pits of southern California are an excellent example of such an occurrence. If the sedimentary rocks which contain the petroleum were formed by Noah's flood, where did Noah get the bitumen he used to seal the joints of the Ark to make it waterproof, BEFORE the flood?

"Make thee an ark of gopher wood; rooms shalt thou make in the ark, and shalt pitch it within and without with pitch." (Genesis 6:14)

The English word *pitch* is from the Hebrew word *kopher,* כפר which is bitumen, an asphalt-like form of petroleum.

Speaking of the formation of hydrocarbons like petroleum, here is another interesting fact that the Young Earth Creationists' theories on Noah's flood cannot address: If you add up all of the fossil fuels (coal, natural gas, and oil) consumed on the Earth since 1751 A.D. (roughly the start of the Industrial Revolution), human beings have burned an amount of fossil fuels equal to that which would have required all the plants growing on the Earth over a time span of 13,300 years[1].

---

[1] Discover Magazine April 2004, page 11, "What's in a Gallon of Gas?"

Conclusion: When you honestly think through all these considerations, it becomes quite clear that the fossils of the Earth's sedimentary rock layers have been there a long, long time. Those creatures were dead and buried, and the strata was already present on the planet when we find the Earth without form and void at Genesis 1:2. No other interpretation meets all the criteria of truth. Are we saying that Noah's global flood did not happen? No! What we are saying is that the Earth's sedimentary rocks were not made by Noah's flood and are not the evidence of Noah's flood. The real indirect evidence for Noah's flood is discussed in the chapter titled *Global Dust Spikes and Paleoclimate Indicators*.

Chapter 6

Global Dust Spikes and Paleoclimate Indicators

In July, 1993, the Greenland Ice Sheet Project Two (GISP2) completed drilling down 3,053.44 meters through the ice and 1.55 meters beyond into the underlying bedrock. From this was recovered the deepest ice core record to date. The European Greenland Ice Core Project (GRIP) recovered a core to a depth of 3,028.8 meters at a site 30 kilometers east of GISP2 one year earlier. Comparative data between these two deep cores have allowed scientists to develop an ice core-derived paleoenvironmental record dating back more than 110,000 years BP. (BP means *before present*, and BP is defined as 1950.)

The establishment of this 100,000+ year BP record of Earth's atmospheric history in the ice has been fairly well calibrated with proxy dating methods. The annual layer counting of visible ice stratification, when compared to radiocarbon extracted from the CO_2 gas trapped within the ice and other measurement techniques, has yielded an age error factor of about 2% from present to 11.64 years BP; about 5% to 17.38 years BP; and 10% to about 40,000 years BP. In other words, the ice has been confirmed to be as old as the collective measurements indicate. These data alone destroy the core doctrinal theory held by Young Earth Creationism that the Earth is only about 6,000 years old.

In addition to the actual age of the ice at any given depth in the core, scientists can also determine the mean temperature of the Earth's past climate for different times and ages by measuring the ratio of the isotopes of oxygen (O_{16} and O_{18}) gas present in the CO_2. Full details of this and other techniques as well as further references to GISP2 and GRIP projects can be read in full on the Internet at *The GISP2 Ice Core Record - Paleoclimate Highlights* website.

Secular critics of Young Earth Creationism cite the very existence of the Greenland Ice Sheet and the paleoenvironmental record it contains (as well as the data found in ice cores from the glaciers on Kilimanjaro in Africa and Huascaran in Peru) as absolute proof that the Earth is older than 6,000 years and that Noah's flood did not occur, since there are no indications of a flood in the ice core layers. They are absolutely correct on the first point. On the second point, we disagree that the lack of direct evidence in the ice proves that a global flood did not take place at all. There is certainly much *indirect* evidence to consider.

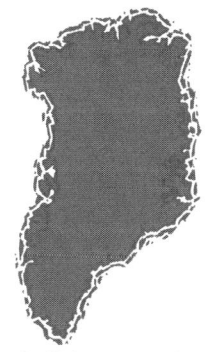

GREENLAND ICE SHEET AND NOAH'S ARK

4,300 *B.P.   4,295 *B.P.

Did the bulk of the material, which constitutes the basement of the present Greenland Ice Sheet somehow survive two floods?

*BP MEANS "BEFORE PRESENT" AND "BP" IS DEFINED AS 1950

The ice core records, whether in Greenland or mountaintop glaciers around the globe, are replete with melt indicators. These are layers in which an indeterminate amount of the surface ice has been melted between accumulations. The resolution of the layer dating at GISP2 is about 3.8 years. Therefore, pinning down a one-year flood sequence to definitively prove or disprove Noah's flood in the ice core record is problematic. It would make no difference whether the ice was floated off its anchor rock by Noah's flood or remained stuck fast to the rock and was submerged by the floodwaters. In either scenario, the top layers would have been washed over by fresh (not salt) water, resulting in a melt layer or hiatus in accumulation. In the former case, this would have occurred by rains, in the latter case, through inundation by a rapidly-rising fresh water lens. (See the chapters on Noah's flood for fresh water explanation.) What is important is the fact that the Greenland Ice Sheet and mountain glaciers exist and have calibrated dated layer points between them. We can learn from these if we know what to look for and where.

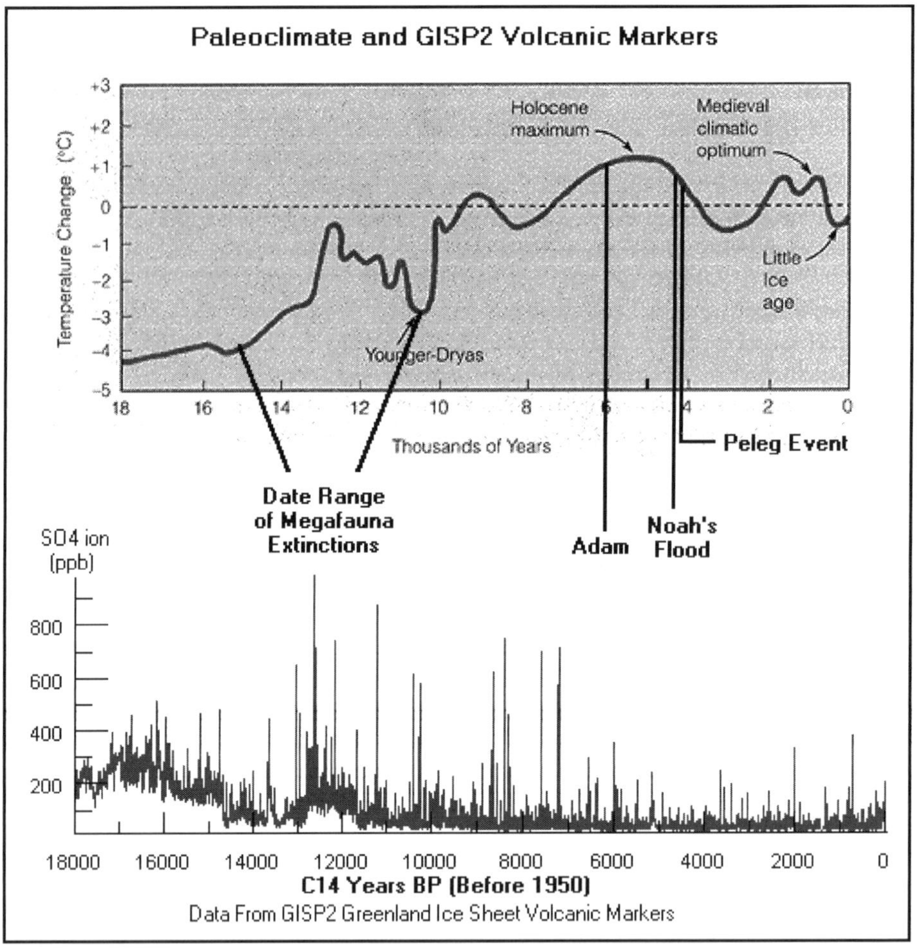

Paleoclimate and GISP2 Volcanic Markers
Temperature Change (°C)
+3
+2
+1
0
-1
-2
-3
-4
-5
Holocene maximum
Medieval climatic optimum
Little Ice age
Younger-Dryas
18
16
14
12
10
8
6
4
2
0
Thousands of Years
Peleg Event
Date Range of Megafauna Extinctions
Adam
Noah's Flood
SO4 ion (ppb)
800
600
400
200
18000
16000
14000
12000
10000
8000
6000
4000
2000
0
C14 Years BP (Before 1950)
Data From GISP2 Greenland Ice Sheet Volcanic Markers

(Top-half of composite Graphic base image from "Meteorology Today" by C. Donald Ahrens © 1994 West Publishing Co.)

If our Bible is true when it tells us Noah's flood was a real and global event that according to the Biblical chronology occurred about 2,345 B.C. (roughly 4,295 BP), and if the GISP2 and GRIP data are also true, the only possible explanation is that the bulk of the material which constitutes the basement of the present Greenland Ice Sheet somehow survived that flood. Actually, it would have needed to survive two floods, as the Earth was also flooded before the six-day regeneration (Genesis 1:2). If that is true, the Paleoclimate data from the ice cores can give us insight into environmental conditions not only *after* the six days of Genesis 1, but also *before* the six days. What has accumulated on the ice since Noah's flood can tell us about the environment from that time until the present.

The top portion of the graphic shows the global temperature trends across 18,000 years before the present as determined by Paleoclimate proxy data. The black lines on the lower left side show where in the timeline the last great mass extinction episode took place according to Paleontology. The black lines on the lower right indicate where Biblical history and events fit into the Earth's Paleoclimate record. The bottom half of the graphic on the previous page shows the GISP2 record for levels of SO_4 ions (acid) in the Earth's atmosphere across the same 18,000 years BP. The ion concentrations reflect relative levels of global volcanic activity at given intervals across the timeline.

The information on the composite graphic reveals several very important things. From the days of Adam until Noah's flood (Holocene Maximum), the Earth's average temperature was about 1° C higher than in the years after the flood. An average temperature elevation of only 1° will translate into temperatures several degrees warmer in the higher latitudes of the Earth. For what it is worth, even with all the millions of tons of so called *greenhouse gases* that have been added to the atmosphere over the last two centuries, the measured greenhouse effect has so far only increased average global temperatures approximately less than half a degree C of what they were before Noah's flood. It is therefore safe to conclude that the world between Adam and Noah was relatively much warmer than our world today.

It should also be pointed out that at the time of Noah's flood (roughly 4,300 years BP), there is no large spike of volcanic markers. This suggests that the Young Earth flood models, all of which are based on suppositions of massive global underwater tectonic and volcanic upheavals, have no basis in fact in the Paleoclimate record. If you will closely examine the bottom section of the chart, you will see that the SO_4 ion concentration at 4,300 years BP shows the very lowest levels measured across the entire 18,000 BP-year timeline. This is in sharp contrast to the heightened volcanic activity on the Earth at the time of the Pleistocene extinctions and through the period immediately before the creation of Adam and the six days of the Earth's regeneration. This level of volcanic markers is unequaled in the period 6,000 years to the present. This volcanic activity was obviously a contributing factor (or at least a component) to the death of the old world order.

Returning to the graph at the top of the chart, we see the Earth's climate temperature rapidly dropping roughly 1.8° C beginning about 4,300 BP. That is well within the exact time frame directly following Noah's flood. This would be consistent with a relatively sudden and dramatic climate change, the introduction of very pronounced yearly weather seasons, or both. The Bible alludes to such a change occurring directly after the flood. *"While the earth remaineth, seedtime and harvest, and cold and heat, and summer and winter, and day and night shall not cease."* (Genesis 8:22)

It is extremely interesting that the Greenland Ice Sheet, the Mount Kilimanjaro glacier in Africa, the Huascaran glacier in Peru, and even the undersea sediments of the Gulf of Oman, all have anomalous indicators that correlate to approximately 4,300 to 4ka years BP. These have been interpreted as markers that suggest extreme climate changes theorized to have precipitated the collapse of many ancient civilizations. The Old Kingdom of Egypt and the Akkadian Empire of Mesopotamia are two examples that appear in published works.

In these papers on historical environmental extremes (which can be *Googled* on the Internet), there appears to be a recurring pattern of great drought, abandonment of settlements, and delayed reoccupation of the abandoned settlements. Google the Internet article titled *Climate change and the collapse of the Akkadian Empire: Evidence from the deep-sea.* In another article titled *Sea Floor Dust,* the following are noted:

1. The time frame, determined by radiocarbon dating, is 4,170 BP +/- 150 cal yrs. That fits the time of Noah's flood (within the dating margin of error).

2. Note the sharp spike in $CACO_3$ and dolomite in the sediments of the Gulf of Oman and their abrupt spike date of 4,194 BP. Again, taking the margin of error into account, it fits the post-flood times.

3. Note that the author attributes the sediments in the Gulf of Oman to dust blown in from neighboring land areas, thus the conclusion that it indicates a great drought.

4. Note the observation that the settlements remained abandoned for nearly 300 years.

The author of the paper correctly deduced from the data that a sudden and dramatic climate change occurred, severe drought conditions began, and the settlements were abandoned, all at about the time indicated by the radiocarbon measurement of the organic artifacts cited. The author did not identify the cause of climate shift or prove that the drought caused the abandonment of the settlements, but he made an assumption on the latter based on the evidence and the thesis of the work.

Needless to say, the author never even considered the possibility that the cause of the sudden and extreme climate shift may have had something to do with Noah's flood.

You ask, "What can a drought and dust possibly have to do with a global flood?" Everything!!!

Applying the same data to a different thesis, I submit that following a global flood, the Earth would have experienced catastrophic drought conditions shortly after the waters abated; the dust anomaly is evidence of this. It can be argued that it was not the drought that caused the sudden abandonment of the Akkadian Empire settlements. It was Noah's flood that caused it, drowning out the inhabitants. The drought conditions (which would have followed the flood because much of the Earth's vegetation had perished, leaving little or nothing with living root systems to hold the soil down) would be predictable. The settlements would have remained abandoned for many years until the descendants of Noah's family multiplied and began to spread out across the Earth. Eventually they would have migrated back into the area and occupied it when conditions were again favorable for sustaining an agricultural-based city-state.

If this were the true scenario, those climate effects would be almost global, and there would be similar climate and dust anomalies elsewhere on Earth corresponding to the same historical time frame.

There is just such evidence found in the ice cores extracted from Mount Kilimanjaro in Africa and across the Atlantic in the Huascaran glacier, high in the Peruvian Andes of the southern hemisphere.

On the following page are two graphs. The top graph shows three data sets from the Huascaran glacier. Notice the extremely pronounced dust spike and the time frame, roughly 4.3ka (the time of Noah's Flood). The second graph shows a similar dust signature found in the Gulf of Oman. As you can see, the dust signature found in Huascaran, several thousand miles and an ocean away from the Gulf of Oman, and the common nature of the indicator (dust) and its time frame (>4ka), match closely enough within the margin of error to be more than a coincidental correlation. The event-sequence timeline of the Akkadian Empire settlement (Imperialization, Collapse, and Resettlement) also matches exactly as it should.

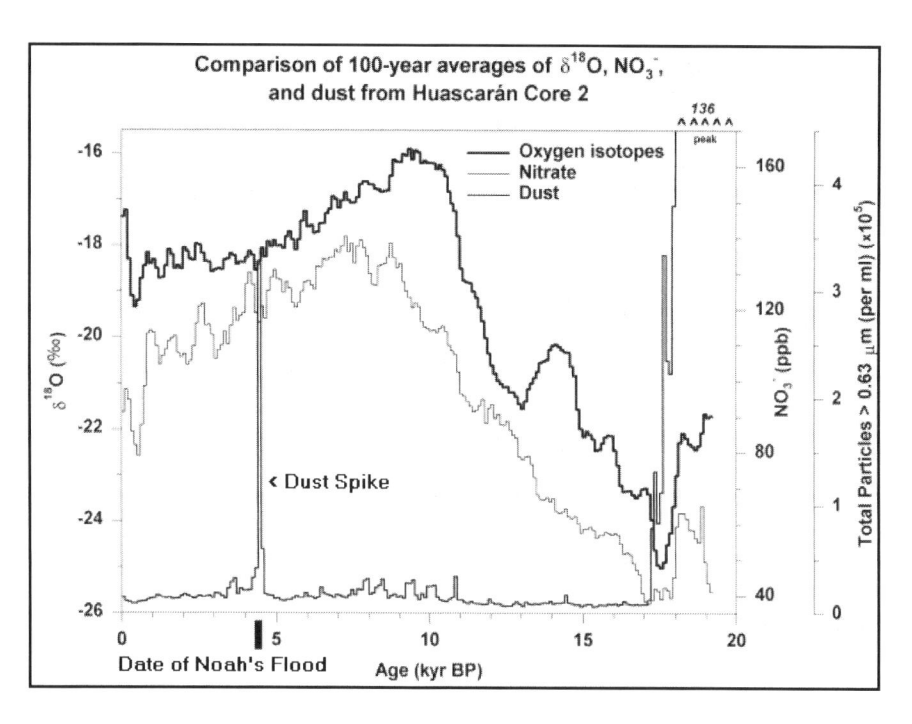

Adapted from chart at:
http://www.ngdc.noaa.gov/paleo/pubs/thompson1995/huascaran.html *website.*

The data presented in another Internet article about the Mount Kilimanjaro Ice Core also show evidence of a dust indicator in the same time frame and suggest that the climate event was connected to the collapse of several ancient civilizations, including the Old

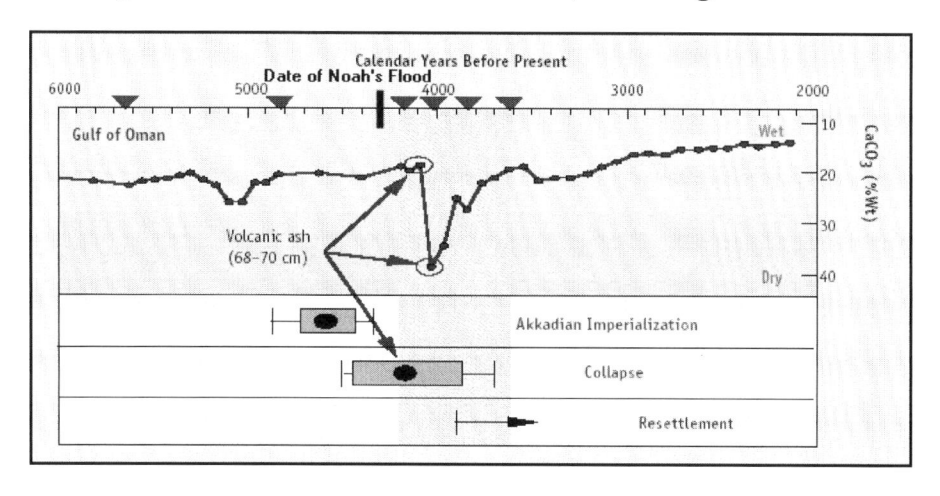

Kingdom of Egypt. Additional supporting evidence is found in sediment samples from beneath the waters of Lake Tana, high in the Ethiopian Highlands. This lake feeds the Nile, and the samples reveal the lake may have dried up approximately 4,200 years ago.

Note: You will find live links to all these mentioned articles on the Bible, Genesis & Geology website at *http://www.kjvbible.org*

Coincidentally, archeological/astronomical evidence found in the remains of the Old Kingdom of Egypt suggests that the Earth may have also tilted on its axis because of Noah's flood. Physicists say that a flood on the Earth of the magnitude of the Biblical proportions claimed would indeed have caused an axis shift, which would most certainly contribute to global changes in weather patterns.

On the Bible, Genesis & Geology website, we note another link reference to the temple of Karnak in Egypt, where the article indicated that "something happened in 2,345" concerning the tilt of stone markers. This caught our interest because the time of Noah's flood was also about 2,345 B.C. (4,295 years B.P.) You should really read this one.

Because the temple of Karnak obviously survived the flood, this tells us that the flood was relatively tranquil, drowning out the antediluvian population without wholesale destruction of the relics of those antediluvian civilizations. Certainly, that fact alone contradicts all those cataclysmic, hydro-plate sliding, underwater volcano mountain building, Grand Canyon gouging models proposed in most Creation Science flood models floating around today. It just did not happen that way.

A valid argument which deserves a response concerns the Greenland Ice Sheet and the mountain glaciers. How could the ice have survived Noah's flood? Some claim that if there were such a flood, the ice sheet and the mountain glaciers would have floated off from the bedrock and broken up, but the continuity of the ice core record shows no such breakup. Others contend the ice would have remained stuck in place, become submerged, and would have contained flood evidence in the ice strata marking the event.

Keep in mind that in either case, a portion of the top layers of ice and snow would have been melted or washed away, leaving no evidence but an indicator of a melt episode or hiatus in accumulation. The renewed new accumulation that followed Noah's flood would only be indicative of post-flood days. The accumulation of the dust spikes previously discussed would be such a post-flood deposition. But could the ice sheet or glaciers remain fast to the Earth and be washed over?

Ice floats, but not under all conditions.

Try this experiment. Take a cupful of ice cubes from your freezer, pour them into a metal or stoneware bowl, and place the bowl in the freezer for a couple of hours. After a couple of hours, remove the bowl, set it on the counter, and quickly pour a glass of tap water over the ice inside the bowl. You will find that the ice will remain stuck to the bottom of the bowl, completely submerged under the water until the bowl's surface warms enough to melt the bond. If you transfer this concept to something on the scale of a mountain glacier, it takes an extended period of time for the bedrock to warm or for water to seep under in order to dissolve a more extensive bond.

The massive Greenland Ice Sheet may be a little different story. Although the fresh water from Noah's flood would certainly be much less buoyant than heavier sea water (meaning less pressure on the ice to float off), the sheer scale of the Ice Sheet could make a stress breakup unavoidable even if the bottom of the sheet were frozen fast to the continent.

The temperature at the bottom of the GISP2 bore hole is -9° C and indicates that the ice sheet is frozen tight to the bedrock. From the top of the ice sheet down to about 2,790 meters, both the GISP2 and GRIP records are nearly identical. Since these two holes are about 30 km apart, it indicates that the composition of the ice record is consistent across a large area, or at least between those two holes.

However, the continuity vanishes below 2,790 meters. Below is a quote from a portion of the previously-referenced, *The GISP2 Ice Core Record - Paleoclimate Highlights* website:

The climatic significance of the deeper part of the GISP2 ice core, below 2790 m depth and 110 kyr age, is a matter of considerable investigation and controversy. The isotopic temperature records and electrical conductivity records of GISP2 and GRIP, so similar for ice <110 kyr in age, are very different in the lower part [Grootes et al., 1993; Taylor et al., 1993a]. Ice in GISP2 below 2790 m depth is folded and tilted, and shows evidence of unconformities [Gow et al., 1993].

This finding of folded and tilted layers and unconformities gives support to the possibility that the massive ice sheet may have been fractured and was lifted off by the global flood of Noah's time, or possibly the earlier flood found at Genesis 1:2. After floating free, the massive sheet would have remained fairly well within the same northern latitudes during such an event (held relatively stationary due to northward-tending currents induced by Earth's Coriolis Force [effect]), and very little would have melted. As the flood waters receded, the ice sheet would then gently settle back down and eventually fuse over the submerged ice that had not broken away because the remaining bottom ice was still frozen solid to the bedrock.

Bottom line: This question will remain open until further data collection can provide the answers.

Chapter 7

Fountains of the Deep

T he Bible says that the waters of Noah's flood covered all of the Earth to above the peaks of the tallest mountains. *"And the waters prevailed exceedingly upon the earth; and all the high hills, that were under the whole heaven, were covered. Fifteen cubits upward did the waters prevail; and the mountains were covered."* (Genesis 7:19-20)

If this flood was literal and global, then we are confronted with the Mount Everest problem. Located in Nepal, Mount Everest is the

Earth's highest peak. It is also the highest peak in a range of mountains stretching across 1,500 miles and containing more than 1000 peaks higher than 20,000 feet.

Mount Everest is presently at a height of 29,028 feet above sea level and getting taller at the rate of about 3-5 millimeters per year. Assuming the tectonic uplift rate of the Himalayan range has been uniform since the days of Noah's flood, Mount Everest would have been only about forty-three (43) feet shorter (28,985 ft.) back in Noah's day. That is still a considerable height, equal to about 5.5 miles above present sea level. It would take a lot of water for the flood to reach that depth - more water than is presently above the crust of the Earth. Where did so much water come from, and where did it go after the flood?

Before answering that question, let's put this puzzle into perspective. Our Earth is about 25,000 miles in circumference. If it were compared to the size of a basketball, the Earth's crust would be about as thick as a sheet of tissue paper wrapped around it. In a global perspective, 5.5 miles of water above today's sea level is a relatively minute quantity, increasing overall circumference by only 0.044%. Of course, to people approximately five to six feet in stature, 5.5 miles is a lot. The thing to keep in mind is perspective.

Many Young Earth Creationists espouse the theory that most of the Earth's mountains and sedimentary rock strata were formed underwater during Noah's flood by massive global volcanic and tectonic activity. They then conclude that because the mountains formed during the flood, not as much water was needed to cover the Earth to fifteen cubits above the highest mountain as Genesis 7:20 requires. Nice try, but no prize.

That answer does not meet the Scriptural or geophysical requirements, as the Bible clearly says (see the verses above) that the mountains were already there, and by implication, the continents and tectonic plates were in their present-day locations (give or take a hundred yards to account for 4,000+ years of continental drift). Additionally, the alleged underwater volcanic and tectonic activity on such a massive scale as proposed by Young Earth Creation Science models, would have produced a great deal of acid, which would be detectable as SO_4 ions in the Greenland Ice Sheet core record. As you read in the previous chapter, that evidence is simply not there.

Instead of taking the usual approach - that Noah's Flood could not have happened because of this or that fact - let's approach the problem from this angle. Noah's Flood happened because the Bible is true; so let's try to find answers that can fit the facts, both scientific and Biblical. After all, Jesus Himself confirmed that the flood was a real event, so there must be an explanation. First, let us closely examine the exact wording of the Bible to begin determining the correct answers to this mystery.

"And God said unto Noah, The end of all flesh is come before me; for the earth is filled with violence through them; and, behold, I will destroy them with the earth." (Genesis 6:13)

Notice that the Lord says the agency of destruction would be the Earth itself. The planet Earth has three spheres: the core, mantle, crust (lithosphere); the seas (hydrosphere); and the air in the heaven above (several atmospheric levels). All three played a part in the destruction of the antediluvian world, so the complete answer is not necessarily confined to geology alone.

"In the six hundredth year of Noah's life, in the second month, the seventeenth day of the month, the same day were all the fountains of the great deep broken up, and the windows of heaven were opened. And the rain was upon the earth forty days and forty nights." (Genesis 7:11-12)

"The fountains also of the deep and the windows of heaven were stopped, and the rain from heaven was restrained;" (Genesis 8:2)

According to the Scriptures, there were two related sources for the rains and waters of Noah's flood. There were *fountains* of water coming up out of the Earth, and there was water coming down from the *windows* of heaven. We will deal with the matter of the fountains first, as they began first and triggered a complex chain reaction from below the Earth's crust that affected things far into the upper atmosphere.

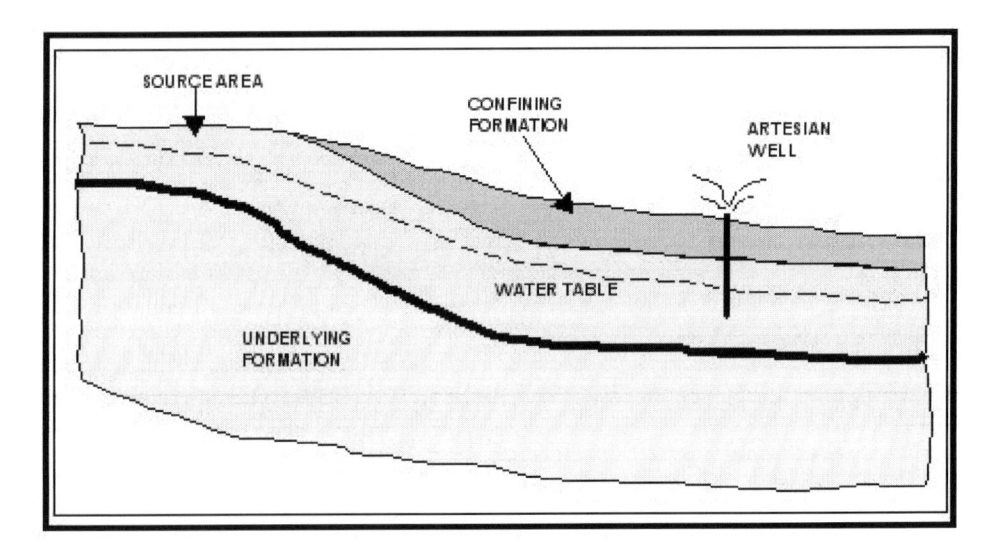

Two types of water fountains occur in nature. One is called an Artesian well/spring. Artesian wells occur when a hole penetrates into the Earth to a region where internal pressure causes the water to flow upward like a fountain.

The internal pressure that drives such fountains is produced when the head of the particular water table penetrated is at a higher elevation than the spring opening. The principle is similar to the gravity pressure that drives water out of your sink tap because the city water supply is stored in an elevated tower.

The second type of fountain is called a geyser. Geysers occur when waters in underground chambers are heated by the surrounding host rock until the pressure and temperature cause them to flash to steam and erupt upward. When the chamber is emptied, replacement water flows back into the chamber, the replacement water is heated, and the cycle repeats. An excellent example of this is seen in Yellowstone National Park's Old Faithful geyser.

According to what is written in the Scriptures, the fountains of Noah's flood may have been a similar form of geyser activity on a massive, world-wide scale, concentrated along the mid-oceanic ridge system. A careful reading of Genesis 7:6-10 seems to indicate that the flood waters were already rising for about seven days before the fountains were broken up (verse 11).

"And Noah was six hundred years old when the flood of waters was upon the earth. And Noah went in, and his sons, and his wife, and his sons' wives with him, into the ark, because of the waters of the flood. Of clean beasts, and of beasts that are not clean, and of fowls, and of every thing that creepeth upon the earth, There went in two and two unto Noah into the ark, the male and the female, as God had commanded Noah. And it came to pass after seven days, that the waters of the flood were upon the earth. In the six hundredth year of Noah's life, in the second month, the seventeenth day of the month, the same day were all the fountains of the great deep broken up, and the windows of heaven were opened. And the rain was upon the earth forty days and forty nights." (Genesis 7:6-12)

Careful parsing of the above passage indicates that great amounts of water were already being added to the Earth's seas at least seven days before the rains even began. This means that sea level was already rapidly rising, flooding low-lying coastal areas, and sending panicked lowland inhabitants inland from the rising seas. Meanwhile, presumably on much higher ground, Noah and his family took shelter on the Ark and waited, while the massive gopher wood vessel remained firmly nested in its construction frame, unmovable and secure until the rising waters lifted it from its resting place.

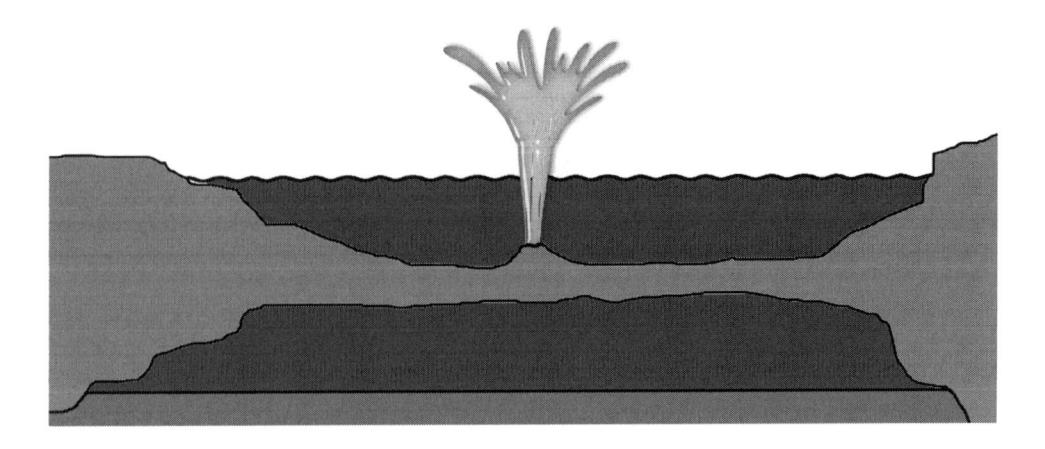

The great volume of water this early in the flood event could only come from massive undersea fountains beginning to breech the crust all along the mid-oceanic ridge system. But this preliminary inflow was still insufficient to breech the ocean's surface. The volume of underwater displacement would, however, be sufficient enough to generate global tsunami (tidal wave) activity, quickly drowning inhabitants who lived near the seas.

Seven days into the flood, the undersea fountains broke through the crust in full fury, and the pressure of the flow sent scalding columns of superheated waters upward, breeching the ocean's surface and erupting skyward as a globe-encircling curtain of steam rocketing into the upper atmosphere. As the steam came into contact with the colder air, it would condense and produce cloud cover and relentless rainfall on a planetary scale. This is precisely the sequence of events described in this part of the passage:

"In the six hundredth year of Noah's life, in the second month, the seventeenth day of the month, the same day were all the fountains of the great deep broken up, and the windows of heaven were opened. And the rain was upon the earth forty days and forty nights." (Genesis 7:11-12)

This first passage (at the beginning of the flood) says that the rains did not begin until AFTER the fountains of the great deep are broken up.

"The fountains also of the deep and the windows of heaven were stopped, and the rain from heaven was restrained;" (Genesis 8:2)

The second passage says the rains ceased only AFTER the fountains stopped. This is fully consistent with the proposed geyser model.

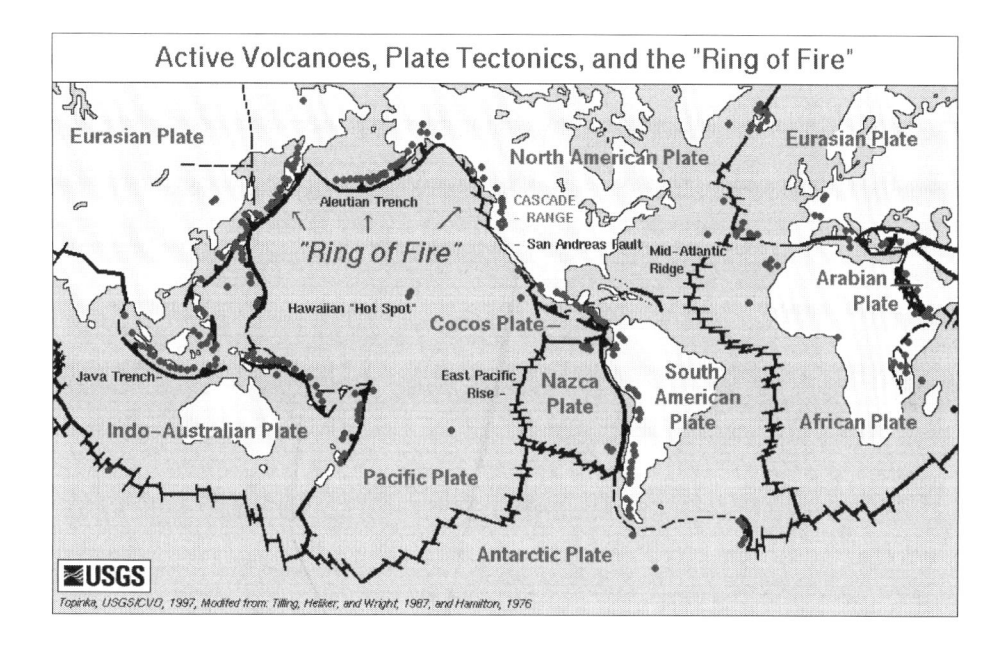

As briefly mentioned earlier, the most likely geological location for the fountains (geysers) was along a narrow, globe encircling series of underwater Tectonic Plate boundaries called the mid-oceanic ridges, where the Earth's oceanic crust is currently spreading apart at the rate of a few centimeters per year. On a map of the Earth's sea floors, this continuous system of faults is seen running south down the middle of the Greenland Sea and the North and South Atlantic Oceans. It then extends eastward into the Indian Ocean basin, onward between Australia and Antarctica, and into the great Pacific Ocean basin. It then continues northward along the eastern side of the Pacific basin.

Editors Note: Scientists are beginning to study what they term as a large *open wound* where the Earth's oceanic crust is missing, deep under the Atlantic Ocean near that ridge system. What scientists are keen to know is whether the crust was ripped away by huge geological faults, or whether it never developed in the first place. Could this be an actual location where the fountains of the great deep were broken up as the Bible indicates? There is a link on the Bible, Genesis & Geology website, where you can read the story titled *Serpentinite not crust, scientists to find out how part of Earth's crust went missing.*

The geysers' source would have been extensive underground reservoirs of magma supersaturated with water that had collected in the regions below the boundary of the oceanic crust and above the underlying mantle region.

Here is an important question to note: Why would magma, supersaturated with water, only accumulate under the crust of the oceans and not under the continents? There are two reasons. First, since water is much lighter than rock, it would have gravitated upward until it was blocked by the crust. It would then have tended to pool between the Crust-Mantle boundaries. Second, because the

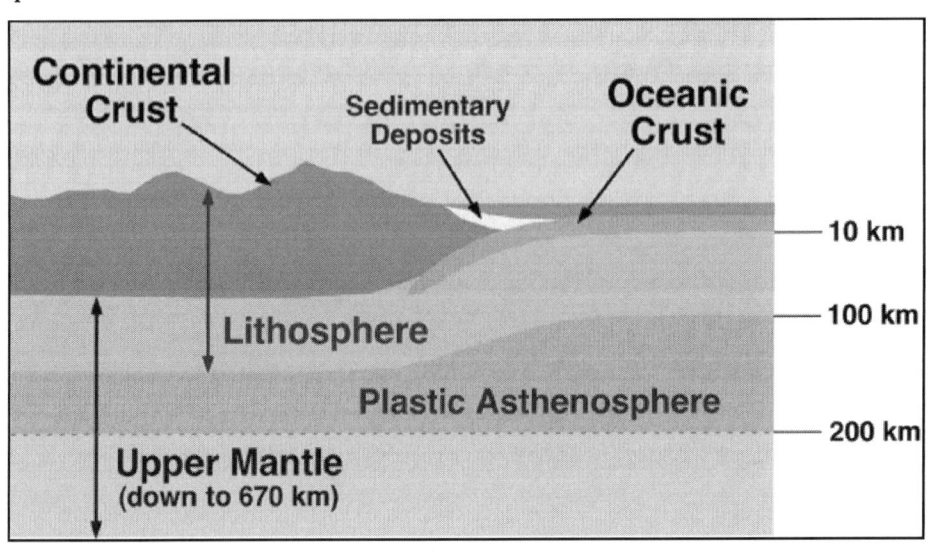

Graphic from http://www.geog.ouc.bc.ca/physgeog/contents/images/lithosphere.gif

Earth's crust is much thinner under the ocean floors (5 - 12 km) than under the continents (35 km average), it would have naturally pooled where the Earth's crust was thinnest - under the basaltic oceanic basins, which ride higher on the mantle. The underground region where this water-saturated magma would have collected is above a zone called the Asthenosphere, commonly known as the Mohorovic discontinuity. The behavior of seismic waves passing through that region appears to show relative liquidity as compared to the rock in the regions above and below it.

Scientists are just now finding evidence to confirm the presence of large volumes of water deep inside the Earth, enough to fill Earth's ocean basins 10 times over. Only a fraction of such an amount would be required to raise sea levels to meet the requirements of Noah's flood. By the way, long before scientists learned there were vast amounts of water under the Earth, the Bible already hinted at this fact (Exodus 20:4).

If a large volume of water-saturated magma had pooled under the Earth's ocean basins, it is probable that the oceans were much shallower then compared to the Post-Flood times of today. Earth's sedimentary geology is replete with evidence of shallow-water depositions. That same geology reveals fluctuations in global sea levels across geologic time that greatly exceed what could possibly be caused by accumulations and melting at the polar caps. One of the possible explanations put forth to explain this mystery is sea floor warping and periodic accumulations and releases of waters from supersaturated magma, as proposed in this model, which could account for this observation. In addition, it would be more likely that a rupture in the crust would occur and these waters would be released if the accumulation of magma below the oceanic crust was placing great upward pressure against the crust.

Therefore, we will assume that at the time just before Noah's flood, the seas were more shallow than today. If this was indeed the case, then explaining how much of the flood waters rapidly receded becomes simple to explain.

Basic law of Physics: For every action there is an equal and opposite reaction.

After the great volumes of flood waters which were formerly trapped below the Earth's oceanic crust jetted upward, condensed, and fell into the regions above the oceanic crust, they quickly began to produce an accumulative great reverse pressure on the thin crust of the ocean floor.

In the meantime, because of the sudden release of great pressure in the supersaturated magma below the crust, there would have been a relative cooling effect on the remaining magma body. This cooling, along with the loss of the volatiles (the waters), would reduce the density of the underlying magma, causing a reduction in volume. In other words, the volume of the magma would shrink. This would further increase the pressure differential.

Combining this with the weight of the released waters accumulating above the crust would then cause the floor of the ocean to bow downward until pressures reached equilibrium. This means that the ocean basins would deepen, and the flood waters would recede from the land as the waters flowed in to fill the enlarged basins.

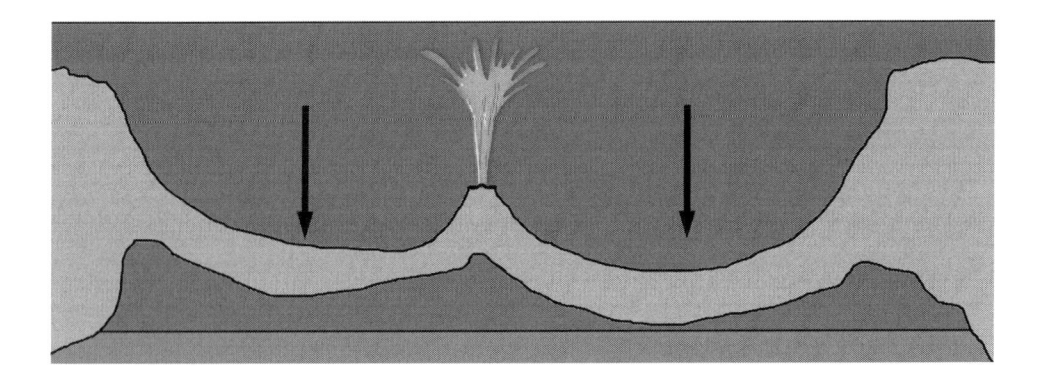

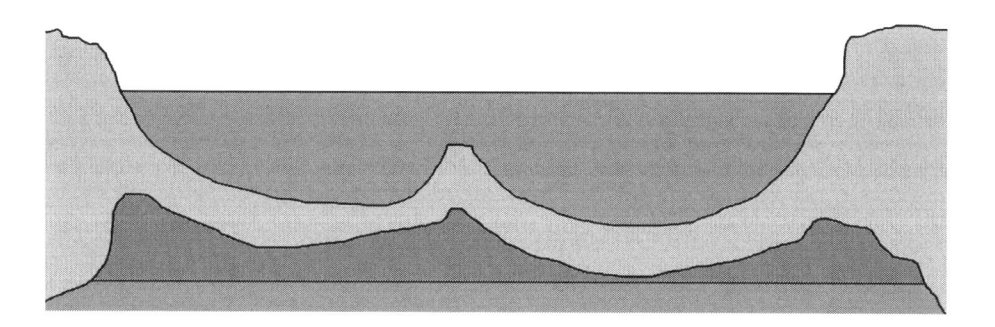

Based on sea mount and Continental Shelf evidence discussed in detail in our chapter titled *Days of Peleg and Sea Level Changes*, sea levels after Noah's flood abated are about 1,000 meters higher today than they were before the flood.

This downward warping of the ocean floors and the mid-oceanic ridge system can be clearly seen in a very detailed, full color Global Relief Map graphic provided by NOAA that can be viewed on the Bible, Genesis & Geology website.

In addition to the downward basin warping, another geological mechanism may have also been at work in drawing down the flood waters. For the first time, scientists have recently documented a new phenomenon at sea floor spreading ridges, where water has been observed being sucked into the porous mix of rock and sediment beneath the ocean. Simply stated, an indeterminate volume of the floodwaters may have been recaptured back into the Earth's subsurface after the geyser activity ceased.

That is the basic proposed geologic component of the Flood Model. In the next chapter, you will learn about the complex chain reaction this triggered in the Earth's atmosphere and the resultant changes that sharply decreased the life span of man on this side of the flood.

Before proceeding to other aspects of the event, we need to address an objection to this geologic model posed by accepted plate tectonic theory. If sea floor spreading and volcanic activity along the mid-oceanic ridge has been ongoing for millions of years, what explains this anomalous eruption of waters at this particular point in the Earth's history? This is a fair question for which I only have a Biblical answer.

Allow me to point your attention back to the seven days of Genesis and the restoration of the Earth and heavens during the six days of the Lord's work. Just before the Lord began His work, the Earth and the solar system were strewn with waters (Genesis 1:2). The Lord then divided the waters from under the firmament from those He placed above the firmament (Genesis 1:6). On the following day, He caused the waters remaining on the Earth's surface to be gathered into one place so that the dry land appeared (Genesis 1:10). Exactly how the Lord accomplished this is not said, but it seems logical that He somehow made some of the water go underground. This is suggested in an obscure comment in the Book of Proverbs that may shed some light on the matter.

In Proverbs chapter eight, the Spirit of Wisdom tells us how she has been with the Lord since before He first created the heaven and Earth, and also with Him at the time He did the regeneration work of the six days. In reference to the latter, the following is said:

"When he prepared the heavens, I was there: when he set a compass upon the face of the depth: When he established the clouds above: when he strengthened the fountains of the deep: When he gave to the sea his decree, that the waters should not pass his commandment: when he appointed the foundations of the earth:" (Proverbs 8:27-29)

This passage seems to indicate that through some agency not clearly understood, the Lord caused some of the waters on the Earth to go underground. The reader will note that in the days of Adam, the vegetation of the Earth was watered by a mist that came up out of the ground.

"And every plant of the field before it was in the earth, and every herb of the field before it grew: for the LORD God had not caused it to rain upon the earth, and there was not a man to till the ground. But there went up a mist from the earth, and watered the whole face of the ground." (Genesis 2:5-6)

This mist seems to indicate that there was a great deal of heated water present under the Earth relatively close to the surface, or at least making its way to the surface at various places in order to produce this mist. These waters may have also been the underground feed source for the river that flowed out of Eden. The Divine reconfiguration of the Earth's geology at this particular time is the only possible explanation. Surely, the Lord knew that He had created an unstable situation that would eventually cause the flood centuries later in the days of Noah. This is not a scientific answer, but it is theologically sound given our understanding of God's omnipotence and foreknowledge.

There is a theoretical scientific possibility. Marvin Herndon, Ph.D., has proposed that there is a naturally-occurring nuclear reactor at the Earth's core. His model proposes that activity cycles of this reactor appear to correspond with the reversals of the Earth's magnetic polls. Perhaps at this point in historic time, this postulated Georeactor at the Earth's core came out of a low activity cycle and began generating higher-than-normal-levels of heat energy, driving large volumes of water upward and, in the course of time, precipitating the Noahic flood anomaly. There were fluctuations in the intensity of Earth's magnetic field at about this time, evidenced by fluctuations in observed C^{14} levels. This would certainly be consistent with the Georeactor model, but that is only conjecture. For your information, we also have a link to Dr. Herndon's paper on the Bible, Genesis & Geology website.

The bottom line is that however they came to be, the geologic conditions that produced the massive geysers of Noah's days no longer exist. Therefore, there can be no repeat of this activity on such a great scale. (See Genesis 9:15 for confirmation.) In other words, the very mechanics and conditions that produced the great flood event self-destructed upon completion of the flood event cycle; thus the geologic changes became permanent. So, unlike the Old Faithful geyser, this was a one-time event.

In our next chapter titled *Windows of Heaven,* we will discuss why the age span of mankind greatly decreased after the flood. We will also explain how Noah and his family, to say nothing of all sea creatures, survived being parboiled by the heat released when the massive geysers erupted in the middle of the Earth's great oceans.

Chapter 8
Windows of Heaven

Before we discuss the atmospheric chain reaction that was triggered by the Fountains of the Deep, and the complexity of the *Windows of Heaven* component of the flood model (Genesis 7:11-12), we need to consider one of the most notable post-flood effects. According to the Bible, the life spans of mankind dropped almost exponentially following the flood. Obviously, something in the Earth's post-flood environment was very different than before Noah's flood because before the flood, man lived to be

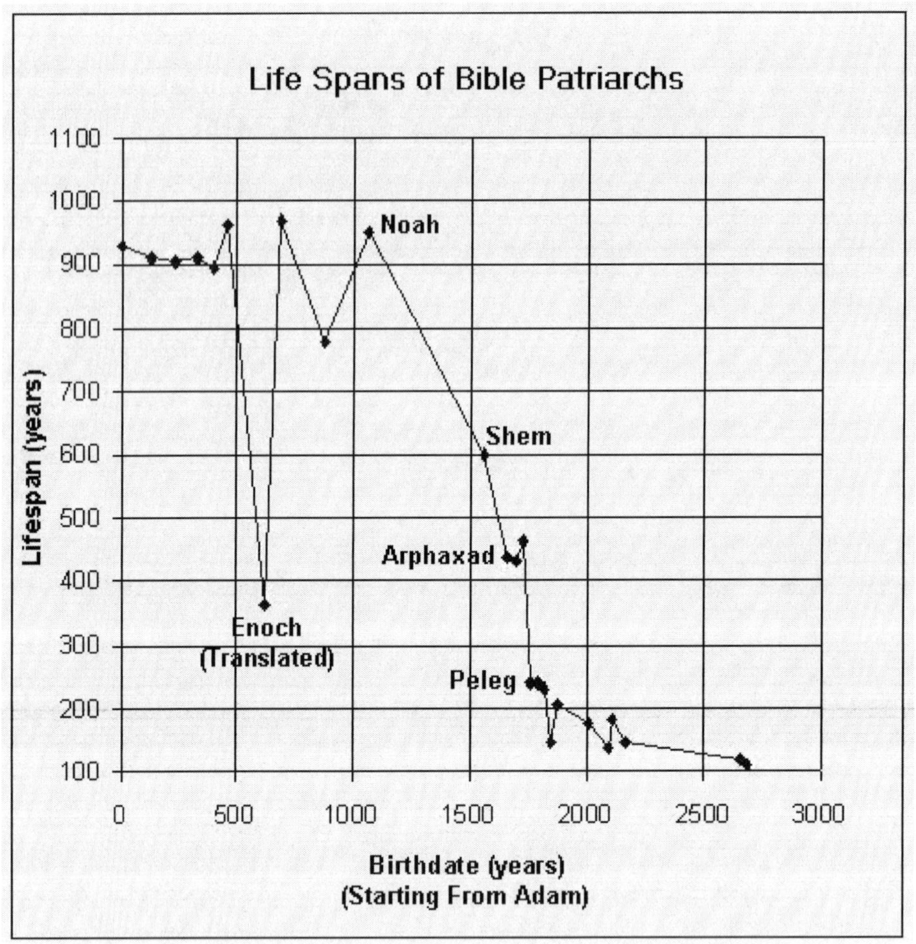
Life Spans of Bible Patriarchs
1100
1000
900
800
700
600
500
400
300
200
100
Lifespan (years)
Noah
Shem
Arphaxad
Enoch
(Translated)
Peleg
0
500
1000
1500
2000
2500
3000
Birthdate (years)
(Starting From Adam)

just short of 1,000 years old. Above is a life span graph showing the ages of 23 men of the Bible from Adam to Joseph.

The life spans drop sharply immediately following and during the 101- year interval between the flood event and the significant post-flood event in the days of Peleg. It then slowly levels out to a less steep decline in the days of the Patriarchs of Israel.

"And unto Eber were born two sons: the name of one was Peleg; for in his days was the earth divided; and his brother's name was Joktan." (Genesis 10:25)

"And unto Eber were born two sons: the name of the one was Peleg; because in his days the earth was divided: and his brother's name was Joktan." (1 Chronicles 1:19)

In attempts to scientifically explain this phenomenon, many agents have been proposed. Possible explanations for the decrease in human life spans range from an increase in the amount of radiation reaching the Earth's surface after the flood to changes in the atmosphere's pressure or composition, or a combination of factors.

An analysis of the graph reveals that Noah, who was born 600 years before the flood, lived only 350 years after the flood but had a total life span of 950 years, only 19 years less than Methuselah. His son, Shem, who was born only 98 years before the flood, lived 500 years after the flood but had a total life span of only 598 years, or about 2/3 the life span of his father. This data suggest that the level of physical body maturity at the time of the flood may hold the key to understanding the long life spans of antediluvian mankind. In other words, children remained children longer, reached puberty later, and their bodies stayed healthier through a greatly-extended adulthood.

Support for this assumption comes from the Bible chronology and the notations of when pre-flood men fathered their first offspring. In the *Book of the Generations of Adam* (Genesis chapter 5), observe the age of listed men and how old they were when they begat their first children: Adam 130 years, Seth 105 years, Enos 90 years, Cainan 70 years, Mahalaleel 65 years, Jared 162 years, Enoch 65 years, etc. See that pattern? It tends to indicate that men did not become sexually mature until at least 60 or 70 years of age. And those who had their first children many years past that maturity point (e.g., Jared 162, Methuselah 187, Lamech 182, and Noah 500), probably restrained from procreation for social or religious reasons. The bottom line is that pre-flood men of the age of 50 to 60 years were physiologically equivalent to today's teenagers.

Did Atmospheric Pressure Keep People Younger, Longer?

Pre-flood men of the age of 50 to 60 years were physiologically equivalent to today's teenagers.

In researching the cause of these greatly-expanded pre-flood age spans, my first inclination was that this must somehow be connected with the functioning of the human pituitary gland. However, what was different after the flood that could cause the aging process to accelerate? I considered increased amounts of solar and cosmic radiation in the post-flood world as a possibility, but the existence of C^{14} in organics dating from before and up to the time of Adam ruled out cosmic radiation. I considered the possibility that perhaps the atmosphere of the Earth back in those days may have filtered out some other form of solar radiation. This could have been part of the answer but did not seem to be enough by itself.

Recently, while reading an article about hyperbaric oxygen (HBO) therapy for treating injuries, the answer came in a bolt of inspiration. Much of the reason men lived longer in pre-flood days was because the Earth's atmospheric pressure was considerably higher, and man was originally made to thrive in a higher-pressure atmospheric environment.

I arrived at this conclusion after studying the subject more closely. In Hyperbaric therapy, a person is placed in a pressurized chamber, and the air pressure is increased 1 to 2 times the normal sea level atmospheric pressure (14.7 psi). Under the increased air pressure, more oxygen gets into the bloodstream. This process seems to accelerate healing of wounds, promote tissue repair, and even favorably affect metabolic rates and the performance of the hormonal systems. In fact, there appears to be a wide range of medical benefits from living in a pressurized environment. It almost seems to be something that should be natural. So why isn't the world like that today if such conditions are so naturally beneficial? Perhaps it was the natural order of things before the flood.

If that was indeed the case, men and women age more rapidly and start dying sooner these days because they are living in conditions that are not optimal for their original biological design, thanks to the great flood.

Note: A comprehensive study of hyperbolic oxygen therapy and benefits is outside the immediate scope of this essay, but I have placed a couple of additional links on the subject at the end of this chapter for your further reading.

If the antediluvian world had a much higher atmospheric pressure, then a large volume of Earth's atmospheric gas has since vanished. How and why? We can assume that the ratio of the various gases in the atmosphere at that time was similar to today (i.e., nitrogen 78.1%, oxygen 20.9%, argon 0.9%, carbon dioxide 0.035%, water vapor, and other gases), otherwise the difference in chemical composition would show up in the polar Ice Core measurements.

Some of our Young Earth Creationist brethren have also reached the conclusion that the antediluvian world had a much higher atmospheric pressure. They also cite the benefits of hyperbaric oxygen as a possible contribution to the longevity of pre-flood mankind. Good for them. Every once in a while they get one right But they attribute the increased pressure to their mythical water canopy they say God placed above the Earth's atmosphere when He divided the waters (Genesis 1:6) and which they claim was the liquid water source for the windows of heaven component of the flood. They are wrong on both latter assumptions.

What is needed is an antediluvian atmospheric model that, unlike their water canopy assumption, does not violate the laws of physics and can explain why the Earth's atmosphere became reduced in volume.

Since we have no idea what the actual atmospheric pressure could have been at that time, let us assume a figure of 2 atmospheres (14.7 psi X 2 = 29.4 psi). That would be a range in which the hyperbaric benefits would be close to optimum without the effects of nitrogen narcosis or oxygen toxicity (about equal to scuba diving in 25-30 feet of water).

We next need to determine the total weight of the additional atmospheric gas. When we do the math, we find that the present weight of the atmosphere is 4.99×10^{14} tons. If you double that, you have the total weight of an additional atmosphere. Of course, about 75% of the additional gas would accumulate close to the ground within the lowest 12 - 15 kilometers, so the total height of the upper atmosphere's edge would still be close to what it is at present. Although that total tonnage is quite mindboggling, it only represents about two millionths of the Earth's total mass; therefore, the Earth's gravitational pull would only be slightly increased.

One possible additional benefit of a thicker atmosphere would be a reduction in the amount of harmful radiation reaching the Earth's surface. Solar radiation is not a simple, single entity. It actually comprises many forms such as electromagnetic radiation, X-rays, gamma rays, and high-speed particles like electrons, protons, neutrons, and atomic nuclei. This factor, combined with the HBO effect, could have been the difference that allowed antediluvian mankind to reach the great ages declared in the Bible. The full verdict is still out on this matter.

Leaving behind this aspect of the Great Flood, we need to address two remaining issues: (1) How did Noah's family in the Ark and the marine life in the seas escape being fried by the tremendous volume of heat released by the global geyser activity? (2) How was the atmosphere reduced to present pressure levels? Let us answer the second question first.

Seven days into the start of the flood sequence, when the fountains (geysers) began creating the worldwide cloud cover and heavy rains, the heat energy from the geysers would have traveled upward in a column as the rain waters condensed from the steam. This would have created soaring thermal air currents on a massive scale, forcing heated lower atmospheric heavy gasses (oxygen, nitrogen, etc.) upward into the higher atmosphere. As this heat accumulated, the sphere of the Earth's atmosphere would have expanded, pushing outward and farther away from Earth's gravity. If the atmosphere had distended enough through this heating, portions of it would have been ripped from Earth's gravitational field by the sun's solar winds. Those gases would have been lost into space. Consequently, following the flood and after the heat source had abated, the upper atmosphere would have begun to cool and shrink back to more normal size. But with great volumes of gas lost through this process, remaining air pressure at sea level would have been reduced to present levels.

As for how Noah's family and Earth's marine life survived, the cloud cover and the heavy rains protected them. For a couple of reasons, the critics are incorrect in arguing that the heat from the geysers would have fried everything on the surface of the Earth. First, heated air rises, and most of the heat from the geysers would have been dissipated high above the Earth's surface. Second, radiant heat (infrared) from the ascending mix would not have traveled far

Heat of Geyser Activity and Noah...

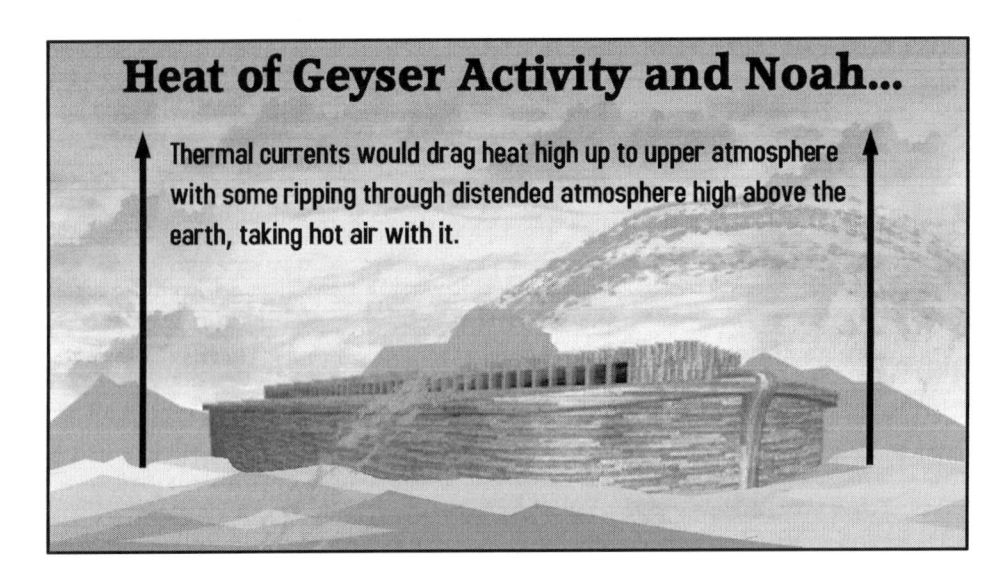

Thermal currents would drag heat high up to upper atmosphere with some ripping through distended atmosphere high above the earth, taking hot air with it.

horizontally because of the heavy precipitation falling below the cloud cover. That cloud cover would have acted as a shield from the heat accumulating in the regions above the cloud cover.

Another important point should be made. All the waters falling from the heavens would have been *fresh* water. Because salt water is denser than fresh water, a large fresh water lens would have formed on top of the flood, especially over submerged continental areas and oceanic areas distant from the points of surface eruption and agitation. This fact can go a long way in accounting for the survival of fresh-water fish and some trees. The Bible says that at least one olive tree survived in the Earth and sprouted fresh leaves after the floodwaters subsided (Genesis 8:11). If olive trees could survive those conditions, certainly the Bristlecone pine could as well. (Let the reader understand.)

That completes this proposed flood model. Farfetched? You be the judge. It is only a theory and requires further refinement. However, it meets the requirements of the literal wording of the Bible and does so through the agency of observable scientific principles.

As promised, below are informative URLs on hyperbaric oxygen therapy:

http://www.hbot4u.com/hom.html
http://en.wikipedia.org/wiki/Hyperbaric_oxygen_therapy

Chapter 9
Days of Peleg and Sea Level Changes

Question: Noah's Ark came to rest on a mountain range in an area which is now called Turkey. How did humans and animals quickly migrate to the other continents like Australia and North America, which are presently separated by the seas?

To begin to answer this important question, we must examine another lesser-known, but important event that occurred on the Earth about one hundred years after Noah's flood. *"And unto Eber were born two sons: the name of one [was] Peleg; for in his days was the earth divided; and his brother's name [was] Joktan."* (Genesis 10:25)

"And unto Eber were born two sons: the name of the one [was] Peleg; because in his days the earth was divided: and his brother's name [was] Joktan." (1 Chronicles 1:19)

In the Hebrew language, the word *Peleg* means *a dividing by a small channel of water* and is also root associated with the meaning of an earthquake. The Hebrew word used as *divided* in the passage means to *split* something. According to the genealogy (Genesis 11:10-17), this man named Peleg was born 101 years after the flood. Undoubtedly, this Peleg was so named because of an event which was greatly significant to the people living at the time he was born.

The fact that the Holy Spirit mentions this dividing event in two places in the Scriptures, and that the exact number of years between this event and the flood is also recorded, allude to the importance of these passages in the interpretation of post-flood history.

Some Creationists have interpreted this event to be the division of the North and South American continents from the European and African continents by the Atlantic Ocean after the flood. But a division of such magnitude at that point in geologic time would invalidate our previously-proposed flood model. It would also invalidate accepted paleomagnetic data, which support gradual sea floor spreading at the mid-Atlantic ridge. Besides, the Atlantic Ocean is no small channel of water between landmasses. Obviously, that is not the answer for which we are looking.

After examining the Hebrew meanings, a more plausible alternative interpretation would be that it describes an Earth-splitting event such as a valley opening in the ground and filling with water. That could have happened anywhere along the Dead Sea Rift zone and may have been associated with a delayed adjustment of the Earth's plates in response to the rapid subsidence of the sea floors by the flood. In theory, when the weight of the waters of the flood forced the sea floors downward to fill the void beneath, strain would have developed between the oceanic and continental portions of the crustal plates. Consequently, tectonic pressures were redistributed. About 100 years later, the strain and pressure redistribution may have caused the Earth's crust to rapidly rent in weaker places, much like a piece of ridged plastic, which can be stretched and deformed. It will eventually snap if the strain remains constant. An abrupt further change in sea levels could possibly accompany such an event.

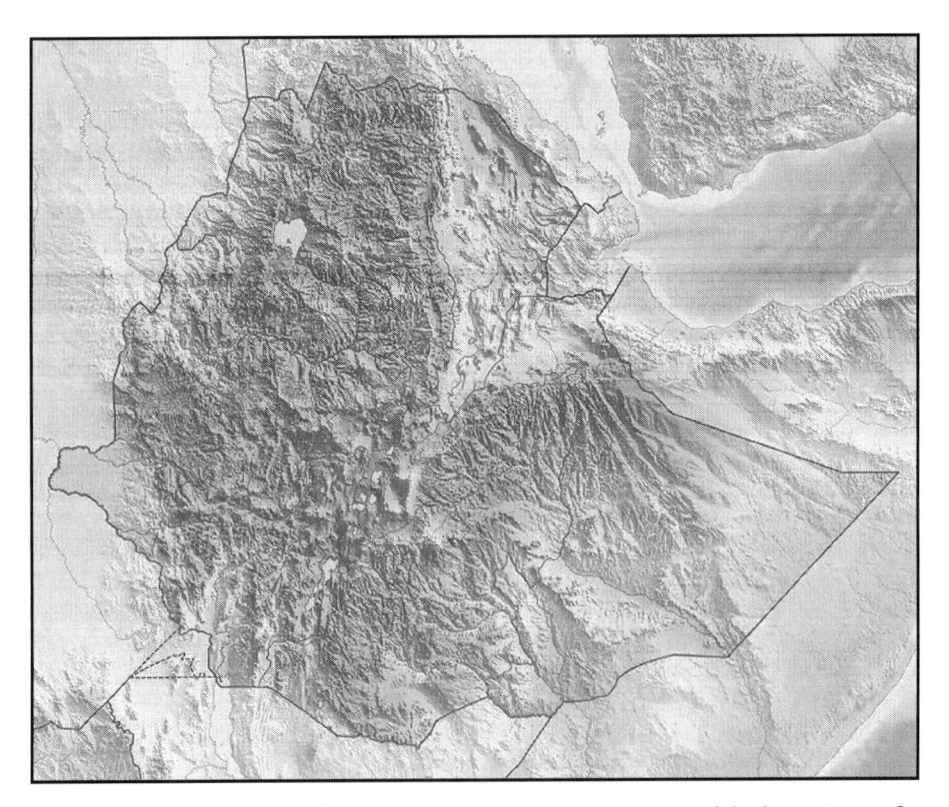

Looking at world relief and tectonic maps, one possible location of the effects of this Peleg event is found in Middle East. It is called the Afar Triangle.

When you examine the relief map above, you can see a geologically-recent rent of Saudi Arabia from Africa. This is a fracture in the continental crust and is different from deep-ocean divergence zones. If you look closely, you can see where a mountain range was sheared and dragged apart.

The Afar fracture is a three-way split, which some geologists believe is caused by an upwelling magma plume, for lack of a better engine. The area on the African continent running south from that fracture locus is the Great African Rift Valley, which runs down into the middle of the African continent. The area going north runs along the bottom of the Red Sea, up into the Dead Sea Rift area of Israel, up the Jordan River valley, and continues northward. This Peleg event is most likely a local reference to a widening of that Rift somewhere near or north of Israel.

In all likelihood, this Rift system was already active before Noah's flood, but the flood triggered renewed activity. I state that because the path of the Rift from Israel continues to run south for the entire length of Ethiopia. It seems to match the described path of the river Gihon, one of four that flowed from the Garden of Eden.

"And the name of the second river is Gihon: the same is it that compasseth the whole land of Ethiopia." (Genesis 2:13)

If that is true, there has been considerable tectonic activity since the Garden of Eden, and Noah's flood may have been just a contributing driver of latter changes.

As for how man and animals got to places like Australia and the Americas, it is possible that they migrated there on dry land during the 101-year interval between the flood and the subsequent plate settling. It is also possible that sea levels had risen quite a bit since the post-flood migrations began, even after the Days of Peleg. An examination of the geology of the region between Indochina and

Australia shows that the sea between the two continental masses is relatively shallow.

The same is true of the Bearing Straits separating Alaska from Russia, where the waters are only about 50 feet deep between the tip of Asia and North America. It is theoretically possible that in the 101 years following the flood, and before the events of Peleg's days, narrow land bridges (which today are submerged) could have existed between many places across the globe. It is also possible that sea levels immediately following Noah's flood were slightly lower than today, and that sea levels could have increased during or following the tectonic adjustment of Peleg's day.

The fact that the ruins of many ancient cities in the Mediterranean Sea area postdate the time of Noah's flood and are found underwater today, tells us that global sea levels have increased by several meters since those cities were built. Therefore, we can say that an appeal to present sea levels is not a valid argument against post-flood migrations to regions now inaccessible across dry land.

It should also be noted that some of the currently-accepted sea level changes across geologic time are in excess of what is possible through climate changes (e.g., melting of vast ice sheets or the accumulation of the same). Sea floor *warping* has been proposed as an explanation. That possibility remains an undemonstrated theory. Your Bible, on the other hand, seems to suggest exactly that, and Noah's flood and the days of Peleg may be good examples.

Assuming that some land bridges existed briefly after the flood by whatever mechanism, the question is whether man and beast had sufficient time to migrate from the resting place of the Ark in Turkey to the other continents before the dividing? Let's do the math.

If you calculate the distance from eastern Turkey to the tip of Australia and divide it by 100 years, you will find that both man and beast would only have to migrate less than 80 miles a year (0.21 miles a day) in order to reach Australia; less than 55 miles a year (0.15 miles a day) to reach North America via the Bearing Straits; and less than 48 miles a year (0.13 miles a day) if a land bridge (or possibly an ice bridge) existed across the northern polar regions. Those average daily distance requirements are much less than most people walk each day in their normal routines. The data support the Scriptures.

"These [are] the three sons of Noah: and of them was the whole earth overspread." (Genesis 9:19)

Shortly after the Ark landed on the mountains of Ararat in Turkey, the families of mankind spread across the world. At that point in time, mankind all spoke a common language.

"And the whole earth was of one language, and of one speech. And it came to pass, as they journeyed from the east, that they found a plain in the land of Shinar; and they dwelt there." (Genesis 11:1-2)

That land of Shinar is Babel (Babylon), and there the Bible says the Lord confounded their language and scattered them across the face of the Earth. Linguistic researchers have recently put forth the results of studies, which tend to indicate that all the Indo-European languages originated in ancient Turkey. Although the given time frame of this occurrence is off by a few thousand years (and is probably conjecture), it is very interesting to see that otherwise it is in close agreement with what the Bible tells us happened in the post-flood world.

Other Evidence of Geologically Recent Sea Level Changes
Geology of the Earth's oceans shows evidence of major (and in some cases rapid) fluctuation in sea levels across recent geologic history. Such evidence can be found in areas near the continental margins. An

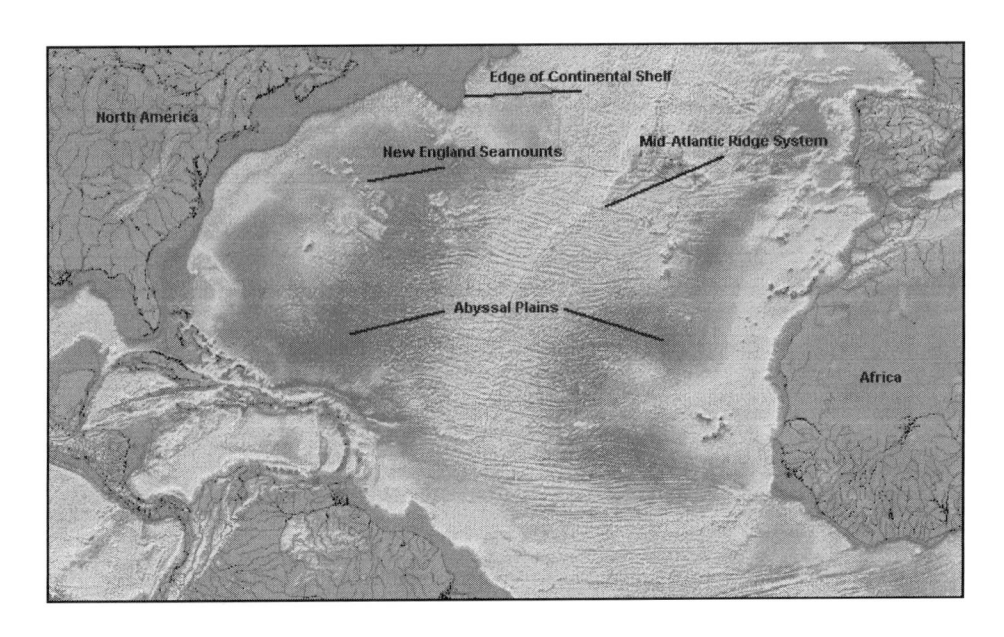

underwater mountain chain in the Atlantic Ocean, just off the New England coast, is a good example..

The New England Seamount chain stretches about 1,600 miles southeast of New England. This chain has more than 30 major peaks, all a kilometer (3,281 feet) or more below the surface. There is evidence to confirm that the tops of these seamounts were once at or above the surface of the ocean in the relatively recent past. Deep-sea dredging of some of these seamounts brought up Eocene (37-58 mya) limestone, which is of shallow-water origin. In a subsequent visit to the seamount in the research submarine Alvin, eyewitnesses reported the first observation of dead coral. (Coral only grows near the surface.) Rock samples containing bits of dead algae were also collected. (Algae only grow within 100 meters of the surface.) The conclusion is that these seamounts have either subsided approximately one kilometer since the Eocene, or that sea levels have changed drastically since the Eocene.[2]

---

[2] J.R. Heirtzler, et al, "A Visit to the New England Seamounts" American Scientist 65 (1977)

This conclusion, however, presents a logical problem to mainline science, as coral reefs grow at known rates that would easily stay ahead of geological subsidence of the seamount. They would stay ahead of sea floor spreading by continental drift, and they would stay ahead of gradual elevations in sea levels, as assumed under Uniformitarism Earth Science paradigms. The New England Seamounts are not unique. Similar occurrences of finding shallow water sediments, reefs, and carbonate platforms in deep-water regions have been recorded in many other places in the Earth's oceans Therefore, the New England Seamounts are not an isolated anomaly. Since gradual processes are inadequate to explain the New England Seamount observations or observations elsewhere, the alternative conclusion is that either the sea floor sank catastrophically, that extraordinary volumes of water were added catastrophically, or both.[3]

A combination of sea floor downward warping AND increased sea

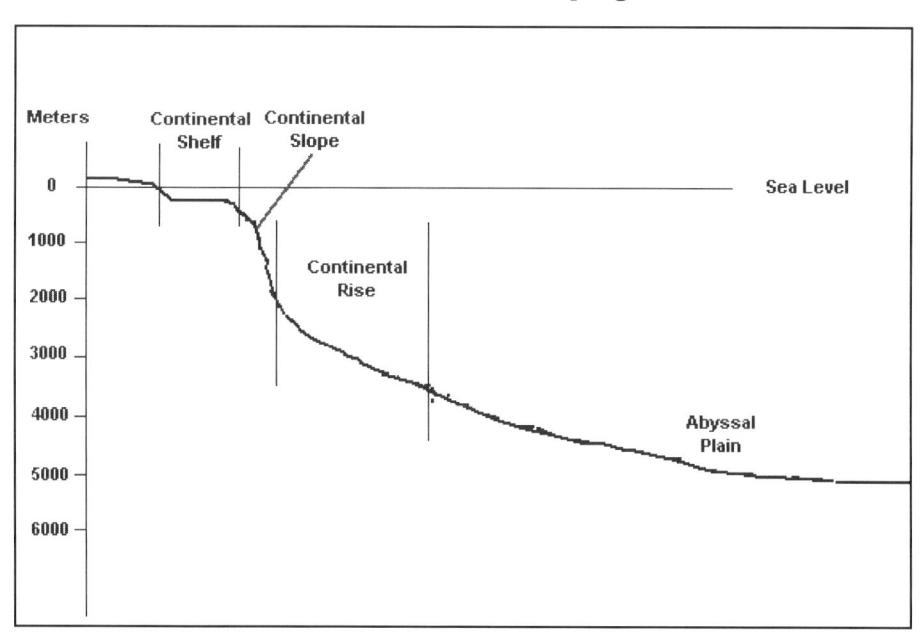

---

[3] Wolfgang Schlager "The Paradox of Drowned Reefs and Carbonate Platforms" Bulletin of the Geological Society of America 92 (1981)

levels, resulting in deeper ocean basins following Noah's flood, would appear a plausible explanation for finding shallow water sediments in deep-water regions today. Is there other undersea evidence to support this theory? Yes! It should be noted that the tops of the submerged New England Seamounts are at the same approximate depth as the edge of the Continental shelf, which is also at a depth of about 1000 meters worldwide.

This edge is called the Continental Slope, a zone where the sea floor plunges sharply downward to the Continental Rise and the even deeper abyssal plains.

This slope's worldwide contour delineates the actual edges of the continents. The continents have their closest *fit* at the 1000-meter depth, where they can be put back together like a giant jigsaw puzzle.[4]

Along the outer edges of the relatively flat Continental Shelf, near the Continental Slope zone, are numerous underwater canyons that cut downward sharply into the floor of the shelf. These canyons are similar to ones cut by fast-flowing waters eroding away rock as observed on land when the flow gradient is very steep. For example, in a portion of a river that drops 800 feet in five miles, the water speed and erosion power is much greater than a portion of river that only drops eight feet in five miles.

Over 80% of the canyons on the edge of the Continental Shelf can be directly traced back across the relatively flat plain of the Continental Shelf, following now-submerged river beds, to the mouths of rivers that exist today.

---

[4] Harold L. Levin "Contemporary Physical Geology", Crustal Deformation and Global Tectonics, page 290, figures 9-38 & 9-39, (1981)

This fact confirms that most of the underwater canyons are clearly extensions of those same present-day rivers, and those canyons were likely cut when the continents stood higher above sea level.

If the Earth's ocean level was 1000 meters lower before Noah's flood, the canyons are easily explained by the force of the river waters running off the flat land of the present Continental Shelf (which would have been above sea level at that time) and down the relatively steep edges of the continental slope.

The rivers would have eroded deep channels in the rock at the edge of the shelf as they plunged sharply downward to the antediluvian sea level. High-velocity turbidity currents carrying silt and rock particles could have further eroded the canyons in post-flood times after they were submerged below today's prevailing sea level.

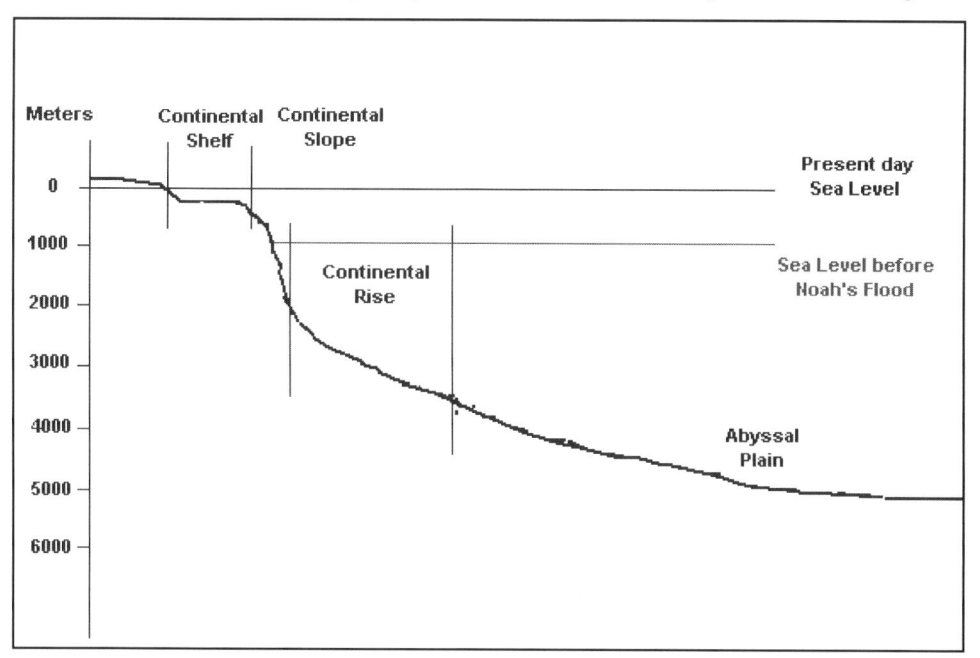

The existence of the submerged river beds across the shelf indicates that at some time in the past, the Continental Shelf was above sea level, and rivers flowed gently across those coastal plains until they reached the edge area. Near the edge zone, the gently-flowing rivers turned into cascading rapids and falls, and the accelerated flow and sediment load further eroded the deep canyons.

Combining the drowned reefs of the New England Seamounts and the submerged riverbeds of the Continental Shelf, we have observable physical evidence that supports the flood model. The data suggest both that the floors of the great ocean basins sank to greater depths and that sea level is about 1000 meters higher today than it was before the flood.

Chapter 10
Relationship of Flesh and Spirit

"...Ye MUST be born again" John 3:7

"Jesus answered, Verily, verily, I say unto thee, Except a man be born of water and [of] the Spirit, he cannot enter into the kingdom of God. That which is born of the flesh is flesh; and that which is born of the Spirit is spirit." (John 3:5-6)

Each man and woman born into this world is a being made of three distinct components. *"And the very God of peace sanctify you wholly; and [I pray God] your whole spirit and soul and body be preserved blameless unto the coming of our Lord Jesus Christ."* (1 Thessalonians 5:23)

1. The BODY. This is your PHYSICAL component of being. It is flesh made from a collection of unremarkable mineral elements (mostly water) and is in harmony with the nature and spirit of this world. It grows, matures, begins to deteriorate, eventually dies, and then decomposes back into its constituent elements and remains as part of the dust of the Earth. The body is a part of you, but is not all of what defines who YOU are.

"And thou mourn at the last, when thy flesh and thy body are consumed," (Proverbs 5:11)

2. The SOUL. This is who YOU are; it is a part of your SPIRITUAL component. This is your individuality, your I AM so to speak (made in God's image), your *heart*. Although your individual soul did not exist before your mother and father procreated you, it will exist forever. It cannot be killed by man.

"And fear not them which kill the body, but are not able to kill the soul: but rather fear him which is able to destroy both soul and body in hell." (Matthew 10:28)

When your body dies, your soul (YOU) will leave the body of flesh. *"And it came to pass, as her soul was in departing, (for she died) that she called his name Benoni: but his father called him Benjamin."* (Genesis 35:18)

3. The SPIRIT. This is the source of power and control for both your body and soul; it is either evil or good, darkness or light, unholy or holy, unclean or clean, of Satan or of God. *"But he turned, and rebuked them, and said, Ye know not what manner of spirit ye are of."* (Luke 9:55)

Where your soul spends eternity after it departs is determined by your personal relationship to God (saved or unsaved). You are an eternal being. You determine your own destiny. In fact, the Bible says that you are a god (small "g"). *"Jesus answered them, Is it not written in your law, I said, Ye are gods?"* (John 10:34)

"So God created man in his [own] image, in the image of God created he him; male and female created he them." (Genesis 1:27. See also Isaiah 41:23 and Psalms 82:6)

The unsaved man or woman (who has only the first birth) is in eternal danger. Since the body and soul of the unsaved man or woman are bonded to the dead spirit of this present world, when this world's physical elements and spiritual components (including death) are cast into the lake of fire (Rev 20:13-15), those eternal souls, living or already dead, will perish with them.

What exactly is the difference between the relationship of the unsaved soul and the saved soul? What does being *born again* actually mean? The answer is something that God does for you at the moment you accept the Lord Jesus Christ as your Savior. An *operation*.

Has a doctor ever operated on you? The doctor uses a knife to cut away something that is diseased. God's operation is similar. Using the Sword of the Lord instead of a scalpel, the Great Physician (Luke 5:31) severs the direct (but unseen) connection between your soul and your flesh. *"For the word of God [is] quick, and powerful, and sharper than any two-edged sword, piercing even to the dividing asunder of soul and spirit, and of the joints and marrow, and [is] a discerner of the thoughts and intents of the heart."* (Hebrews 4:12)

"Buried with him in baptism, wherein also ye are risen with [him] through the faith of the operation of God, who hath raised him from the dead." (Colossians 2:12)

This operation is a spiritual circumcision. Your flesh is cut away from your soul, and you are given God's Spirit. *"But he [is] a Jew, which is one inwardly; and circumcision [is that] of the heart, in the spirit, [and] not in the letter; whose praise [is] not of men, but of God."* (Romans 2:29)

After you have accepted the free gift of salvation through faith in the shed blood of the Lord Jesus Christ, and as you grow and mature in the Lord (your continuing sanctification), you will begin to notice some changes in how you think. You will find that your heart (soul) grows more and more in agreement with God and His law (which is spiritual), but your flesh will still want to go the way of the world. All born again Christians have a split personality so to speak. Even when you work not to sin (you don't work to stay saved), sin still happens along your path of Christian growth. Paul sums it up quite well in the book of Romans. *"I find then a law, that, when I would do good, evil is present with me. For I delight in the law of God after the inward man: But I see another law in my members, warring against the law of my mind, and bringing me into captivity to the law of sin which is in my members. O wretched man that I am! who shall deliver me from the body of this death? I thank God through Jesus Christ our Lord. So then with the mind I myself serve the law of God; but with the flesh the law of sin."* (Romans 7:21-25)

Your soul is saved, but your flesh (your present physical body) is still dead and cannot be salvaged. It will perish and return to the Earth. (You get a new body later.) Your present flesh will still lust to do those things that are unlawful, while at the same time your heart and the Spirit will condemn those thoughts and feelings and empower you to avoid the temptation. No Christian is perfect in the flesh and will sometimes give in to those feelings and will sin in the flesh (but not in his/her heart).

FACT: Christian people DO sin at times (but in the flesh only) after they are saved. *"If we say that we have no sin, we deceive ourselves, and the truth is not in us."* (1 John 1:8)

"My little children, these things write I unto you, that ye sin not. And if any man sin, we have an advocate with the Father, Jesus Christ the righteous:" (1 John 2:1)

When this occurs and the guilt begins to set in, the Christian starts worrying about losing his/her salvation or committing the unpardonable sin. That cannot happen.

FACT: It is NOT POSSIBLE for a Christian's SOUL to sin, because that soul has been born again by His (God's) seed into God's family. *"Whosoever is born of God doth not commit sin; for his seed remaineth in him: and he cannot sin, because he is born of God."* (1 John 3:9)

Physical circumcision is permanent and cannot be reversed; once that flesh is cut away, it is gone forever. The same metaphor applies to circumcision of the heart; once that body of flesh is cut away, your soul can't be reattached to it. Praise God for that! Salvation is the free gift of God and eternal; it is not earned (or retained) by good works. *"For all have sinned, and come short of the glory of God;"* (Romans 3:23)

"Knowing that a man is not justified by the works of the law, but by the faith of Jesus Christ, even we have believed in Jesus Christ, that we might be justified by the faith of Christ, and not by the works of the law: for by the works of the law shall no flesh be justified." (Galatians 2:16)

If you are not good enough to earn it, why do so many Christian people think that they can un-earn it? Once you have given your soul to God, it is His forever! If you have accepted the Lord Jesus Christ, then you are loved of God and don't have to worry about holding onto God because HE WILL HOLD ONTO YOU.

"For I am persuaded, that neither death, nor life, nor angels, nor principalities, nor powers, nor things present, nor things to come, Nor height, nor depth, nor any other creature, shall be able to separate us

from the love of God, which is in Christ Jesus our Lord." (Romans 8:38-39)

"Your lamb shall be without blemish, a male of the first year: ye shall take it out from the sheep, or from the goats: And ye shall keep it up until the fourteenth day of the same month: and the whole assembly of the congregation of Israel shall kill it in the evening. And they shall take of the blood, and strike it on the two side posts and on the upper door post of the houses, wherein they shall eat it. And they shall eat the flesh in that night, roast with fire, and unleavened bread; and with bitter herbs they shall eat it." (Exodus 12:5-8)

This He did for YOU!

"Behold, the Lamb of God!"

Chapter 11

The Pre-Adamic World

"And the earth <u>was</u> ..." (Genesis 1:2)

At the very beginning of the Bible, the reader is confronted with the first mystery of the Holy Scriptures - a mystery which, when fully understood, reveals why the ancient geologic fossil record is fairly accurate, and why the account of the six 24-hour days of creation in the Holy Scriptures is a regeneration of the heaven and the Earth and NOT in direct contradiction to the accepted geologic time scale.

What you will learn here precept-upon-precept (Isaiah 28:10-11) will help you understand many other difficult Biblical passages from

Genesis to Revelation. The Genesis account must be interpreted from God's perspective, not man's (Isaiah 55:8-9). Hold onto your faith; it is about to be tested (1 John 4:1)!

In Genesis 1:2, and in direct contrast to the glorious heaven and Earth of Genesis 1:1 (which, according to Isaiah 45:18, was initially created by the Word of God to be inhabited), the Spirit now speaks of the same Earth as a planet now in ruin and total desolation.

"And the earth was without form [תהו], and void [בהו]; and darkness [חשך] was upon the face of the deep [תהום]. And the Spirit of God moved upon the face of the waters." (Genesis 1:2)

"For this they willingly are ignorant of, that by the word of God the heavens were of old [εκπαλαι], and the earth standing [συνισταω] out of the water and in the water: Whereby the world that then was, being overflowed [κατακλυζω] with water, perished [απoολλυμι] : But the heavens and the earth, which are now, by the same word are kept in store, reserved unto fire against the day of judgment and perdition of ungodly men." (2 Pet 3:5-7)

Genesis 1:2 shows a lifeless and uninhabited planet Earth drifting in the cold and darkness of the chaotic remains of the old universe. The planet is submerged in water, and waters rage around it and across a ruined universal abyssal. Carefully (and prayerfully) consider the import of the Hebrew and Greek word definitions given above. As you study the root word definitions and the English translation of the KJV Bible, a picture emerges of a former world that once existed but now is totally destroyed and dead. Taking the words of the Bible at face value and reading the verses objectively, several facts become clear.

First, the context and time placement of Genesis 1:2 are one verse before God says, "Let there be light." (Genesis 1:3), where He begins the creative process of the famous six days found in Genesis 1:3 through 1:31.

Second, if light (Genesis 1:3) was the very first thing God ever created, then what is all this other stuff already in existence? Specifically, in Genesis 1:2, there is water, composed of hydrogen and oxygen, and there is the Earth, composed of myriads of elements and compounds in a solid form recognizable as a planet which has already been assigned a proper name. Water and Earth are both matter. According to the observations of physics (the equation e=mc² in particular), space must be present in order for matter to exist; space and matter must exist in time; matter, space, and time are directly governed by the speed of light, which is a constant. According to the face value of the exact words of Genesis 1:2 in the KJV Bible, the planet Earth, much water, and a universe in time already existed before God says, "Let there be light" in Genesis 1:3.

Third, and very important, there is something else already present at this time - DARKNESS! And not just physical darkness (an absence of light) but also spiritual darkness (the absence of holiness and harmony חֹשֶׁךְ).

When all these facts are taken into account, the following inescapable truths stand out:

1. *The planet Earth and a universe were already in existence before the creative process of Genesis 1:3 through 1:31 even began. Earth had already existed for an unspecified period of historical time.*

2. *The physics of time, space, and matter were already established, which by extension means that the processes which regulate radioactive decay (the half-life principle) were also functioning and valid.*

> 3. *At some undetermined time in history past, death and the powers of darkness first came into being - before Adam.*

Before we proceed further, we need to firmly establish a governing principle for regulating our interpretation of the Holy Scriptures and the Earth's geology.

- *If the Bible is true and faithful about Jesus and redemption by His shed blood on the cross of Calvary,*
- *If the Bible is true and faithful about man's fall and need for redemption,*
- *If the Bible is true and faithful about heaven, hell, and coming judgment,*
- *If the Bible is faithful and true about the history of Israel and the patriarchs,...*

....then the Bible is also true about Moses and the Lord parting the Red sea. It is true about the Lord making the sundial go backward 10 degrees as a sign to Hezekiah. (Read 2 Kings 20:9-11.) It is also true that the Lord made the sun stand still in the sky for Joshua. (Read Joshua 10:12-14.) It is then true that the Lord made the present heavens and Earth, our world, in just six 24-hour days and only about 6,000 years ago just as the Scriptures say. In other words, we must take the Lord's words as truth.

Also consider this:

- *If the ages of the geologic fossil record are true and faithful as is commonly accepted,*
- *If the principle of radioactive decay and half-life dating is true and reliable,*
- *If those same dating techniques are reliable when they show that the oldest known rocks on the Earth are around 3.8 to 4.5 billion years old, and that the first fossil remains of macro*

> *organic life on this planet were approximately 500 - 700 million years ago,...*

....then all of this means we are confronted with the only logical conclusion:

THE SIX DAYS OF GENESIS ARE THE ACCOUNT OF A RE-CREATION, OR REGENERATION OF A PREVIOUSLY-EXISTING HEAVENS AND EARTH, NOT THE ORIGINAL FIRST- TIME CREATION OF ALL THINGS BY THE LORD, AND THAT GENESIS CHAPTER ONE'S SEVEN CREATIVE DAYS ARE CERTAINLY NOT A GEOLOGICAL HISTORY OF THE EARTH!

There is no other logical answer that makes any sense in light of the true and faithful words of the Bible and the time-tested physical observations (not theories) of the geologic sciences.

If, however, we accept this as the true solution to the Creation vs. Evolution paradox, then the scientists are wrong about every living thing on the face of the planet today being a direct descendent of living things which evolved across those hundreds of millions of years of natural history. The condition of the former world as revealed in Genesis 1:2 is that of a completely dead planet, void of any remaining life forms whatsoever.

On the other hand, it also means that every living thing on the face of the planet today IS directly descended from those life forms which God made when He re-created the heavens and Earth about 6,000 years ago, and that those replacement life forms were patterned after the same kinds of life forms that inhabited the face of the old Earth shortly before it perished. In addition, every man, woman, and child alive on the face of the Earth today is genetically descended from the first man, Adam, who was made in God's image and not "after his kind" like the beasts and vegetation. By extension, this implies that any genetic DNA sampled from known *human* remains older than 6,000 years (like Neanderthal and Cro-Magnon) will be found to have no genetic connection to any people living on the Earth today. Several examples of this evidence are presented in our chapter titled *Life Forms During Ice Age, After Seven Days of Genesis*, in which we also show when all life from the previous world perished.

In essence, what the Scriptures are collectively saying is this:

Long ago, in very distant times past, the Lord God first created the heaven and Earth (Genesis 1:1). At the place in time referred to in Genesis 1:2, there was a vast gap of possibly hundreds of millions of years in historical time. In Genesis 1:1, we have a glorious heaven and Earth, but in 1:2, we see a decimated heaven and Earth. The bulk of the geologic column fits between 1:1 and 1:2, and the geologic time marker at Genesis 1:2 is the very end of the Pleistocene. The end of the Pleistocene (about 12,000 to 14,000 years ago) shows evidence of a global extinction event and a severe drop in global temperatures. We will show from the evidence that all life perished from the face of the Earth for a brief period before God regenerated a new creation from the remains of the old heavens and Earth.

What exactly happened during this great gap of time between Genesis 1:1 and Genesis 1:2? Why was death already in existence before the six days and before Adam sinned? More specifically, how were sin and death on the Earth before Adam was even created if Romans 5:12 is taken as literal truth? For clues to that answer, we must look to the writings of the prophets Isaiah and Ezekiel. In these prophetic Scriptures, the Holy Ghost spoke through these men concerning the origin of Satan, which is the key doctrine to unlocking this great mystery.

What the Spirit of Truth Reveals in the Words of Truth
In the passages below, the prophets are speaking against the King of Babylon (Isaiah 14:4) and the Prince of Tyrus (Ezekiel 28:2), who were renown mortal men of history. Prophetically, the Spirit is also addressing a man yet to come, the Antichrist (2 Thessalonians 2:1-

10). It is clearly evident from the content, however, that the Holy Ghost is also speaking here against a spirit; an ancient, unholy, and malevolent spirit that motivated the evil deeds of these historical and mortal men.

*"**How art thou fallen from heaven**, O Lucifer, son of the morning! [how] art thou cut down to the ground, which didst weaken the nations! For thou hast said in thine heart, I will ascend into heaven, I will exalt my throne above the stars of God: I will sit also upon the mount of the congregation, in the sides of the north: **I will ascend above the heights of the clouds; I will be like the most High**. Yet thou shalt be brought down to hell, to the sides of the pit. They that see thee shall narrowly look upon thee, [and] consider thee, [saying, Is] this the man that made the earth to tremble, that did shake kingdoms;"* (Isaiah 14:12-16)

*"Thou hast been in Eden the garden of God; every precious stone [was] thy covering, the sardius, topaz, and the diamond, the beryl, the onyx, and the jasper, the sapphire, the emerald, and the carbuncle, and gold: the workmanship of thy tabrets and of thy pipes was prepared in thee in the day that thou wast created. Thou [art] the anointed cherub that covereth; and I have set thee [so]: thou wast upon the holy mountain of God; **thou hast walked up and down in the midst of the stones of fire**. Thou [wast] perfect in thy ways from the day that thou wast created, till iniquity was found in thee. By the multitude of thy merchandise they have filled the midst of thee with violence, and thou hast sinned: therefore I will cast thee as profane out of the mountain of God: and I will destroy thee, O covering cherub, **from the midst of the stones of fire**. Thine heart was lifted up because of thy beauty, thou hast corrupted thy wisdom by reason of thy brightness: I will cast thee to the ground, I will lay thee before kings, that they may behold thee."* (Ezekiel 28:13-17)

The highlighted words speak of things that could *not possibly* be attributed to the actual acts of any human king or prince. No man in history has ever walked up and down in the midst of the stones of fire or fallen from heaven.

The name Lucifer means *light bearer* or *brightness* in the Hebrew sense of the word. This creature was the first King of the Kingdom of Heaven in the day when the Lord God created the heaven and Earth (Genesis 1:1). It is important to understand that the Kingdom of Heaven is not something that just begins with the Gospels of the New Testament. The saga for control and Kingship of the Kingdom of Heaven is the Bible's core theme from Genesis through Revelation. The geography of this Kingdom is from the Earth below up to all things within the bounds of the firmament of heaven, the physical universe. This topic is discussed more in depth in the chapter titled *Kingdom of Heaven and Kingdom of God, the Doctrinal Differences.*

For now we must learn about a created being that the Lord God first placed in charge and stewardship over the Kingdom of Heaven long ago at the very beginning of time. This angelic being, a cherub named Lucifer, was second only to the throne of God and was the choir leader of the universe in the day when the Lord God first made all things.

"Where wast thou when I laid the foundations of the earth? declare, if thou hast understanding. Who hath laid the measures thereof, if thou knowest? or who hath stretched the line upon it? Whereupon are the foundations thereof fastened? or who laid the corner stone thereof; When the morning stars sang together, and all the sons of God shouted for joy?" (Job 38:4-7)

Spiritual harmony and continuity were part of the original creation in the physical realm of the Kingdom, from the surface of the Earth upward to the throne of the triune eternal God. Physical matter and spirit were one under the stewardship of Lucifer, this anointed cherub. He was second only to the Lord God in power and authority over the realm of the whole Kingdom. Lucifer was a created being, created by God to serve Him as ruler of the Kingdom and leader of worship to the Lord.

You should also note that Lucifer was covered in a detail of 10 precious stones. These are not the exact same 12 stones that the High Priest of Israel wore on his Breastplate, but the similarities of such a covering signify that Lucifer was a priestly ruler over the old world of those ancient times. However, he was not satisfied with his glorious appointed station over all things in the Kingdom and eventually desired to be God himself. "I will ascend above the heights of the clouds; I will be like the most High."

Lucifer rebelled, transgressed against the Lord God, and became the first created being to sin. Lucifer sinned a long, long time ago before Adam was even created. The earliest (thus first) documented sin (and documented in the Holy Scriptures we should add) occurred countless eons ago. It certainly happened before the Cambrian geologic period (about 500 -600 million years ago) because that is where we see an explosion of well-developed life forms in the fossil record. Except for what has been interpreted as bacteria or primitive cell remains, no antecedent fossils exist in the more ancient Precambrian. Consequently, what appears in the fossil record to the evolutionist as an explosion of life is, to the creationist, an explosion of death. The sudden appearance of the remains of extremely complex life forms does not mean those ancient life forms were only as old as the Cambrian times. They could have been living in the geologic times long before the Cambrian. Things that are alive don't leave remains until they die. The Cambrian marks the first record of death of complex life forms in the Earth's history, not the very beginning of complex life itself.

There is another extremely noteworthy geologic event that took place on the ancient Earth just before the Cambrian Explosion. Scientists have accumulated evidence through observations that seem to suggest the Earth was frozen over completely at the end of the Precambrian. Since the 1960s, scientists have hypothesized that the Earth was subjected to severe glacial action between 750 million and 580 million years ago. This is called the Snowball Earth hypothesis and has been put forth to explain a number of observations in the geological record. It proposes that a severe ice age at that time caused the Earth's oceans to completely freeze over.

How is this event directly connected to the Cambrian Explosion that followed? Is it a coincidence that the Earth's continents began to break apart following the Snowball Earth and Cambrian Explosion events? At that time in Earth's history, the world's continental landmass was locked together in the configuration of a supercontinent called Rodinia, which was clustered near the Earth's equator. This sequence of events - a super Ice Age, the Cambrian Explosion of life, and the breakup of Rodinia - all occurred in the time frame between 750 million to 500 million years ago. This is the most likely point in Earth's natural history for Lucifer's rebellion and the domino effects it precipitated on all creation.

Allow me to digress and inject some parenthetical thoughts. Make note of the association of Lucifer with the stones of fire, and keep in mind that fire can be a physical and/or spiritual component.

"And Elisha prayed, and said, LORD, I pray thee, open his eyes, that he may see. And the LORD opened the eyes of the young man; and he saw: and, behold, the mountain [was] full of horses and chariots of fire round about Elisha." (2 Kings 6:17)

"And out of the throne proceeded lightnings and thunderings and voices: and [there were] seven lamps of fire burning before the throne, which are the seven Spirits of God." (Revelation 4:5)

"For our God [is] a consuming fire." (Hebrews 12:29)

In the Hebrew language concordance, the word for the stones spoken of as the stones of fire is **eben *eh'-ben***, which suggests that these stones were more akin to building blocks or masonry than to natural rocks or burning volcanic brimstone. I believe this is significant, as it may be telling us that this covering cherub, Lucifer, was in the setting of some sort of spiritual structure of fire. A *temple* of fire on the Earth? After all, this Lucifer also had a covering of diverse gemstones similar to the breastplate of gemstones worn by the High Priests of the tabernacle and the temple in Old Testament times. Are these similarities a coincidence? But, I digress.

With his initial act of sin and rebellion, death and corruption, like leaven, began to permeate the physical realm that was under Lucifer's stewardship to rule. It started in Eden, the Garden of God on the Earth. The ancient Earth became cursed, and death spread like a cancer upon all the ancient living creatures on the Earth at that time. The effect spread out across the cosmos. Every life form then present, as well as those that afterward came forth across Earth's natural history, held the sentence of death. Fossilized remains are the testimony, written in stone, of life's struggle under that sentence across the geologic ages. Throughout those vast geologic ages, the physical universe and all things in it eventually decayed, and the whole system finally ran down and died (entropy).

Scientists use the term *Evolution* to describe the observed progress of life forms on this planet as revealed in the fossil record. Darwin called it the survival of the fittest, and it does appear that more and more complex organisms took their place on the stage of history; they did so by killing and adapting to the struggle against death. The dinosaurs came and went. All things died, and those creatures that came after them also died. So it continued across millenniums of historical time until the spirit of death overtook all things, including the stars in the universe. A few million years ago, coldness and darkness began to increase. This was the onset of the last Ice Age, and it is the universe's eventual cold, dark, and completely dead condition that the Spirit describes in the words of the time period of Genesis 1:2:

"And the earth was without form, and void; and darkness [was] upon the face of the deep. And the Spirit of God moved upon the face of the waters." (Genesis 1:2)

At this point in historical time (Genesis 1:2), with the ancient world in total ruin, the Lord God draws a clear distinction in the cosmos between spiritual and physical light and the darkness. At the very beginning of this regeneration work, He sets an impassable and fixed boundary between His Holy throne on high and the corrupted physical realm of matter below.

"And God said, Let there be a firmament [רקיע] in the midst of the waters, and let it divide the waters from the waters. And God made the firmament, and divided the waters which [were] under the firmament from the waters which [were] above the firmament: and it was so. And God called the firmament Heaven. And the evening and the morning were the second day." (Genesis 1:6-8)

This firmament, the reconfiguration as structured here, contains three heavens; specifically, the Earth's atmosphere as the first, and outer space as the second. The Third Heaven is above it all, beyond the realm of the physical cosmos. Between the second and third heaven, the Lord God now places a Sea which is a point of division. This Sea is above the cosmos but below the third heaven. These waters above the firmament are spoken of in the following references: Gen 1:6-10, Rev 4:6, Rev 21:1, and others including Ezekiel 1:22.

This is a partition He established between Himself and His abode (Holy and pure) and the physical cosmos below (now purged from uncleanness, yet still bearing the buried scars of death's previous effects - the fossil record). You will notice that this partition work, the work of the second day, is not pronounced as good. The work of the second day is the only work that is not called good, but it was necessary and good only in respect to the whole regeneration scheme for reasons that will become more evident later in this study.

"And he said unto them, Ye are from beneath; I am from above: ye are of this world; I am not of this world." (John 8:23)

"Far above all principality, and power, and might, and dominion, and every name that is named, not only in this world, but also in that which is to come:" (Ephesians 1:21)

The impassable barrier of that firmament would not be breached until the death, burial, and resurrection of the Lord Jesus Christ. Just like the veil of the Temple that was rent when the Lord Jesus died, signifying that He had broken down the wall of partition between God and man, that firmament in type is similar to the veil or curtain between the Holy place and the Holy of Holies through which only the high priest could enter to make the atonement. (You should now be starting to get the picture.) In other words, there was nobody from the profane world below who was going to get up to the Third heaven through the firmament until Jesus made the way.

Having drawn the lines between the profane and holy worlds, the Lord God proceeds to renew the face of the old planet Earth with replacement vegetation (Day 3: Genesis 1:11-12), regenerate the second heaven, the cosmos (Day 4: Genesis 1:14), and fill the Earth with living creatures (Days 5 and 6: Genesis 1:20-25) similar to the kinds of life forms that had previously been on the Earth. He then proceeds to create Adam, the first true man (also made on Day 6), made in the image of God, to be God's next appointed King of the Kingdom of Heaven.

Lucifer and those sons of God (Genesis 6:1-4) who followed him in the ancient rebellion were still around but could now only have indirect influence in the new world the Lord God had made on the face of the old planet, and they had temporarily lost control of the power of death. In order for Satan to communicate with Eve, he had to become incarnate in the physical Serpent that was in the Garden of Eden. It appears from the verse below that the sons of God (we are assuming here the ones who had not followed Lucifer in rebellion) had access to the new world and were known to Adam and Eve; otherwise where did they get their knowledge of gods? Read carefully:

"And the serpent said unto the woman, Ye shall not surely die: For God doth know that in the day ye eat thereof, then your eyes shall be opened, and ye shall be as gods, knowing good and evil." (Genesis 3:4-5)

It seems that the innocent and sinless man and woman were familiar with other beings in their world known as gods, and they must have been some kind of marvelous creatures to behold in their goings and comings; otherwise, why would the serpent use such as comparison to tempt her? This passage also shows that Evil was lurking there, and that a clear distinction had already been made between good and evil (Genesis 1:4) in the new world, although Adam and Eve were blind to it in their initial innocence.

As for death, the Scriptures tell us it was also present and dormant in the background of the new world as well. This is shown by the fact that Adam and Eve, although innocent and sinless, were not immortal beings. Since they were created from the dust of a temporal world, they would have to eat of the Tree of Life (Genesis 2:9) in order to have full physical immortality; otherwise, why the necessity of there even being a Tree of Life in the garden? If nothing happened before Adam and Eve like death or sin, as Young Earth Creationists claim, what would be the purpose of the Tree of Knowledge of Good and Evil in the first place?

"And the LORD God said, Behold, the man is become as one of us, to know good and evil: and now, lest he put forth his hand, and take also of the tree of life, and eat, and live for ever:" (Genesis 3:22)

When the Lord God made Adam, He made him from the physical elements of the planet Earth.

"And the LORD God formed man of the dust of the ground, and breathed into his nostrils the breath of life; and man became a living soul." (Genesis 2:7)

Although Adam was a living soul created in the image of God, his physical body was made from the dust of the same Earth which, at this point in time, also had the fossilized remains of the planet's past history buried under it. The soil was not pure and undefiled, but Adam was formed from it.

You must keep in mind that in the Old Testament, before Calvary and the new birth through the Lord Jesus Christ, the physical body of man and his soul are spoken of as a single entity stuck together, although we know that there is a distinctive difference between the soul and the flesh.

"And it came to pass, as her soul was in departing, (for she died) that she called his name Benoni: but his father called him Benjamin." (Genesis 35:18)

Although Adam was made innocent (he was not born) and without sin, he was not immortal at this point. Had he not eaten of the Tree of the Knowledge of Good and Evil, his flesh would have eventually died unless he and Eve had eaten from the Tree of Life that was in the garden. When Adam and Eve transgressed, their eyes were opened (Genesis 3:7), their innocence was lost, and they died spiritually and in due course, physically.

"Jesus said unto them, If ye were blind, ye should have no sin: but now ye say, We see; therefore your sin remaineth." (John 9:41)

Satan regained control of the Kingdom by their transgression, and the power of death entered full force into and upon the world of mankind. Because Adam was the appointed steward of the new world, all the creation of that new world was subjected to death through his act of disobedience.

"Wherefore, as by one man sin entered into the world, and death by sin; and so death passed upon all men, for that all have sinned:" (Romans 5:12)

"Forasmuch then as the children are partakers of flesh and blood, he also himself likewise took part of the same; that through death he might destroy him that had the power of death, that is, the devil;" (Hebrews 2:14)

Lucifer, now Satan, regained control of the newly-regenerated physical realm of the Kingdom of Heaven by deceit.

"And the devil, taking him up into an high mountain, shewed unto him all the kingdoms of the world in a moment of time. And the devil said unto him, All this power will I give thee, and the glory of them: for that is delivered unto me; and to whomsoever I will I give it. If thou therefore wilt worship me, all shall be thine." (Luke 4:5-7)

"And from the days of John the Baptist until now the kingdom of heaven suffereth violence, and the violent take it by force." (Matthew 11:12)

The Lord Jesus Christ, through His sacrificial death on the cross and His resurrection from the dead, reclaimed the title and ownership of the Kingdom of Heaven. One day in the not-too-distant-future, He will come back to take possession of what is rightfully now His, purchased by His shed blood. *"Jesus answered, My kingdom is not of this world: if my kingdom were of this world, then would my servants fight, that I should not be delivered to the Jews: but now is my kingdom not from hence."* (John 18:36)

"And Jesus came and spake unto them, saying, All power is given unto me in heaven and in earth." (Matthew 28:18)

"At that time they shall call Jerusalem the throne of the LORD; and all the nations shall be gathered unto it, to the name of the LORD, to Jerusalem: neither shall they walk any more after the imagination of their evil heart." (Jeremiah 3:17)

"But those mine enemies, which would not that I should reign over them, bring hither, and slay [them] before me." (Luke 19:27)

The Kingdom and who will rightfully rule it is the CENTRAL THEME of the Scriptures and all history of the ages. Every Christian knows how the story will end (Revelation chapters 19-22), but few know or understand exactly how, why, and when the story began.

Final Notes on Lucifer and matters pertaining to the Kingdom: When prayerfully studying these matters, note the close association of the anointed Cherub with crystalline minerals and elements, including metals, which are physical things.

"Thou hast been in Eden the garden of God; every precious stone was thy covering, the sardius, topaz, and the diamond, the beryl, the onyx, and the jasper, the sapphire, the emerald, and the carbuncle, and gold: the workmanship of thy tabrets and of thy pipes was prepared in thee in the day that thou wast created." (Ezekiel 28:13)

Man is made from the dust of the Earth. Our flesh is composed of water and many of the same mineral elements that are found in some of these stones (primarily carbon, as in the case of the diamond). The Scriptures say that Satan has power to work through the flesh.

"Wherein in time past ye walked according to the course of this world, according to the prince of the power of the air, the spirit that now worketh in the children of disobedience: Among whom also we all had our conversation in times past in the lusts of our flesh, fulfilling the desires of the flesh and of the mind; and were by nature the children of wrath, even as others." (Ephesians 2:2-3)

In the next chapter, we will study the structure of the regenerated heavens.

Chapter 12
The Firmament

On the second day in the Genesis narrative, the Lord calls for there to be a firmament in the midst of the waters to divide the waters. *"And God said, Let there be a firmament in the midst of the waters, and let it divide the waters from the waters. And God made the firmament, and divided the waters which were under the firmament from the waters which were above the firmament: and it was so. And God called the firmament Heaven. And the evening and the morning were the second day."* (Genesis 1:6-8)

Because of its Hebrew definition, the term *firmament* and its identity have been among the greatest puzzles concerning the Creation account.

Strongs Hebrew Definition # 7549: eyqr raqiya` raw-kee'-ah from 7554; properly, an expanse, i.e. the firmament or (apparently) visible arch of the sky:--firmament.

Strongs Hebrew Definition # 7554: eqr raqa` raw-kah' a primitive root; to pound the earth (as a sign of passion); by analogy to expand (by hammering); by implication, to overlay (with thin sheets of metal):-- beat, make broad, spread abroad (forth, over, out, into plates), stamp, stretch.

Most people interpret this to mean just the expanse of the sky (the atmosphere) or outer space, or both (which it is), but the full meaning goes well beyond that simplistic interpretation. The creation of the firmament is associated with the placement of some sort of structure.

Many modern scholars consign the term firmament as a relic of a pre-scientific culture and translate the Hebrew word *raqia* (rendered as firmament in the KJV) as a *dome* or *vault* in some modern Bibles. The problem that puzzles people is the implication in the Hebrew language that the firmament is a firm, fixed structure (FIRMament). That structure can be explained in the context of the Ruin-Reconstruction interpretation of Genesis.

Young Earth Creationists have interpreted the waters above the firmament as a theoretical water canopy which once surrounded the Earth but no longer exists (their source of the waters of Noah's flood). This is an incorrect concept that does not exactly hold water (pun intended) when closely examined within the literal framework of the Genesis narrative. The reason is because of what is said in this passage: "*And God said, Let there be lights <u>in the</u> firmament of the* *heaven to divide the day from the night; and let them be for signs, and for seasons, and for days, and years: And let them be for lights in the firmament of the heaven to give light upon the earth: and it was so. And God made two great lights; the greater light to rule the day, and the lesser light to rule the night: he made the stars also."* (Genesis 1:14-16)

This verse says that the Sun, Moon, and Stars are IN the firmament. Therefore, applying the rules of grammar and logic, those waters that are above the firmament must be above the Sun, Moon, and Stars. That means these waters are above the visible cosmos. For some, this is a hard pill to swallow, but that is exactly what the Bible is saying.

"Praise him, ye heavens of heavens, and ye waters that [be] above the heavens." (Psalms 148:4)

The Bible says that in the Lord Jesus Christ, the incarnate Word of God, all wisdom and knowledge are found (Colossians 2:3). The same holds true for the Holy Scriptures, the written Word of God. According to the Scriptures, there is a physical/spiritual structure to the universe. The Apostle Paul makes reference to the importance of this knowledge in the book of Ephesians where he wrote, *"That Christ may dwell in your hearts by faith; that ye, being rooted and grounded in love, May be able to comprehend with all saints what [is] the breadth, and length, and depth, and height; And to know the love of Christ, which passeth knowledge, that ye might be filled with all the fulness of God."* (Ephesians 3:17-19)

Pay close attention to the structure of the grammar. Paul is speaking about two different things in this passage. The first is the structure of things (the breadth, and length, and depth, and height;), and the second is to know the love of Christ, which passeth knowledge. The important key word here is the conjunction "And" which separates the two clauses.

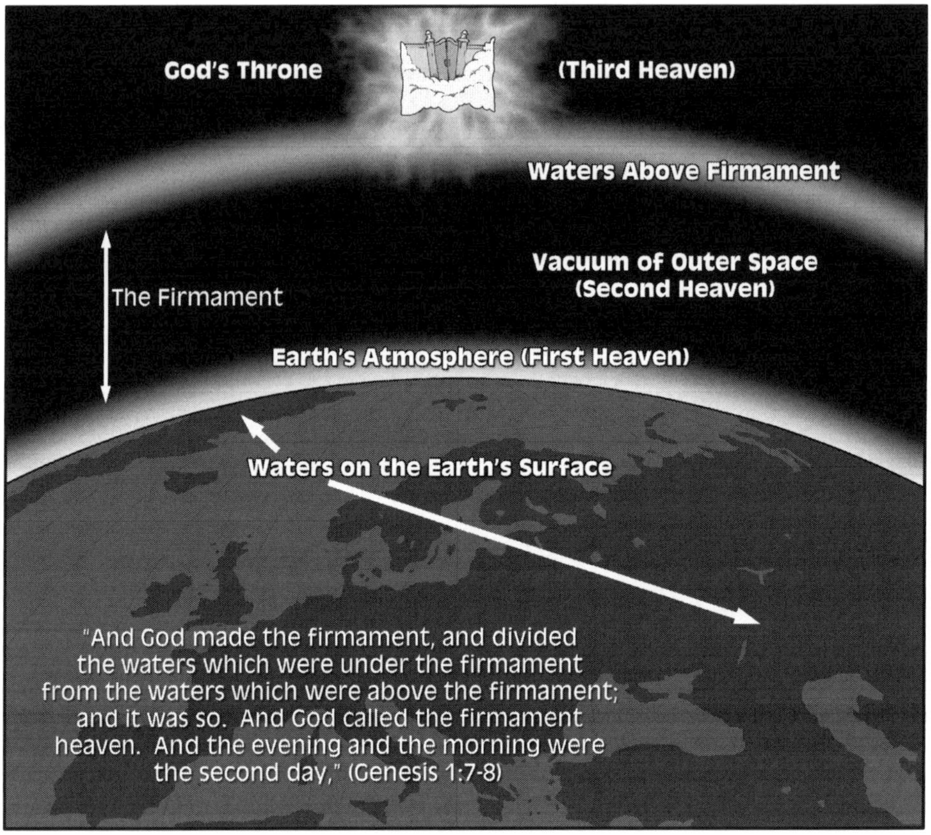
God's Throne
(Third Heaven)
Waters Above Firmament
Vacuum of Outer Space
(Second Heaven)
The Firmament
Earth's Atmosphere (First Heaven)
Waters on the Earth's Surface
"And God made the firmament, and divided the waters which were under the firmament from the waters which were above the firmament; and it was so. And God called the firmament heaven. And the evening and the morning were the second day," (Genesis 1:7-8)

In other words, Paul is saying there are two things the believer can and should know. (1) The dimensions and structure of all things, which can be defined. (2) The love of Christ, which man is unable to fully comprehend. A corollary to the truth of this passage is found in an Old Testament proverb.

"*The heaven for height, and the earth for depth, and the heart of kings [is] unsearchable.*" (Proverbs 25:3)

The firmament deals with the structure of the present heavens and Earth (Genesis 2:1) as opposed to the structure of the original heaven and Earth (Genesis 1:1). There is presently a three-heavens structure. A different configuration existed in the old world of the original creation. Let's look back to Genesis 1:6 again and more closely examine that verse to determine that present structure. *"And God said, Let there be a firmament in the midst of the waters, and let it divide the waters from the waters. And God made the firmament, and divided the waters which [were] under the firmament from the waters which [were] above the firmament: and it was so."* (Genesis 1:6-7)

On the second day of the creation, the Lord God divided the waters (plural) of the great deep into two parts with a firmament in the midst. According to Genesis 1:10, both the waters that were upon the face of the Earth and the waters which He placed *above* the firmament He called Seas:

"And God called the dry [land] Earth; and the gathering together of the waters called he Seas: and God saw that [it was] good." (Genesis 1:10)

This is important to understand. We know that the waters on the Earth are called Seas in the Bible, but there is also another Sea that is spoken of in the Scriptures, and that one is above the firmament. (Special note: Notice that the word Sea is capitalized at Genesis 1:10 in the KJV Bible). But, exactly where is above the firmament? During the six days of the Genesis regeneration, the Lord God defined Three Heavens. The first heaven is the Earth's atmosphere. *"And God said, Let the waters bring forth abundantly the moving creature that hath life, and fowl [that] may fly above the earth in the open firmament of heaven."* (Genesis 1:20)

The second heaven is the vast expanse of the physical universe, which we call outer space. *"And God said, Let there be lights in the firmament of the heaven to divide the day from the night; and let them be for signs, and for seasons, and for days, and years:"* (Genesis 1:14)

These two heavens constitute a *continuum* called the firmament, and this firmament is collectively called Heaven. *"And God called the firmament Heaven. And the evening and the morning were the second day."* (Genesis 1:8)

The Third Heaven is above this higher Sea, and this higher sea is before and below the Throne of God. *"And before the throne there was a sea of glass like unto crystal: and in the midst of the throne, and round about the throne, were four beasts full of eyes before and behind."* (Revelation 4:6)

Therefore, this particular Sea above the firmament is above the known physical universe. Since the sun, moon, and stars are *in* the firmament, this Sea must be above them. This is difficult for the science of man to fathom, but it is a Scriptural fact on cosmology. It represents a firm and impassable barrier between the world of man (below) and the abode of God (above). Here are some additional verses in the Bible which refer to this particular Sea: *"Praise him, ye heavens of heavens, and ye waters that [be] above the heavens."* (Psalms 148:4)

This is the sea that John saw in his visions. *"And before the throne [there was] a sea of glass like unto crystal: and in the midst of the throne, and round about the throne, [were] four beasts full of eyes before and behind."* (Revelation 4:6)

This is a present Sea of separation that will no longer exist when God destroys the old world and makes all things new after the 1,000-year Kingdom of Heaven and the final judgment that follows. *"And I saw a new heaven and a new earth: for the first heaven and the first earth were passed away; and there was no more sea."* (Revelation 21:1)

This is the sea that is spoken of in Exodus 20:11 and frequently quoted by Young Earth Creationists as a proof text to support their doctrine. *"For in six days the LORD made heaven and earth, the sea, and all that in them is, and rested the seventh day: wherefore the LORD blessed the sabbath day, and hallowed it."* (Exodus 20:11)

That reference to the sea in the above verse is a reference to the Sea established above the firmament, NOT to any sea on the Earth. Look at the English grammar of the verse. The heaven and Earth are set apart as separate and complete entities as is *the sea.* That Sea above the firmament was not made until the second day. There is something even more important to notice about these waters above the firmament. Look again at the passage concerning the second day. *"And God said, Let there be a firmament in the midst of the waters, and let it divide the waters from the waters. And God made the firmament, and divided the waters which were under the firmament from the waters which were above the firmament: and it was so. And God called the firmament Heaven. And the evening and the morning were the second day."* (Genesis 1:6-8)

Something is missing there. Do you know what it is? Ok, I'll tell you. This work on the second day is the only day in the Genesis narrative where the Lord does not say it was good. Therefore, when you consider the statement the Lord makes in Genesis 1:31, where He says that all that was made was very good... *"And God saw every thing that he had made, and, behold, it was very good. And the evening and the morning were the sixth day."* (Genesis 1:31)...

...it must be considered so in the context of circumstances. The context is the overall work of Reconstruction from Ruin and the preparation of the Earth and a new world for Man. The term *very good* does not mean *perfect*, and the sea of separation placed between the world above and the world below was not good, but necessary. It would not be until the work of the Lord Jesus Christ on the cross that a way would be made for crossing that barrier (the Sea, or waters, above the firmament).

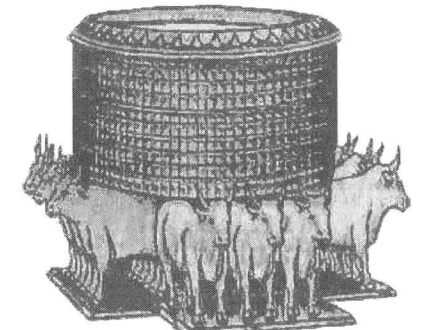

That particular Sea is represented (in type) in a part of the design of Solomon's

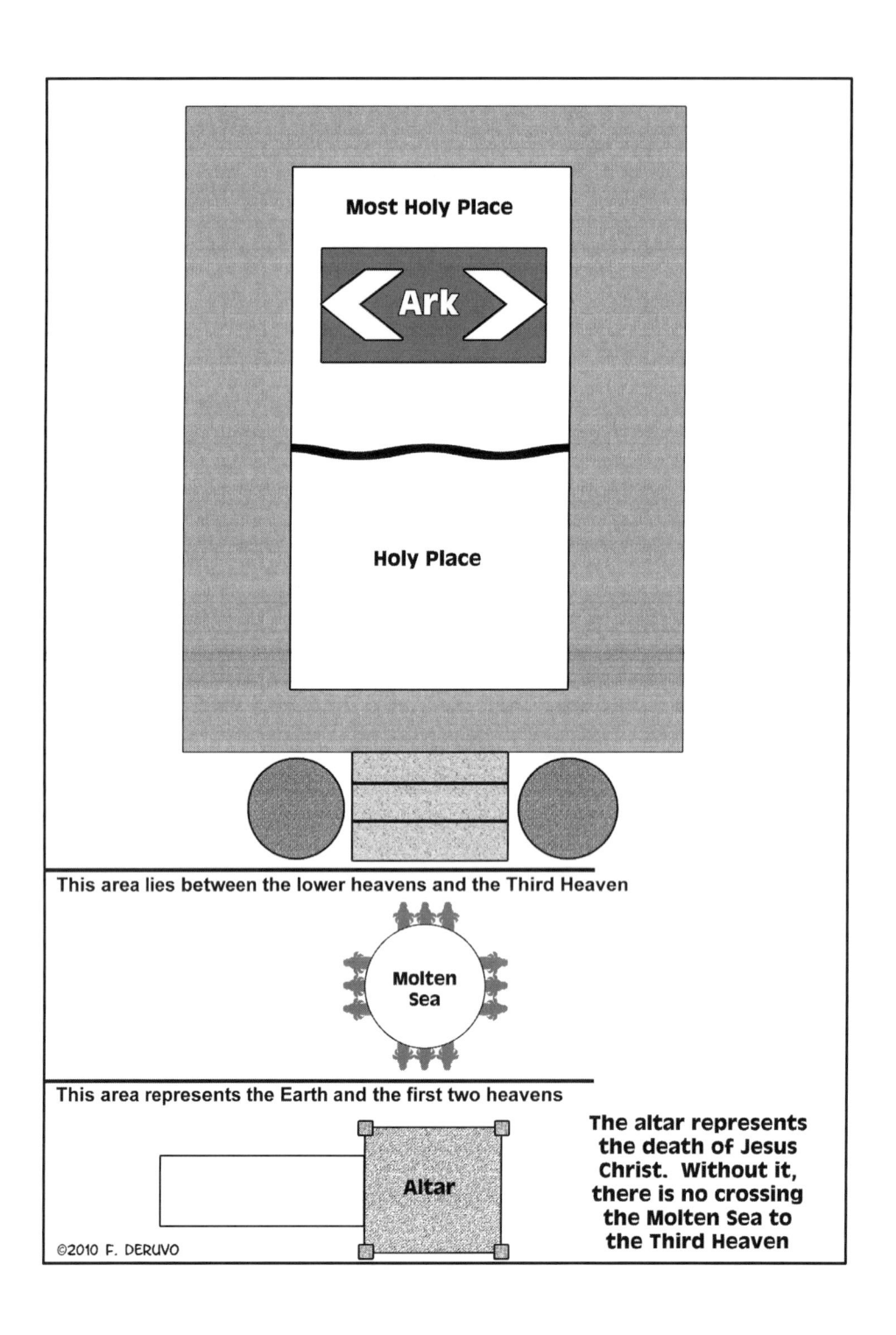

Most Holy Place

Ark

Holy Place

This area lies between the lower heavens and the Third Heaven

Molten Sea

This area represents the Earth and the first two heavens

Altar

The altar represents the death of Jesus Christ. Without it, there is no crossing the Molten Sea to the Third Heaven

©2010 F. DERUVO

Temple known as the Molten Sea (1 Kings 7:23; 2 Chronicles 4:2). If you look at a diagram layout of the Temple, you will see that this Sea is between the Altar and the main part of the Temple where the Holy Place and Most Holy Place were.

The structure of all things in type can be found in schematic form in the design of the Temple.

The Altar where the sacrifices were made represents where the Lamb of God was sacrificed. It represents the world that is below (the Earth & the first and second heavens).

The Molten Sea is between those two lower heavens and the Third Heaven where the true Temple of God is located.

Third Heaven
This now gives us a better understanding of what the Apostle Paul was talking about in II Corinthians 12:2, where he speaks of the Third Heaven. *"I knew a man in Christ above fourteen years ago, (whether in the body, I cannot tell; or whether out of the body, I cannot tell: God knoweth;) such an one caught up to the third heaven."* (2 Corinthians 12:2)

Although the Third Heaven is not directly mentioned in the Genesis narrative, the established structure of all things is defined in Genesis chapter one and, when understood, allows us to comprehend exactly where and what Paul was talking about when he mentions it in his letter. It also gives the reader a better understanding of John's vision in Revelation chapter four. When the Lord God divided the waters, He created a boundary, which presently exists between the two lower heavens (the firmament) and the Third Heaven (where the throne of God is). That boundary is that Sea, and that sea is above the two heavens of the firmament. It is also likened in places to crystal or smooth glass. *"And the likeness of the firmament upon the heads of the living creature was as the colour of the terrible crystal, stretched forth over their heads above."* (Ezekiel 1:22)

The reason it appears like a smooth, crystal surface is because it is frozen. *"The waters are hid as [with] a stone, and the face of the deep is frozen."* (Job 38:30)

"And they saw the God of Israel: and there was under his feet as it were a paved work of a sapphire stone, and as it were the body of heaven in his clearness." (Exodus 24:10)

It is also likened to glass. *"And I saw as it were a sea of glass mingled with fire: and them that had gotten the victory over the beast, and over his image, and over his mark, and over the number of his name, stand on the sea of glass, having the harps of God."* (Revelation 15:2)

With this understanding of what the Firmament is and the structure of all things that God made during the seven days, many things that were previously obscure suddenly take on real meaning and enrich the reader's understanding.

In summary, here is the structure of the physical world as it now exists from the face of the Earth upward:

- *The lower sea of physical waters (our seas and oceans)*
- *The first heaven (the atmosphere)*
- *The second heaven (outer space)*
- *The sea above outer space and below the Third Heaven (a sea of separation)*
- *And above it all, there is the Third Heaven.*

"That Christ may dwell in your hearts by faith; that ye, being rooted and grounded in love, May be able to comprehend with all saints what [is] the breadth, and length, and depth, and height; And to know the love of Christ, which passeth knowledge, that ye might be filled with all

the fulness of God."
(Ephesians 3:17-19)

The structure of the heavens is a recurring theme throughout the Bible and is reinforced in typology. For example, it is likened to the floors of a building, which we call stories, and the same word is even used in the KJV Bible.

1. To describe the design of the heavens: *"[It is] he that buildeth his stories in the heaven, and hath founded his troop in the earth; he that calleth for the waters of the sea, and poureth them out upon the face of the earth: The LORD [is] his name."* (Amos 9:6)

2. This pattern of three levels is also found in some other important things in the Bible, an example of which is the description of the design of Noah's Ark: *"A window shalt thou make to the ark, and in a cubit shalt thou finish it above; and the door of the ark shalt thou set in the side thereof; [with] lower, second, and third [stories] shalt thou make it."* (Genesis 6:16)

3. To describe the construction of the Temple: *"The door posts, and the narrow windows, and the galleries round about on their three stories, over against the door, cieled with wood round about, and from the ground up to the windows, and the windows [were] covered;"* (Ezekiel 41:16)

There were three main parts in the construction of Moses' Tabernacle in the wilderness. (1) The outer court, where the brazen altar of sacrifice was. (2) The Holy Place, where the candlestick, table of shewbread, and golden altar of incense were. (3) The Holy of Holies where the Ark of the Covenant was. Also note that between parts two and three was a curtain for a partition, which matches the Sea above the firmament (in type) in the structure of the Three Heavens. It is no coincidence that all these Biblical things have a similar three-tiered structure. There is much spiritual insight to be gained in further study of those things:

- *Three Heavens*
- *Three levels inside Noah's Ark*
- *Three floors in a section of the Temple*
- *Three sections to Moses' Tabernacle*

Regarding the design of the Temple, keep in mind that Moses' tent Tabernacle and Solomon's Temple both had three main parts:

- *The outer court*
- *The holy place (where the table, lamp and incense alter were, outside the veil)*
- *The Most Holy Place (where the Ark was, behind the veil)*

As you can see, this theme of structure based on threes is consistent throughout the Bible. Even the structure of the Earth has three main divisions: the core, the mantle, and the crust.

Does the Universe really have a structure? When you go into outer space, is there really any such thing as up or down? Is there a top or bottom? Does the cosmos have a definite shape? We cannot observe such in our three-dimensional view of the universe.

I found an interesting article in volume 25, number 1, of *Discover* Magazine (page 37) in which this subject is briefly discussed. Using observations from the Wilkinson Microwave Anisotropy Probe (WMAP), which observes the faint cosmic microwave background of space, scientists have been able to reconstruct the "exact proportions" of the cosmos. They found that there is only 4% "normal" matter, 23% "dark" matter and 73% "dark energy" out there. To quote the article, "Those figures indicate that the universe is flat and will most likely continue to expand forever."

This is what can be observed, but is that all that is really out there? Not according to the Bible! In the words of the Lord Himself, there is a world above the one we live in and can observe. *"And he said unto them, Ye are from <u>beneath</u>; I am from above: ye are of <u>this world</u>; I am not of this world."* (John 8:23)

Just because we cannot observe or understand something does not disprove its existence.

Chapter 13
The Fourth Day of Genesis: A Paradox?

Throughout this book, we have sought to provide both Biblical and Scientific answers to the many issues that have evaded reconciliation of Geology and Genesis and the doctrinal conflict between Old Earth and Young Earth Creationism. Having demonstrated that the Ruin-Reconstruction (Gap Theory) interpretation provides the superior, Biblically-credible answer to what the Bible says and the Earth's geology reveals, we must now tackle a final and elusive issue in the reconciliation process, specifically, the sun and stars of the 4th Day of the Genesis narrative. *"And God said, Let there be lights in the firmament of the heaven to divide the day from the night; and let them be for signs, and for seasons, and for days, and years: And let them be for lights in the firmament of the heaven to give light upon the earth: and it was so. And God made two great lights; the greater light to rule the day, and the lesser light to rule the night: he made the stars also. And God set them in the firmament of the heaven to give light upon the earth, And to rule over the day and over the night, and to divide the light from the darkness: and God saw that it was good. And the evening and the morning were the fourth day."* (Genesis 1:14-19)

Young Earth Creationists claim that the Sun and Stars were first *created* about 6,000 years ago on the 4th Day of Genesis. This claim runs counter to empirical observations and the Biblical text. In fact, the word *create* is nowhere in the above passage. The word used is *made* and comes from a different Hebrew word with a different meaning. Of course, the YECs will argue that the words are interchangeable, but we will not address that argument on this page.

The scientific fact of the matter is that most of the stars we see in the sky are old - much older than just 6,000 years. In order to defend their Young Earth Creationist position against this widely-accepted fact, Young Earth Creationists have proposed every counter-argument imaginable. These arguments range from changes in the speed of light, to time-dilation, to God deliberately making everything appear old just to trick all the evil evolutionists into believing the lies of science and receiving damnation for their unbelief. Of course, that latter explanation would also make God a liar and a deceiver, but they never think that one through.

In Gap Theory Old Earth Creationism, we postulate that there was a previous world on the ancient Earth long, long before the world of Adam. Of course, such an ancient world had to have a Sun (and stars) shining in the sky from ancient times. From that interpretive perspective alone, the events of Genesis Day 4 cannot possibly be the first-time creation of the Sun and Stars. The Bible says there were stars and a heaven of old (II Peter 3:5-7). Those stars had to exist (and then perish?) before the seven days of Genesis, otherwise why the requirement for the Sun and Stars to be regenerated (made) on the 4th Day?

When you look up into the sky at any distant star, you are in effect looking backward into historical time. What you see when you look at a star one million light years away is what that star looked like one million years ago. In reality, it may no longer be there. It could have exploded 500,000 years ago, and you would not see that from Earth for another 500,000 years from today. Light travels at a velocity of 299,792,458 m/s, and the distances between the Earth and the stars are measured in light-years.

So, if by looking up into space we are actually looking back into time, why can't we see the old heavens that were here long before the seven days of Genesis? Actually, we are seeing them! We are also seeing light from stars that were regenerated 6,000 years ago. What we are not presently seeing, however, is the light from what I will call The Event Horizon from historical time past, when the old heavens perished into a state of ruin. We do not see the light from that event because that light is yet to reach us here on the Earth. Confused? Let's try to explain it another way.

In several places within this book, we present our evidence that indicates the old Earth and heavens perished (passed into a state of coldness and ruin) about 12,000 radiocarbon years ago at the end of the Pleistocene. We also postulate that when the stars in the heavens went dark and cold, some of the hydrogen from those dying stars produced great quantities of waters across the cosmos.

Such a universal event would have produced a spectacular light show in the heavens (stars expanding into Red Giants and imploding into

White Dwarfs, etc.) before the darkness and cold settled in. One day soon, we who presently live on the face of the Earth may look up into the night sky and see this very wondrous and terrible past event as it appeared 12,000 years ago. It will look to us like it is happening in real-time, but this will not be the case.

The coming great universal light show certainly didn't occur instantaneously, but most likely at an accelerated rate. There would have been signs of this coming event beginning shortly before it happened. We know that it apparently ended about 12,000 years ago. The heavens and Earth evidently were in darkness and ruin for approximately 6,000 years before they were regenerated about 6,000 years later. Consequently, the light from just before the start of that ancient event is still approaching Earth. It is coming from over 12,000 light years away, and the predicted arrival of that light just so happens to coincide with the generally-predicted time of the coming Great Tribulation. Look what the Bible says about those coming days:

"And there shall be signs in the sun, and in the moon, and in the stars; and upon the earth distress of nations, with perplexity; the sea and the waves roaring; Men's hearts failing them for fear, and for looking after those things which are coming on the earth: for the powers of heaven shall be shaken." (Luke 21:25-26)

As the light from this ancient view of the heavens passes the Earth, the particles of energy from that event wave may also begin to interact with the magnetic fields of the Sun and the Earth, producing other wonders in the sky. *"And I will shew wonders in the heavens and in the earth, blood, and fire, and pillars of smoke. The sun shall be turned into darkness, and the moon into blood, before the great and the terrible day of the LORD come."* (Joel 2:30-31)

Could the prophet have seen visions of massive red Auroras in the night skies of the Tribulation period? Are you aware of what can happen up in the sky when a strong surge of the solar wind hits the

Earth's magnetic field and ionizes the gasses aloft? You get Auroras, and depending on the gasses affected and the strength of the magnetic storm, you can get ones that are blood red.

There are historical accounts of Auroras being visible in the lower latitudes during unusually strong solar storms. Many people who had never seen such things before thought it was the end of the world.

The passing of this predicted event horizon and the energies of the event wave will certainly fill the sky with terrible sights in both the star field and the Earth's upper atmosphere. Imagine you were viewing the Earth's moon through the light of such an Aurora. Would the moon not appear blood red as well?

"And great earthquakes shall be in divers places, and famines, and pestilences; and fearful sights and great signs shall there be from heaven." (Luke 21:11)

Keep in mind that an event horizon strong enough to affect Earth's magnetic field will also affect the magnetic field of the sun and may precipitate other anomalous activity within the sun and the fundamental forces that govern nature. Almost anything is possible, and some of the events prophesied in the Bible are almost impossible for man to imagine.

In summary, if this basic prediction is accurate, we have the answer to the paradox of the stars being made (not created) on Genesis Day 4. If the old state of the universe (what we see now) went out in a blaze of stellar activity approximately 12,000 years ago, we should be seeing the start of that fossil event sometime soon, just as the Bible says. In any event, it should be quite a light show when it gets here. If you understand this, you will not be one of those perplexed at the sight.

Chapter 14
Geologic Evidence: Death of the Ancient World

The geologic and fossil records are the surviving evidence, written in stone, that testify to the truth that the Earth is very old and was populated long before the seven days of Genesis chapter one. But does that record provide evidence of the sudden end of the old world by a universal destructive event before the seven days and before Noah's flood?

"And the earth was without form, and void; and darkness was upon the face of the deep. And the Spirit of God moved upon the face of the waters." (Genesis 1:2)

This certainly would appear to be the case. Throughout the geologic record, there is evidence of mass extinction and geologic catastrophes. The theory that a giant asteroid struck the Earth about 65 million years ago and thus precipitated the demise of the dinosaurs is now widely accepted as a fact. As recently as a few years ago, that theory was scoffed at until the remains of an ancient crater were found in the Yucatan. That same school scoffed at Alfred Wegner's theory about plate tectonics, *The Origin of the Continents and Oceans,* back in the early days of the 20th century, but today that theory is considered the grand unifying theory of the geological sciences.

One of the greatest remaining mysteries to modern geology is found within the most recent episode of mass destruction which occurred in the Pleistocene, the age just before the Holocene, which is the age of Man. This extinction event appears to be linked with the Ice Age. The evidence consists of vast animal cemeteries found in many places around the world, which seem to show a catastrophic and sudden destruction of life all across the planet only a few thousand years ago.

This little-known evidence was documented by many back in the 19th century, but this evidence was mostly ignored by the leading scientists of the day because it did not fit into the prevailing scientific paradigm. This evidence is still mostly ignored today, although the Young Earth Creationists have seized upon it as proof of Noah's flood. It is actually proof of the flood, which happened just before the time of Genesis 1:2, the time when all life on the surface of the Earth had been wiped out.

The best collection of the documentation on this event can be found within the paper, *Catastrophe and Reconstitution,* by the late Arthur Custance. I recommend you take time to read this paper. For those of you in a hurry, here is a sampling of references by several scientists cited within that paper:

On the general topic of animal cemeteries, one source wrote:

"The great problem for geological theories to explain is that amazing phenomenon, the mingling of the remains of animals of different species and climates, discovered in exhaustless quantities in the interior parts of the earth so that the exuviae of those genera which no longer exist at all, are found confusedly mixed together in the soils of the most northerly latitudes. . . The bones of those animals which can live only in the torrid zone are buried in the frozen soil of the polar regions." Penn, Granville, A Comparative Estimate of thc Mineral and Mosaical Geologies, Vol. II, 2nd ed., London, 1825, p. 81.

In a reference to a site in Italy, another wrote:

"In this sandy matrix bones were found at every depth from that of a few feet to a hundred feet or more. From the large and more apparent bones of the elephant, the rhinoceros, the megatherium, the elk, the buffalo, the stag, and so forth, naturalists were led by the elaborate studies of Cuvier and other comparative anatomists to the remains of the now living bear, tiger, wolf, hyena, rabbit, and finally the more minute remains even of the water rat and the mouse. In some places so complete was the confusion . . . that the bones of many different elephants were brought into contact, and on some of them even oyster shells were matted." Fairholme, George, New and Conclusive Physical Demonstrations of the Fact and Period of the Mosaic Deluge, n.p., 1837.

In one of his early writings, even Charles Darwin commented on what he saw in the fossils of South America:

"The mind is at first irresistibly hurried into the belief that some great catastrophe has occurred. Thus, to destroy animals both large and small in South Patagonia, in Brazil, in the Cordillera, in North America up to the Behring Straits, we must shake the entire framework of the globe. Certainly no fact in the long history of the world is so startling as

the wide extermination of its Inhabitants." Darwin, Charles, Journal of Researches, Ward Lock, New York. 1845, p. 178.

A contemporary of Darwin commented:

"We live in a zoologically impoverished world, from which all the hugest and fiercest, and strangest forms have recently disappeared.... Yet it is surely a marvelous fact, and one that has hardly been sufficiently dwelt upon this sudden dying out of so many large mammalia not in one place only but over half the land surface of the globe."

"There must have been some physical cause for this great change, and it must have been a cause capable of acting almost simultaneously over large portions of the earth's surface." Wallace, Alfred Russell, Geographical Distribution of Animals, Vol. 1, Hafner, New York, 1876, pp. 150, 151.

From a book titled *The Mammoth and the Flood*, by Sir Henry Howorth, the following are excerpts about data he gathered first hand in Siberia:

"In the first place, it is almost certain in my opinion that a very great cataclysm or catastrophe occurred ...by which the mammoth with his companions was overwhelmed over a very large part of the earth's surface. This catastrophe, secondly, involved a widespread flood of waters which not only killed the animals but also buried them under continuous beds of loam or gravel. Thirdly, that the same catastrophe was accompanied by a very sudden change of climate in Siberia, by which the animals that had previously lived in fairly temperate conditions were frozen in their flesh under the ground and have remained there ever since."

"When the facts are stated, they are of such a nature as to be almost incredible and they are drawn from the works of such men as Wrangell, Strahlenberg, Witzen, Muller, Klaproth, Avril, Erman,

Hedenstrom, Betuschef, Bregne, Gemlin, Brandt, Antermony, Liachof, Kusholof, Chamisso, Maljuschkin, Ides, Baer, Schmidt, Bell, Tatishof, Middendorf, von Schrenck, Olders, Laptef, Sarytschef, Motschulsky, Schtscukin, Maydell, besides the official documents of the Russian Government." Howorth, Sir Henry, Thc Mammoth and thc Flood: Uniformity and Geology, London, 1887. p. 47.

Henry Howorth had this to say about animal cemeteries:

"The most obvious cause we can appeal to as occasionally producing mortality on a wide scale among animals is a murrain or pestilence, but what murrain or pestilence is so completely unbiased in its actions as to sweep away all forms of terrestrial life, even the very carriers of it--the rodents-- including the fowls of the air, the beasts of the field, elephants, tigers, rhinoceroses, frogs, mice, bison and snakes, landsnails, and every conceivable form of life, and this not in one corner only but, as far as we know, over the whole of the two great continents irrespective of latitude or longitude."

"The fact of the bones occurring in great caches or deposits in which various species are mixed pell-mell is very important, and it is a fact undenied by geologists that whenever we find such a locality in which animals have suffered together in a violent and instantaneous destruction, the bones are invariably mixed and, as it were, 'deposited' in a manner which could hardly be explained otherwise than by postulating the action of great tidal waves carrying fishes and all before them, depositing them far inland with no respect to order." Howorth, Sir Henry, Thc Mammoth and thc Flood: Uniformity and Geology, London, 1887, p.180.

In concluding remarks, Howorth had this to say:

"If animals die occasionally (in large numbers) from natural causes, different species do not come together to die, nor does the lion come to take his last sleep with the lamb! The fact of finding masses of animal

remains of mixed species all showing the same state of preservation, not only points to a more or less contemporary death, but is quite fatal to the theory that they ended their days peacefully and by purely natural means."

"If they had been exposed to the air, and to the severe transition between mid-winter and mid-summer, which characterizes Arctic latitudes, the mammoths would have decayed rapidly. But their state of preservation proves that they were covered over and protected ever since."

"It is almost certain in my opinion that a very great cataclysm or catastrophe occurred by which the mammoth and his companions were overwhelmed over a very large part of the earth's surface. And that the same catastrophe was accompanied by a very great and sudden change of climate in Siberia, by which the animals which had previously lived in fairly temperate conditions were frozen ... and were never once thawed until the day of their discovery. No other theory will explain the perfect preservation of these great elephants."

In summarizing his comments on Howorth and the other sources cited, Arthur Custance made these observations:

"Howorth even recorded a whale which was found entombed with the elephants, a discovery which Pallas confirmed--mentioning also buffalo in situ with the heads of large fishes."

"In spite of the fact that many of these authorities would now be considered quite out of date, so that their interpretations would almost certainly be rejected, the evidence itself remains undeniable; and it is difficult to explain it satisfactorily in any other way."

"Such, then, is the kind of evidence which is to be found all over the world of the sudden death of an enormous number of animals of very recent and modern times. Some of these creatures died in latitudes that were almost at once plunged into an Ice Age which preserved them by

freezing. Some of them died in more temperate zones and were accumulated by the action of torrents of water sweeping hither and yon as the earth reeled, before the waters had been sufficiently gathered together in one place to expose the dry land. And, finally, some were accumulated and rammed together forcibly and indiscriminately into clefts in the rocks which served to sieve them out of the draining waters."

"The suddenness of the event is everywhere attested, in the Arctic by the extraordinary state of preservation of mammoths and other creatures, and in the more temperate zones by the very fact that predators and preyed upon came to a sudden end together. Even within the waters, the movements of silt and water-washed materials were sometimes so sudden and overwhelming that fishes were trapped before they had the few seconds necessary to react in a characteristic defensive way. Some bivalved forms, in fact, were overwhelmed so rapidly that they did not have time to close."

"Furthermore, we may conclude, I think, that the catastrophe which was worldwide profoundly affected world climate."
Custance, Arthur, "Catastrophe and Reconstitution" Custance Library Doorway Papers & Books on Interface between Faith and Science

Although I do not personally subscribe to all the doctrines the late Arthur Custance put forth in his vast collection of papers, I do feel that he presented a good argument for the evidence of a great universal catastrophe in the days before true man was placed upon the Earth.

Although the exact mechanics of the total event are not yet understood, there is ample supporting evidence for a vast and violent flood as the destructive agent - a flood before the flood of Noah's day. This would be consistent with the gap of Genesis 1:2 and the condition of the Earth at that point in time.

A nuclear scientist named Richard Firestone recently reported finding impact regions on mammoth tusks found in Gainey, Michigan, which were caused by high-velocity magnetic particles rich in elements like titanium and uranium. Firestone says that based on his discovery of similar material at a North American Clovis site, he estimates that comets (possibly produced by a relatively close supernova) struck the solar system during the Clovis period roughly 13,000 years ago. This time frame, of course, closely correlates with the other evidence presented.

Chapter 15

Life Forms of the Ice Age, After Seven Days of Genesis

Your attention is called to the particular phrasing, *after their kind* and *after his kind*, throughout the narrative of Genesis chapter one. When the Lord God made the new world on the face of the old Earth during those six days, the Scriptures seem to tell us that He filled it with many of the same *kinds* of plants and animals that had previously been on the face of the Earth. Many were not replaced after their kind, however, but new ones were introduced in their place.

Paleoclimate and GISP2 Volcanic Markers

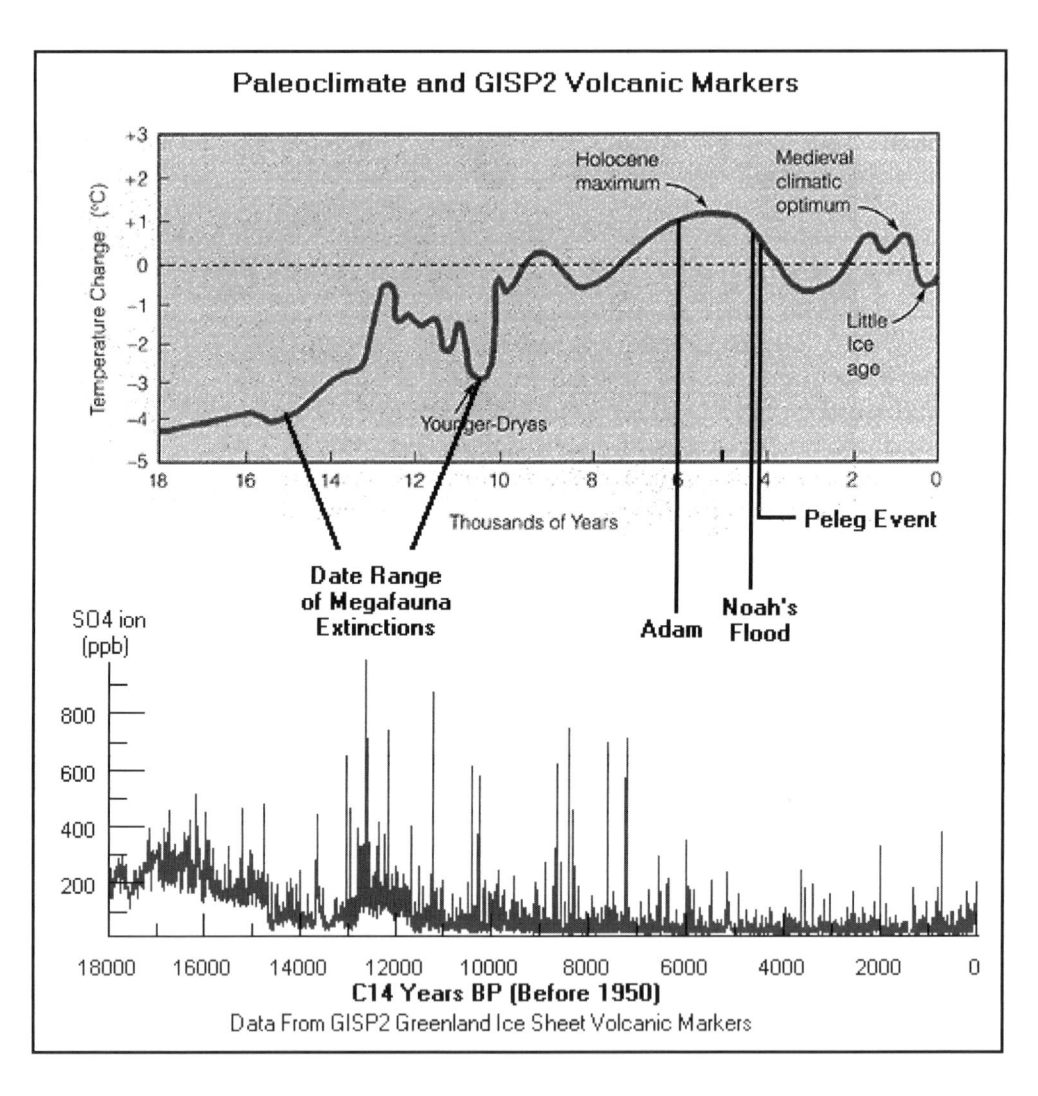

(Top-half of composite Graphic base image from "Meteorology Today" by C. Donald Ahrens © 1994 West Publishing Co.)

The geologic time frame preceding the six days of Genesis correlates roughly with the end of the great Ice Age at the Pleistocene/Holocene epoch boundary, which dates to about 10,000 - 14,000 C$_{14}$ years before present (BP = 1950). The geologic record reveals a mass extinction episode at this time, in which hundreds of large and unusual forms of megafauna mysteriously perished from the face of the Earth. Gone are the Mammoths, Mastodons, giant ground sloth, woolly rhinos, rats the size of dogs, armadillos the size of Volkswagens, and about 200 other known species, including some very weird-looking creatures that raise thoughts of radioactive mutations. By the end of the Ice Age, (geologically recent), they had all disappeared. Their replacement kinds of today's world are quite different in both size and morphology.

The leading scientific theory was that humans hunted these animals to extinction, but that theory is losing favor for lack of direct evidence.

Two important things should be noted from the composite graphic on the previous page, which shows the Earth's average atmospheric temperature (top) and volcanic activity markers (bottom) for the past 18,000 years BP. (1) There is a pronounced increase in indications of volcanic activity between the time when the megafauna extinctions begin (about 14,000 BP) that ends just slightly before the date of the regeneration of the heavens and Earth (about 6,000 years ago- Genesis 1:2). (2) The end of the extinction phase terminates in a relatively sudden and dramatic drop in global temperatures, marked by the Younger-Dryas cooling event.

Clearly, the data indicate there were rapid temperature changes, an onset of intensive geologic activity, and probable changes in the levels of solar activity at this point in Earth's history. The latter fact is supported by reported fluctuations in radiocarbon concentrations in the Younger-Dryas cold period between 12,700 and 11,500 years BP. In sum, this was anything but a normal pattern of events.

Why would so many animals perish at one time (at the end of the Ice Age, when things were warming up) after surviving several thousand years through the harsh glacial conditions in the Pleistocene epoch? The scientific community is greatly divided on the issue. Some hold that they were killed off by *man* for food, by disease, their inability to adapt to a changing post-glacial climate, or some combination of all.

This form of causal reasoning precipitates from a uniformitarian paradigm that is colored by our culture's preoccupation with environmental issues like Global Warming. There is no agreement on this mystery.

A new theory on the cause of the Megafauna extinctions may hold the answer. Abundant tiny particles of diamond dust have been found in sediments dating back 12,900 years at six North American sites. This adds strong evidence for Earth's impact with a rare swarm of carbon-and-water-rich comets or carbonaceous chondrites, precipitating the Younger-Dryas. (An Internet link to the article on that theory can be found at *www.kjvbible.org.*)

Needless to say, the Biblical notion of a universal catastrophic destruction of all living things in the recent past and a Supernatural regeneration of the world by the Lord God is not something many men and women of science today would ever consider. Expect even more new theories to emerge as scientists continue to wrestle with this problem.

Would it not seem logical that a global event of this magnitude and severity, which wiped out the giant mammals, would also wipe out the humanoids that hunted them? Could a population of nomadic hunters quickly switch to an agriculturally-sustained society, especially at a time when the Earth's average temperatures had plummeted sharply? I don't think so.

Keep in mind that, according to the Bible, Adam and his linage began as tillers of the soil and herdsmen after Adam's fall. The first indication of hunting does not appear in the Bible until after Noah's flood. (See Nimrod in Genesis 10:9.) Consequently, if the Paleoclimate data are valid, and the Biblical timeline of Adam and modern mankind is valid, we must conclude it was not the descendants of Adam and Eve who hunted the now-extinct mammoths. Those who did so were a race of manlike beings, which were on the Earth before Adam and Eve - the Pre-Adamite race of hominids not made in the image of God. This fact which raises the following question: In whose image were these hominids made?

With the recent advent of the science of DNA testing, the supporting proof for this incredible hypothesis is coming to light, much to the consternation of the evolutionary uniformitarian school of human origins. For example, DNA testing of Neanderthal remains clearly shows that modern man is NOT descended from the Neanderthal. The DNA from three different sets of Neanderthal remains showed there is no genetic link between modern man and the Neanderthal. More recent studies of Neanderthal DNA and Neanderthal Skull Characteristics further confirm this finding. This is forcing the evolutionists to start looking even farther back in the fossil record for a common ancestor or missing link branch from the primates. They will not find it.

Recently, the remains of an anatomically modern human (Cro-Magnon) found in Australia have revealed that it was at least 60,000 years old and had a mitochondria DNA generic marker which is now extinct. That is, nobody today is descended from that particular line of beings, at least on the female side. This find has raised serious debate between the Out of Africa and Regional Continuity evolutionary camps. Will future testing of other Cro-Magnon remains reveal similar DNA surprises? If the Bible is true, the prediction is that they will.

Even more recently, and closer to our time in natural history, strands of very well preserved *human* hair were found in a Pleistocene age deposit in Oregon. These strands were dated to be between 10,000 - 12,000 years old. They present a mystery to science because DNA analysis has shown that they are not genetically related to any modern humans. See the story link, *12,000-Year-Old Human Hair DNA Has No Match With Modern Humans,* at *www.kjvbible.org*.

Evolutionary mainline science still cannot provide a fully satisfactory answer to origins of modern man. As the tools of science improve (e.g., DNA analysis), the mysteries only become more mysterious as is demonstrated by the above cases. Reasoning from a uniformitarian paradigm, and in reference to the above-cited cases of no DNA connections to present humans, secular scientists will say that this only means those particular lines of humans must have been a branch of mankind that perished. As Evolutionary Theory demands, they would have to make the claim that there was continuity of the human race. However, the link between the evidence from the past and present is still yet to be scientifically established. In fact, evolutionary research is finding just the opposite. Scientists today are claiming that human evolution has greatly accelerated, particularly since about 10,000 years ago. The truth is that there are big morphological differences between modern man and primitive man, and pronouncing a sudden acceleration of evolution is their only way to explain the findings within the accepted evolutionary paradigm. The Bible has a better answer: Modern man is a new creation.

In a recently-released study that compared Neanderthal and modern human bone structures with those of the earliest members of the genus Homo, it was found that Neanderthals were a more normal match than modern humans. This is just one more bit of accumulating data that supports the suggestion that modern humans are not descended from evolutionary ancestors; modern man is a unique and a special creation, just as the Bible states.

The concisely-parsed words of the Holy Bible say that there is a gap, or discontinuity, between the ancient world of the past (which included the Neanderthal) and the present world of modern man. The very existence of such a gap in the Genesis narrative is the unifying factor between the Bible narrative and all available empirical data. Specifically, all life on the planet perished near the

Younger-Dryas marker, and the planet was lifeless for a brief period. Then, in a special Creative event (the 7 days of Genesis), the Lord God restored the Creation and made the world of true man, Adam. Without knowledge that a gap existed, mainline science assumes that there was a continuum of life and attempts to fill in the blanks with the available evidence.

For review purposes, here is the Biblical sequence of events:

(1) In Genesis 1:1 we have a general proclamation by the Spirit that God created the heaven and the Earth. It did not evolve and achieve self conscience awareness. God made it. He made it to be inhabited (Isaiah 45:18). Exactly when in time it was first created is not revealed in the Scriptures.

(2) In Genesis 1:2 we find the Earth in ruin, in darkness, and in the waters, which indicate a state of ruin and destruction but, nonetheless, the Earth. Waters and darkness are already there before God says, "Let there be light." Exactly how long it was in that state is also not revealed by the Scriptures. However, the data from the Greenland ice sheet alone confirm that the Earth had already been around for at least 110,000 years. The rest of the Earth's geology reveals an even more ancient age.

(3) In Genesis 1:3 we have the Lord God making a new world out of the ruins and restoring the face of the Earth and the functioning of the heavens.

Before dismissing this scenario as science fiction or Creationist pseudo science, let's put this time in the Earth's geologic history into perspective in relation to a remarkable coincidence of historical findings, which date to the same period of time near the end of the last Ice Age, the Pleistocene/Holocene boundary:

a. This was the time when the long period of the Ice Ages abruptly ended and the Earth's climate suddenly warmed up considerably.

b. This was the time when Neanderthal vanished and Modern man appeared.

c. If man has been evolving for a couple of million years, and there were modern humans 60,000 years ago, why did it take him so long to develop things like city states, agriculture, arts, writing, and structured social order, all of which only go back about 6,000 years?

d. Why did a few hundred very hardy species of megafauna, which had survived through the bitter conditions of the entire Pleistocene epoch, suddenly die off when things were just warming up?

e. Why is there global evidence of great volcanic activity in the late Pleistocene (including massive flood basalts), and why is there evidence of great tidal waves and vast animal death deposits in high mountain regions?

Is it just coincidence that all these things seem to have a common nexus in time? I don't believe so. All the facts and coincidences seem to point to a cataclysmic end of the world at the end of the Pleistocene epoch, which lends considerable support to the Bible's chronology of the seven days of Genesis and the special Creation of true man.

Leaving behind the obscure and still mysterious events of the Pleistocene epoch and the geologic ages that came before it, let us now examine the six-day work of regeneration of life on the face of the Earth according to the Bible. Since we have previously commented on the restored structure of the cosmos, we will now concentrate on the restoration of life forms:

On the third day, God replenished the Earth with vegetation.

"And God said, Let the earth bring forth grass, the herb yielding seed, [and] the fruit tree yielding fruit after his kind, whose seed [is] in itself, upon the earth: and it was so." (Genesis 1:11)

"And the earth brought forth grass, [and] herb yielding seed after his kind, and the tree yielding fruit, whose seed [was] in itself, after his kind: and God saw that [it was] good." (Genesis 1:12)

On the fourth day God made the sun, moon, and stars from the ruins of the old cosmic order. The fact that the Bible says God made the vegetation on the third day and the sun on the fourth day causes Bible critics to point out that plants need sunshine to grow (photosynthesis), so the sequence can't possibly be true. Is this a mistake or unscientific? If the six days of Genesis were literal 24-hour days, there is no problem. Since there were less than 24 hours between the placement of the vegetation (day 3) and the making of the sun (day 4), any farmer will tell you that all plants can survive 24 hours without any sunlight. This order (plants before sunshine) disallows the notions that the six days are long periods of time or that the Genesis account roughly parallels the evolutionary record. It does neither. Think about that one.

On the fifth day He filled the oceans with fish and aquatic mammals and filled the skies with birds.

"And God said, Let the waters bring forth abundantly the moving creature that hath life, and fowl that may fly above the earth in the open firmament of heaven. And God created great whales, and every living creature that moveth, which the waters brought forth abundantly, after their kind, and every winged fowl after his kind: and God saw that [it was] good." (Genesis 1:20-21)

Note of Interest: The wording of the passage says that the birds in our present world came forth from the waters, *not* the land. This shows that modern birds are not the direct descendants of the dinosaurs. Latest study: Scientists say no evidence exists that therapod dinosaurs evolved into birds.

According to the fossil record, there have been life forms in the Earth's oceans for millions of years. Many are long since extinct, and new kinds took their place throughout the geologic ages. Fish that scientists thought were extinct have been found alive in southern oceans. The Coelacanth is the best-known example. However, scientists have recently compared the fins of a fossilized Coelacanth with the fins of those recently caught off the coasts of Africa and Indonesia, hoping to demonstrate Evolutionary development in the species over time. Guess what! It turns out that it's not really the same primitive fish! Yep, that old fellow also appears to have been made after his kind, as well.

Although the void and dark Earth as found in Genesis 1:2 roughly correlates with the end of the Ice Ages, we cannot be exactly sure when (before the six days) all prior marine life forms perished. The most likely marker would again be the Younger-Dryas time frame, the same as when the last of the megafauna perished on land.

In His creative restocking of the oceans on that day, God saw fit to include the old Coelacanth kind along with other kinds of fish which had populated the Earth's seas in the times immediately prior to the old world's destruction. On the other hand, many other ancient marine species were not reintroduced in the reconstruction.

Then there is the sea creature that God created that was not made after his kind but was introduced new and unique to this creation - the great whale.

"And God created great whales, ..." (Genesis 1:21)

Notice in the sentence structure of Genesis 1:21 that the creation of the great whales is set apart from the making of the rest of the sea creatures by a comma. Is this great whale a specific species of whale such as the gigantic Blue Whale, a general reference to the suborder Baleena, or a particular size range? I'm not sure. There are small whales that look like dolphins, e.g., the Beluga Whale. There is also a larger animal we call a killer whale, or Orca, which is actually the largest dolphin. The Whale Shark is not a mammal like the whale or dolphin; it is a really big fish. So the Biblical term *great whale* is somewhat ambiguous. Regardless, we can say with a high degree of confidence that according to the Bible, there are great whales swimming in today's oceans that were not on the Earth in the previous world.

At this juncture, we should mention that there is a whale of a controversy these days about the evolution of the whale. Mainline science argues that the whale evolved from a wolf-like (some argue a hippopotamus-like) land creature and did so in an accelerated period of time (about six million years) very recently, geologically speaking. This is inconsistent with and opposed to the evolutionary paradigm that all land creatures evolved from ancestors that originally came from the seas. Could it be that God's creation of the great whales threw such a monkey wrench into the fossil record of whale species that evolutionary scientists had to create a special rapid macro evolutionary scenario to explain the disconnect? In any case, the Young Earth Creationists point to this specific inconsistency as a proof for the Young Earth argument. Both arguments are incorrect. The wording of Genesis 1:21 specifically addresses the issue and has done so for a few thousand years, long before it even became an issue.

On the sixth day the Lord filled the new world with the land animals.

"And God said, Let the earth bring forth the living creature after his kind, cattle, and creeping thing, and beast of the earth after his kind: and it was so. And God made the beast of the earth after his kind, and cattle after their kind, and every thing that creepeth upon the earth after his kind: and God saw that [it was] good." (Genesis 1:24-25)

All these living creatures and the vegetation are said to be made after their kind or after his kind, and there seems to be a great emphasis placed on that point in the narrative. Now (and this is very important) see what else the Lord God did NOT make after his kind - Man: *"And God said, Let us make man in our image, after our likeness: and let them have dominion over the fish of the sea, and over the fowl of the air, and over the cattle, and over all the earth, and over every creeping thing that creepeth upon the earth."* (Genesis 1:26)

This last use of the word *after* in relation to the creation of Man provides the true sense of interpretation of the word as used elsewhere in Genesis chapter one. If Man was made after God's likeness, the likeness of which was a pre-existing form or pattern, this gives credibility to the notion that the vegetation and animals were made after the patterns of previously-existing forms which were on the face of the Earth in the old world. This would explain the emphasis and number of references to *after his kind*, much like the term *a thousand years* is stated and restated six times in Revelation chapter 20 to define the exact length of Christ's future Kingdom on the face of the Earth. Even after repeating the term a thousand years six times to make the point, amillennial and postmillennial eschatologists still overlook that truth. As far as some people are concerned, the same can be said about the meaning of *after their kind* in Genesis.

It should also be pointed out that Man was the only living thing in Genesis (other than the whale) that was not said to be made after his kind; therefore he was new and unique. That uniqueness was in respect to being made in the image of God, which refers not to a physical, bodily trait but to the soul and mind. Unlike all the other creatures God made during the six days, only Man was told to replenish the Earth (Genesis 1:28), which indicates that Man, made in God's image, was to replace the humanoids of the old creation. These humanoids obviously had a physical form biologically very similar to true man in physical structure but not in mind and soul, *which is defined as being "after our [God, the Trinity's] likeness."*

"And God blessed them, and God said unto them, Be fruitful, and multiply, and replenish the earth, and subdue it: and have dominion over the fish of the sea, and over the fowl of the air, and over every living thing that moveth upon the earth." (Genesis 1:28)

Summation: The truth of these passages and the emerging evidence affirm that true Modern Man is a newcomer to the face of this old planet. True man, made in the image of God, has only been on the Earth about 6,000 years. He is a created creature - he did not evolve. Although he was preceded on the face of the Earth by lineages of humanoids of varying morphology closely approaching modern anatomical similarity, Adam and his descendants (us) are unique. That uniqueness is defined as creation in the *image of God*, and that definition eludes scientific quantification.

Chapter 16

Sevens of the Bible in Time and Nature

Why did the Lord God take seven days to make the present world, when surely an omnipotent God could have done so instantly with a single word? The answer is so simple that it may astound you.

The Scriptures say that there are seven Spirits of God (Revelation 3:1, 4:5, 5:6). There are numerous places in the Scriptures where God denotes things in sevens or multiples of seven. The Bible also shows us that God uses sevens throughout the Scriptures to denote prophetic time. Below are just a few examples.

"Behold, there come seven years of great plenty throughout all the land of Egypt:" (Genesis 41:29)

'And there shall arise after them seven years of famine; and all the plenty shall be forgotten in the land of Egypt; and the famine shall consume the land;" (Genesis 41:30)

"And thou shalt number seven sabbaths of years unto thee, seven times seven years; and the space of the seven sabbaths of years shall be unto thee forty and nine years." (Leviticus 25:8)

"And they that dwell in the cities of Israel shall go forth, and shall set on fire and burn the weapons, both the shields and the bucklers, the bows and the arrows, and the handstaves, and the spears, and they shall burn them with fire seven years:" (Ezekiel 39:9)

"Seventy weeks are determined upon thy people and upon thy holy city, to finish the transgression, and to make an end of sins, and to make reconciliation for iniquity, and to bring in everlasting righteousness, and to seal up the vision and prophecy, and to anoint the most Holy." (Daniel 9:24)

The very first use of sevens to denote time is found in Genesis, chapters one and two. That very first group of sevens has delineated the days of the week since the beginning of human history. Man certainly has messed with the years and the calendars (so no man today can know *exactly* what year it really is), but that seven-day week system has survived from Adam until today. No wonder - it was ordained by God from the beginning of this creation. The 7th Day was proclaimed as something very special from the first two chapters of the Biblical account. Let us look closer at the importance of the Seventh Day in relation to time.

"And on the seventh day God ended his work which he had made; and he rested on the seventh day from all his work which he had made. And

God blessed the seventh day, and sanctified it: because that in it he had rested from all his work which God created and made." (Genesis 2:2-3)

"For [in] six days the LORD made heaven and earth, the sea, and all that in them [is], and rested the seventh day: wherefore the LORD blessed the sabbath day, and hallowed it." (Exodus 20:11)

"It [is] a sign between me and the children of Israel for ever: for [in] six days the LORD made heaven and earth, and on the seventh day he rested, and was refreshed." (Exodus 31:17)

"Six days shall work be done, but on the seventh day there shall be to you an holy day, a sabbath of rest to the LORD: whosoever doeth work therein shall be put to death." (Exodus 35:2)

"And he said unto them, The sabbath was made for man, and not man for the sabbath:" (Mark 2:27)

"For the Son of man is Lord even of the sabbath day." (Matthew 12:8)

With the context of those verses in mind, look at the following verses:

"But, beloved, be not ignorant of this one thing, that one day [is] with the Lord as a thousand years, and a thousand years as one day." (2 Peter 3:8)

"And I saw thrones, and they sat upon them, and judgment was given unto them: and [I saw] the souls of them that were beheaded for the witness of Jesus, and for the word of God, and which had not worshipped the beast, neither his image, neither had received [his] mark upon their foreheads, or in their hands; and they lived and reigned with Christ a thousand years." (Revelation 20:4)

The latter verse speaks of a time yet future, when the Lord Jesus Christ will reign on the Earth with man for a period of 1,000 years before the final judgment, the final destruction of Satan and death, and the beginning of eternity future. What these verses tell us is that the seven 24-hour days of Genesis are a prophetic type which, when multiplied by 1,000, gives us the length of time of the Biblical history of man from Adam until the end of time as we know it. In other words, 7,000 years is the length of all human history (but not all natural history) both past and future on this present Earth. According to the Biblical chronology, the past part of that human history to the present is roughly 6,000 years. That means there are yet another 1,000 years ahead, which equate to a 1,000-year Sabbath of rest (Day 7. See Hebrews 4:9), when the Lord Jesus Christ will return, reign, and rest from His redemptive work on the Earth as the King of Kings and Lord of Lords.

"Blessed and holy [is] he that hath part in the first resurrection: on such the second death hath no power, but they shall be priests of God and of Christ, and shall reign with him a thousand years." (Revelation 20:6)

"And when the thousand years are expired, Satan shall be loosed out of his prison," (Revelation 20:7)

"And cast him into the bottomless pit, and shut him up, and set a seal upon him, that he should deceive the nations no more, till the thousand years should be fulfilled: and after that he must be loosed a little season." (Revelation 20:3)

"Jesus answered, My kingdom is not of this world: if my kingdom were of this world, then would my servants fight, that I should not be delivered to the Jews: but now is my kingdom not from hence." (John 18:36)

Following that glorious 7th Day 1,000 years of time, the day which follows will be a new first day, a new eternal beginning without end, the next octave up the musical scale (more on that in a moment) so to speak.

"And I saw a new heaven and a new earth: for the first heaven and the first earth were passed away; and there was no more sea." (Revelation 21:1)

"And he that sat upon the throne said, Behold, I make all things new. And he said unto me, Write: for these words are true and faithful." (Revelation 21:5)

It has been about 2,000 years (prophetic days 5 and 6) since the Lord first came to save us from the power of sin and death. That means that his return is very close. Keep in mind that although our modern calendar is already past the year 2,000, it has not really been a full 2,000 years since the first coming of the Lord Jesus Christ. The history of the Gregorian calendar reveals that there are years missing. Even before that, a year was skipped between 1 B.C. and 1 A.D. (There was no 0 year.) Although we can't set an exact date, we can be sure that the seventh prophetic day is soon to dawn upon this sin-cursed world, and the Great Tribulation (seven years) could begin at almost any time. Is this a faithful prediction? Certainly, because observance of the seventh day Sabbath was a part of the Ten Commandments, a part of the law of God. *"And it is easier for heaven and earth to pass, than one tittle of the law to fail."* (Luke 16:17)

"An instructor of the foolish, a teacher of babes, which hast the form of knowledge and of the truth in the law." (Romans 2:20)

"For the law was given by Moses, [but] grace and truth came by Jesus Christ." (John 1:17)

Sevens in Nature
The Sevens of God can also be observed in the things of Nature. It appears that the physics and chemistry of nature are structured on such a base system. Nearly everyone can relate to music. All the songs you hear on the radio are based on a musical system of just seven major notes.

Notice that the seven notes repeat, with the eighth key a higher or lower octave above or below the first as you go up or down the keyboard. All other minor notes, sharps, and flats fit within the structure of the basic seven.

If you pass sunlight through a prism, it produces seven colors - three primary colors and four secondary.

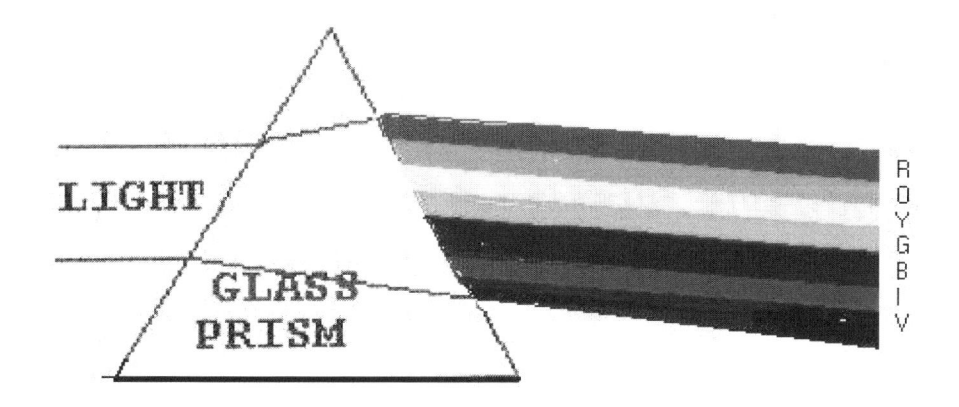

In the realm of Minerals and Geochemistry, there are seven crystal systems:

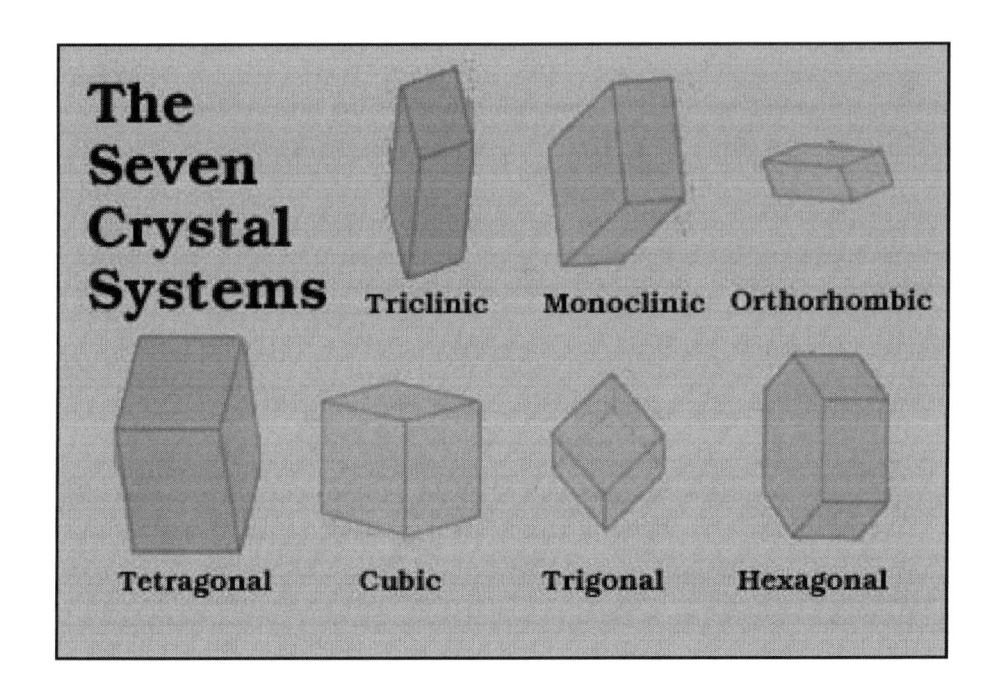

Here is a picture of example minerals from each of the seven systems:

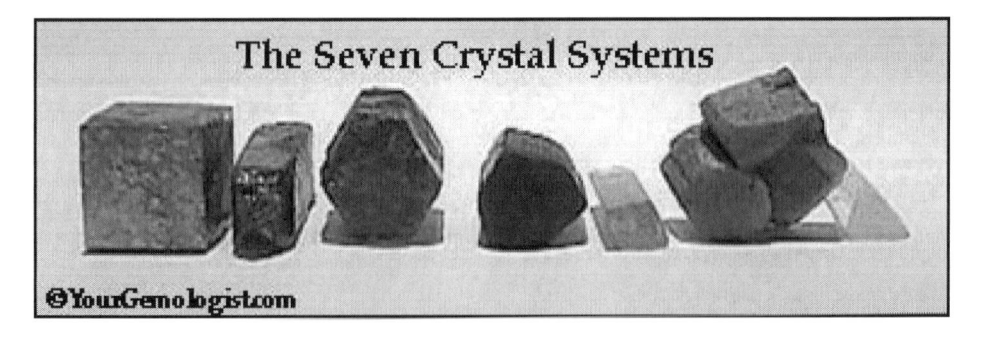

(Picture courtesy of http://yourgemologist.com)

Even the Periodic Table of the known Elements appears to have seven levels of periodicity:

We can see from these examples that God has ordained a pattern of sevens in Nature. All things, be they matter, energy, time, or space, were designed and ordained by the Lord God. Therefore, rest assured that our Holy Bible is the infallible Master Textbook of true science. Scientists can only elaborate on the observed details.

"For by him were all things created, that are in heaven, and that are in earth, visible and invisible, whether [they be] thrones, or dominions, or principalities, or powers: all things were created by him, and for him: And he is before all things, and by him all things consist." (Colossians 1:16-17)

Chapter 17

Doctrinal Differences: Kingdom of Heaven and Kingdom of God

Knowing the doctrinal difference between the terms *Kingdom of Heaven* and *Kingdom of God* is the key to understanding the complete timeline of Biblical history past, present, and future, the proper place of the Church, and the prophetic future of Israel. The Bible is about the struggle for a Kingdom, the Kingdom of Heaven, with its Capital City (Jerusalem) on this Earth.

Israel rejected the Lord Jesus Christ as the Messiah when He first came because Israel was looking for a political King who would make Israel the world-ruling kingdom spoken of by their prophets (Jeremiah 23:5; Psalms 48:2). They were expecting a military deliverance from the Romans and the rest of the heathen. This is easy to understand, as they were expecting carnal deliverance. However, they were missing the point about spiritual deliverance and righteousness, which led them to ask of Jesus: *"And when he was demanded of the Pharisees, when the kingdom of God should come, he answered them and said, The kingdom of God cometh not with observation: Neither shall they say, Lo here! or, lo there! for, behold, the kingdom of God is within you."* (Luke 17:20-21)

In that statement, Jesus was declaring a spiritual truth that Israel did not see. When Pontius Pilot asked about His Kingdom on another occasion, He gave a somewhat different answer: *"Jesus answered, My kingdom is not of this world: if my kingdom were of this world, then would my servants fight, that I should not be delivered to the Jews: but now is my kingdom not from hence."* (John 18:36)

In this particular passage, the word *now* is not speaking about the spiritual Kingdom of God (within you) but of a literal political Kingdom yet to come on the Earth. You should also note that the word now has been removed from many newer translations (NASB, AMP, NLT, ESV, CEV). The reason is because most of the translators of today's Bibles are amillennial in their position on prophecy. In other words, they do not accept the literal return of the Lord Jesus Christ to reign on the Earth for a thousand years as foretold in Revelation.

Although that truth is rejected by a major portion of Christianity today, His disciples knew it and were asking when the literal Kingdom would come. *"When they therefore were come together, they asked of him, saying, Lord, wilt thou at this time restore again the kingdom to Israel? And he said unto them, It is not for you to know the times or the seasons, which the Father hath put in his own power. But ye shall receive power, after that the Holy Ghost is come upon you: and ye shall be witnesses unto me both in Jerusalem, and in all Judaea, and in Samaria, and unto the uttermost part of the earth."* (Acts 1:6-8)

The disciples are clearly asking about a literal Kingdom, and the Lord says it is not for them to know the time when that literal Kingdom (the Kingdom of Heaven) will take place. Until that time, the disciples were given power to preach the Kingdom of God and righteousness through faith in the risen Savior, who will return and rule over the whole Earth from Jerusalem.

This is one of the most hated and least understood doctrines of the Bible, yet it is one of the most important in rightly dividing the truth - the separation of Church doctrine from Tribulation doctrine. Some churches do not want to hear this because they think the Church has replaced Israel. Certainly, the whole world reviles at the prospect of hated Israel becoming the head of the Kingdoms. A hatred of Christians and Jews exists on a spiritual level that is beyond their own comprehension. Satan hates the Jews, and the world is under Satan's control. Hate and envy are the root reasons the word now is removed from John 18:36 in some translations. The world does not want the Lord Jesus Christ to return and rule over them, and that's why the Jews killed their King the first time He came. Here is what their King will say about that when He returns: *"But those mine enemies, which would not that I should reign over them, bring hither, and slay [them] before me."* (Luke 19:27)

There will be a big attitude difference between the Lord's first coming as the gentle Lamb of God and His Second Coming as the warrior King, the Lion of Judah. *"And I saw heaven opened, and behold a white horse; and he that sat upon him [was] called Faithful and True, and in righteousness he doth judge and make war. His eyes [were] as a flame of fire, and on his head [were] many crowns; and he had a name written, that no man knew, but he himself. And he [was] clothed with a vesture dipped in blood: and his name is called The Word of God."* (Revelation 19:11-13)

The Lord Jesus Christ came to His own and preached a dualistic message. To the Jews, the heirs of the promised political Kingdom, the Lord preached the Gospel of the Kingdom of Heaven - a literal physical Kingdom soon to come. *"From that time Jesus began to preach, and to say, Repent: for the kingdom of heaven is at hand."* (Matt. 4:17)

To the entire world, He preached the coming Kingdom of God - righteousness and holiness. *"Now after that John was put in prison, Jesus came into Galilee, preaching the gospel of the kingdom of God, And saying, The time is fulfilled, and the kingdom of God is at hand: repent ye, and believe the gospel."* (Mark 1:14)

Because the Lord used the terms Kingdom of Heaven and Kingdom of God interchangeably in places in the four Gospels, most Christians think they are one and the same. They will be, but not until the Second Coming of the Lord Jesus Christ, when He rules the world for a thousand years on the throne of His father David (His father in the flesh, His human side) at Jerusalem. Again: *"Jesus answered, My kingdom is not of this world: if my kingdom were of this world, then would my servants fight, that I should not be delivered to the Jews: but now is my kingdom not from hence."* (John 18:36)

If you rightly divide the Bible, you will see that Jesus was preaching about two components of the Kingdom. He preached that the political kingdom (Kingdom of Heaven) was coming, and if the Jews had accepted Him after His death and resurrection, He would have come back and established it after seven years of tribulation as foretold in the prophecies. *"Seventy weeks are determined upon thy people and upon thy holy city, to finish the transgression, and to make an end of sins, and to make reconciliation for iniquity, and to bring in everlasting righteousness, and to seal up the vision and prophecy, and to anoint the most Holy. Know therefore and understand, [that] from the going forth of the commandment to restore and to build Jerusalem unto the Messiah the Prince [shall be] seven weeks, and threescore and two weeks: the street shall be built again, and the wall, even in troublous times. And after threescore and two weeks shall Messiah be cut off, but not for himself: and the people of the prince that shall come shall destroy the city and the sanctuary; and the end thereof [shall be] with a flood, and unto the end of the war desolations are determined. And he shall confirm the covenant with many for one week: and in the midst of the week he shall cause the sacrifice and the oblation to cease, and for the overspreading of abominations he shall make [it] desolate, even until the consummation, and that determined shall be poured upon the desolate."* (Daniel 9:24-27)

In fact, when Stephen was preaching to the Pharisees as they were stoning him, the Lord Jesus was standing up from His seat in the Third Heaven ready to come back, save the Jews, and establish the Kingdom *"But he, being full of the Holy Ghost, looked up stedfastly into heaven, and saw the glory of God, and Jesus standing on the right hand of God, And said, Behold, I see the heavens opened, and the Son of man standing on the right hand of God."* (Acts 7:55-56)

To show by the Scriptures the difference between the terms Kingdom of Heaven and Kingdom of God, the Holy Spirit has put this little nugget of truth within the Gospel of Matthew: *"And from the days of John the Baptist until now the kingdom of heaven suffereth violence, and the violent take it by force."* (Matthew 11:12)

Ask yourself this question: If the Kingdom of God is within you, and if the Kingdom of God and Kingdom of Heaven are one and the same, how could anyone take it out of you by violence? And if that righteousness, i.e., the Kingdom of God within you, could not possibly be there until after the cross and the resurrection, what is Jesus saying to the Jews here *before* the cross and the resurrection? The answer is the Kingdom of Israel, which is God's people and Jerusalem, the Lord's chosen place from which to rule. *"But I say unto you, Swear not at all; neither by heaven; for it is God's throne: Nor by the earth; for it is his footstool: neither by Jerusalem; for it is the city of the great King."* (Matthew 5:34-35)

Israel rejected their King when He came the first time. In the nearly two millenniums since then, His Kingdom has been in a mystery form, the Lord Jesus Christ reigning in the heart of the believer and yet seated on the right hand of the Father in the Third Heaven...

"[Even] the mystery which hath been hid from ages and from generations, but now is made manifest to his saints: To whom God would make known what [is] the riches of the glory of this mystery among the Gentiles; which is Christ in you, the hope of glory:" (Colossians 1:26-27)

...while Satan still holds the physical throne over this world. *"And the devil said unto him, All this power will I give thee, and the glory of them: for that is delivered unto me; and to whomsoever I will I give it. If thou therefore wilt worship me, all shall be thine."* (Luke 4:6-7)

Although Satan has now lost the war, the final battle for physical possession is yet to come. This is the present status of the Kingdom of Heaven.

In the more than 1,900 years since His own people rejected His salvation, God has been chastising Israel, while blessings and salvation have gone out to the Gentiles. However, God is not finished with Israel, but He IS just about finished with the Gentiles. The Gentiles' time is running out. The Apostle Paul said this: *"For I would not, brethren, that ye should be ignorant of this mystery, lest ye should be wise in your own conceits; that blindness in part is happened to Israel, until the fulness of the Gentiles be come in. And so all Israel shall be saved: as it is written, There shall come out of Sion the Deliverer, and shall turn away ungodliness from Jacob:"* (Romans 11:25-26)

We are living in the last days of the blessing to the Gentiles. The Jews are back in the land of Israel (although the Arab world does not recognize it as Israel but insists on calling it Palestine). Regardless of the name, it is still the land God promised to Abraham and his seed through Isaac and Jacob, not through the line of Ishmael. That is the ancient root of contention still festering today over the issue of the land.

The Jews have returned to the land as prophesied in the Scriptures, but they are still in unbelief about Jesus. Although they are the enemies of the Gospel of Grace by the Lord Jesus Christ...

"As concerning the gospel, they are enemies for your sakes: but as touching the election, they are beloved for the fathers' sakes. For the gifts and calling of God are without repentance. For as ye in times past have not believed God, yet have now obtained mercy through their unbelief." (Romans 11:28-30)

...they are still God's people, and He will use the present evil world to chastise them, open their eyes to the truth they rejected, and bring them again to Himself. That is the truth of the matter - a truth that is bitterly denied by the whole world. Jerusalem and the Middle East are the crucible and iron furnace that will soon wax hotter as the prophecies unfold before us.

Beware! There are two things to watch for which must come to pass before the Lord's return. First (and this is directly related to the relationship of Jerusalem to Israel, the Arab world, and the Palestinians) there will be some kind of contract among all parties on the matter of Jerusalem in an effort to establish peace. This is spoken of by the prophet Daniel. *"Then shall he return into his land with great riches; and his heart shall be against the holy covenant; and he shall do exploits, and return to his own land. At the time appointed he shall return, and come toward the south; but it shall not be as the former, or as the latter. For the ships of Chittim shall come against him: therefore he shall be grieved, and return, and have indignation against the holy covenant: so shall he do; he shall even return, and have intelligence with them that forsake the holy covenant. And arms shall stand on his part, and they shall pollute the sanctuary of strength, and shall take away the daily sacrifice, and they shall place the abomination that maketh desolate."* (Daniel 11:28-31)

Second, there is going to be a new Temple built in Jerusalem in the future. Notice that the context above is about the exploits of the coming Antichrist, whom unbelieving Israel and the unbelieving world will welcome as the Messiah. Take note of the daily sacrifice, the sanctuary, and the abomination that maketh desolate. There cannot be a daily sacrifice without a Temple. This is a cross reference to what the Apostle Paul spoke about in 2 Thessalonians. *"That ye be not soon shaken in mind, or be troubled, neither by spirit, nor by word, nor by letter as from us, as that the day of Christ is at hand. Let no man deceive you by any means: for that day shall not come, except there come a falling away first, and that man of sin be revealed, the son of perdition; Who opposeth and exalteth himself above all that is called God, or that is worshipped; so that he as God sitteth in the temple of God, shewing himself that he is God."* (2 Thessalonians 2:2-4)

These things are future and yet to be fulfilled, but they will come to pass. The Holy Bible says so. Believe it!

The entire theme of the Holy Bible is about the battle over a Kingdom and the rightful ruler of that Kingdom. This controversy goes back long before Abraham and long before Adam. It began sometime after the Lord first created the heavens and the Earth. Lucifer (Satan) was the first ruler in the Kingdom of Heaven in the ancient past. *"Thou [art] the <u>anointed</u> cherub that covereth; and I have set thee [so]: thou wast upon the holy mountain of God; thou hast walked up and down in the midst of the stones of fire. Thou [wast] perfect in thy ways from the day that thou wast created, till iniquity was found in thee."* (Ezekiel 28:14-15)

When he rebelled and sinned against God, unrighteousness was introduced into the physical realm, and death came upon the ancient world.

Remember, the story of the whole Bible from the very beginning until the end is about the spiritual battle for the Kingdom. The eventual triumphant ruler of that Kingdom, both in the literal world and over the spiritual forces, will be the KING of KINGS; the Lord Jesus Christ, The Son of the Living God of Israel, who first came as a Lamb but is soon coming as the Lion of Judah.

Chapter 18

Exact English KJV Wording: Is It Important?

U pon close and honest observation, the literal wording of the Holy Bible does not support the doctrine of Young Earth Creationism. When the words of Genesis are taken at face value and Rightly-Divided against the major doctrines of the Bible, it is found that the Bible actually supports the scientifically-accepted evidence for an Old Earth. The hundreds of millions of years of the Geologic time scale and the fossil evidence of death on the face of the Earth, stretching far back into antiquity, are God's preserved evidence written in stone that the Earth is very old, and that death has been around for a long time. Acceptance of these facts does not contradict or nullify the events chronicled in the seven days of Genesis because that particular evidence is from a time well before the seven days of Genesis. When you insert that ancient natural history into the time-gap between Genesis 1:1 and Genesis 1:2, you have placed it into the proper Biblical context. That now brings you forward in time to about 6,000 years ago and the actual start of God's work of the seven days. That starting point begins where the Lord God says, "Let there be light."

Why was light needed? Because something bad had happened to the original Creation, and the Spirit of God is plainly telling you so in Genesis 1:2, where the Earth has become without form, void, and dark. The seven days of Genesis were not the original creation of the universe and all things. They were a regeneration, a new generation of the heavens and Earth. As fantastic as that may seem, it is the only answer that makes sense when you compare the Earth's geological history with the literal wording of the Bible. Let me emphasize that we are weighing the Earth's Geological history against the literal wording of the Bible, not against traditional interpretations of that wording.

It is the purpose of this book to point out inaccurate assumptions using both the Scriptures and common sense, and to affirm the Holy Bible as the final authority on all questions of natural history and spiritual truth. We have chosen to use the literal wording of the old King James Authorized Version of the Bible (based on the original translation work of 1611) because it predates today's denominational Christian movements. Thus it is a translation free from contamination by modern Christian Scholarship and textual bias. It is also a translation free of scientific contamination, as it predates all works of the founding fathers of the Geological sciences (Nicholas Steno (1638-1686), James Hutton (1726-1797), Charles Lyell (1797-1875), and William Smith (1769-1839) and predates the inception of Darwin's Theory of Evolution by over 200 years. If the written words of the English language Bible of 1611 were truth back in 1611 (just short of 400 years ago), then those same written words will still be truth in our English language today. It is from this standard of written authority that the material in this book is presented and defended.

Although the King James Version of the Holy Scriptures is just one of many translations of the Scriptures, it is a self-interpreting whole with its own internal set of terminology and concepts. Additional insight into the choice of English wording can be gained from reviewing the Hebrew and Greek definitions and/or comparing translations in other languages, and I recommend doing so. Understanding of it all is provided by the Holy Spirit of Truth.

When studying His Scriptures, it is important to keep these points in mind:

1. *The Scriptures are self interpreting when correctly translated. Every single word, tense, and phrase is structured to convey PRECISE meaning.*

2. *Things that are different are NOT the same. Things that are the same ARE the same.*

3. *There are NO real contradictions in the Scriptures (John 10:35). For every apparent contradiction, there is a Scriptural resolution. The Scriptures cannot be broken.*

When man communicates with his fellow man, lawyers draw up contracts, which use precise word meanings. Legislatures draft laws and regulations on the same principles, as do diplomats, who must convey their nations' positions with concisely-worded documents that effectively communicate across language and cultural differences. The use of a word to convey a particular nuance of meaning can speak volumes. Recipients parse words closely for determination of intent and subtly of meaning. Should we not therefore apply the same principle and understanding in respecting and interpreting what God has to say to man in all matters? Of course!

With respect to the doctrine that the six days of Genesis are describing a regeneration of the heavens and Earth to replace a previous world destroyed by God, there are several comparisons of Scripture with Scripture that suggest this doctrine:

Compare: ..the generations of Adam (Genesis 5:1) with ...the generations of the heaven and the Earth (Genesis 2:4)

In Genesis 5:1-5, the Bible accounts the generations of Adam, but the genealogy begins with Seth and makes no mention of Cain and Abel. This is in spite of the fact that Cain and Abel were previously mentioned. Why? Because it denotes a new beginning for the Messianic line from Adam to Christ. The rebellion of Cain (who was of the wicked one) and the murder of his brother, Abel, destroyed the first natural order of things. Seth was the appointed replacement. The importance of this will be explained shortly when we discuss the Rule of First Mention of Bible interpretation.

Compare these two verses:

"In the beginning God created the heaven and the earth." (Genesis 1:1)

"Thus the heavens and the earth were finished, and all the host of them." (Genesis 2:1)

Notice the singular tense of the word *heaven* in the first verse and the plural rendering of the word in the second verse. In both instances the word is from the same dual tense Hebrew word. For that reason, critics of the AV say it is a mistranslation and thus render the word in Genesis 1:1 as plural in other contemporary English translations.

Remember: Things that are different are not the same, and by this one letter difference in rendering the word as singular in Genesis 1:1

and plural in Genesis 2:1 of the KJV, the Spirit is directing your attention to something very important - a subtle difference in the meaning of the term and its context. Why? To make you search for the significance of that subtle difference, because it leads to more perfect understanding of the rest of the Bible in our own language (English). This difference supports the interpretive import of the comparison we made between Genesis 5:1 and Genesis 2:4 and between Cain and Seth. It fits the intent of meaning.

By the way, that minor difference of an "s" or no "s" at the end of the word heaven is also directly connected to interpretation of other key concepts in passages, including Genesis 1:10, Isaiah 65:17, and Revelation 21:1.The difference also plays a major part in understanding the term *Third Heaven* that the Apostle Paul wrote about in 2 Corinthians 12:2. It should not be lightly dismissed and is explained in great detail elsewhere. .(See chapter titled *The Firmament.*)

Compare these verses:

"And God blessed them, and God said unto them, Be fruitful, and multiply, and replenish the earth, and subdue it: and have dominion over the fish of the sea, and over the fowl of the air, and over every living thing that moveth upon the earth." (Genesis 1:28)

"And God blessed them, saying, Be fruitful, and multiply, and fill the waters in the seas, and let fowl multiply in the earth." (Genesis 1:22)

"And God blessed Noah and his sons, and said unto them, Be fruitful, and multiply, and replenish the earth." (Genesis 9:1)

The word *replenish* in 1:28 and the word *fill* in 1:22 are also from the same Hebrew word (*male*) as is the word replenish in Genesis 9:1. Critics of the AV text are quick to point out that this Hebrew word can have different meanings, such as to fill something for the first time or to fill up something again. They are correct in pointing that out, but they are incorrect when they call it an unfortunate translation and insist that it should also be changed to fill in Genesis 1:22 and Genesis 9:1. The Spirit had a good reason when He moved the translators of the AV1611 Bible to make this particular nuance of distinction. When you compare the word replenish as spoken in Genesis 1:28 with the meaning of its rendering in Genesis 9:1 concerning Noah, we begin to see that the Spirit is saying something very important. As Noah and his family were told to go forth from the Ark and repopulate a new world (because the former one and all its population had been destroyed), God was also telling Adam something very similar, specifically, to repopulate a new world after the former one had been destroyed. This point will also be explained and expanded upon shortly.

Compare:

"And the earth was without form, and void; and darkness was upon the face of the deep. And the Spirit of God moved upon the face of the waters." (Genesis 1:2)

" I beheld the earth, and, lo, it was without form, and void; and the heavens, and they had no light. I beheld the mountains, and, lo, they trembled, and all the hills moved lightly. I beheld, and, lo, there was no man, and all the birds of the heavens were fled. I beheld, and, lo, the fruitful place was a wilderness, and all the cities thereof were broken down at the presence of the LORD, and by his fierce anger." (Jeremiah 4:23-26)

The context of the first verse is the past time immediately before God says, "Let there be light" on the first day in Genesis. The context of the second verse is the future time immediately after the Great Tribulation, at the second coming of the Lord Jesus Christ. The first verse above speaks about the Earth's condition before it is prepared for the first Adam. The second verse speaks about the Earth's condition before it is prepared for the second Adam, the Lord Jesus Christ.

"And so it is written, The first man Adam was made a living soul; the last Adam was made a quickening spirit. Howbeit that was not first which is spiritual, but that which is natural; and afterward that which is spiritual. The first man is of the earth, earthy: the second man is the Lord from heaven." (1 Corinthians 15:45-47)

Having defended the Gap Theory argument on the basis of these arguments, let us now review them and test them against a commonly-accepted rule of Biblical Interpretation, The Rule of First Mention.

This rule states that the first mention of a word in Scripture sets the tone for the use of that particular word throughout the rest of the Bible. There are at least three such applications of this rule in the King James Bible that confirm support for the Ruin-Reconstruction (Gap Theory) interpretation. Let us begin by examining the first and second mention of the word *generations* in the Bible:

1st Mention: *"These [are] the generations of the heavens and of the earth when they were created, in the day that the LORD God made the earth and the heavens, And every plant of the field before it was in the earth, and every herb of the field before it grew: for the LORD God had not caused it to rain upon the earth, and [there was] not a man to till the ground."* (Genesis 2:4-5)

2nd Mention: "*This [is] the book of the generations of Adam. In the day that God created man, in the likeness of God made he him; Male and female created he them; and blessed them, and called their name Adam, in the day when they were created. And Adam lived an hundred and thirty years, and begat [a son] in his own likeness, after his image; and called his name Seth:*" (Genesis 5:1-3)

Notice that the second mention of the term *generations* in the Bible chronicles the family line of Adam. However, this verse begins the start of Adam's family line with Seth and not with Cain or Abel. This is extremely instructive, as anyone who reads the Bible knows that Eve gave birth to Cain and Abel *before* Seth. So why does this particular verse of Scripture and the genealogy of Adam deliberately skip over Cain and Abel? Let's look at the Bible for the answer.

"And Adam knew his wife again; and she bare a son, and called his name Seth: For God, [said she], hath appointed me another seed instead of Abel, whom Cain slew." (Genesis 4:25)

This prior verse says that Seth was a replacement for the first seed (Abel), who was destroyed by the evil deed of his brother (Cain), but neither the one replaced nor his brother is mentioned in the genealogy of Genesis 5:1-3; they are skipped over. There is a gap in the generations of Adam from that point forward in time. Applying the Rule of First Mention to the first mention of the word generations in Genesis 2:1 (aided with the additional insight gained in observing the word's use in the second mention at Genesis 5:1-4), we can be confident there must also a gap at the first mention.

In other words, the generations of the heavens and of the Earth beginning at Genesis 2:4 are also a replacement for a previous heaven and Earth which, as alleged in the Gap Theory interpretation, were eventually destroyed as a consequence of Lucifer's rebellion in the ancient past. In order for this interpretation to be true and the Rule of First Mention to remain valid, every use of the word generations in the Bible (all 114 references) must refer to a starting point in time, which skips over a previous generation or generations. That appears to be the case. The third mention of generations begins with Noah:

"These [are] the generations of Noah: Noah was a just man [and] perfect in his generations, [and] Noah walked with God." (Genesis 6:9)

Noah was the beginning of a new generation because he was the father of every descendant who survived the flood and the father of us all. The destruction of the old world by the flood was a new starting point for reckoning the generations, as all before him from Adam to Lamech are skipped over in that verse. You will observe that every reference to generations which follows in the Bible sets a specific point of reference in historical time, which always runs forward (never backward).

This brings us to the application of the Rule of First Mention, which we find in our next word, replenish (Genesis 1:23 & Genesis 9:1)

1st Mention: "*And God blessed them, and God said unto them, Be fruitful, and multiply, and replenish the earth, and subdue it: and have dominion over the fish of the sea, and over the fowl of the air, and over every living thing that moveth upon the earth.*" (Genesis 1:28)

2nd Mention: "*And God blessed Noah and his sons, and said unto them, Be fruitful, and multiply, and replenish the earth.*" (Genesis 9:1)

In the second mention of the word replenish in the KJV Bible, the Lord God is commanding Noah to repopulate and refill the Earth after all the its previous land inhabitants were destroyed by a flood. Noah is the starting point of a new generation. The command to replenish follows these event specifics:

1. The old world was flooded with water.

2. It was a judgment from God upon a world in which the cumulative state of evil that began with a single act of disobedience (in this case Adam's sin) had led to a world filled with death and violence.

3. Noah was the starting point for repopulation of the new world after the flood.

Referring back to the 1st mention of replenish where God commanded Adam to do so, we find these similarities:

1. The world was also flooded with water (Genesis 1:2).

2. This would infer that this flood was also a judgment from God upon a previous world in which the cumulative state of evil that began with a single act of disobedience (in this case Lucifer's sin) had led to a world filled with death and violence. The Earth's geology is consistent with a long history of death and violence.

3. Adam was therefore the starting point for repopulation of the new world created in six days after a flood. He replaced a race of beings that had populated the previous world.

If the Rule of First Mention is valid, these things must be so. We now will show you a third application of this rule that confirms this truth:

1st Mention: *"And the earth was without form, and void; and darkness [was] upon the face of the deep. And the Spirit of God moved upon the face of the waters."* (Genesis 1:2)

2nd Mention: *"I beheld the earth, and, lo, [it was] without form, and void; and the heavens, and they [had] no light. I beheld the mountains, and, lo, they trembled, and all the hills moved lightly. I beheld, and, lo, [there was] no man, and all the birds of the heavens were fled. I beheld, and, lo, the fruitful place [was] a wilderness, and all the cities thereof were broken down at the presence of the LORD, [and] by his fierce anger. For thus hath the LORD said, The whole land shall be desolate; yet will I not make a full end. For this shall the earth mourn, and the heavens above be black: because I have spoken [it], I have purposed [it], and will not repent, neither will I turn back from it."* (Jeremiah 4:23-28)

In the second mention of *without form and void* in the Bible the prophet is describing the condition of the Earth and heavens, not in the past but in the future; and that future time is following the Great Tribulation and the return of the Lord Jesus Christ to this Earth. We know this is future (and not a reference to Genesis 1:2 as some Gap Theory advocates allege) because of the following facts:

1. There is mention of cities being destroyed, but we know there were no cities built on the Earth before Adam was created and men began to multiply.

2. The Lord is both physically present and angry.

3. The tense of the phrase "the whole land shall" makes this a reference to a future, not a past event.

Following the heavens and Earth found without form and void in Jeremiah, the Lord will regenerate the heavens and Earth for His Earthly 1,000-year Kingdom. You see, the Lord Jesus Christ is the SECOND ADAM. (Read 1 Corinthians 15:22-47.) This second Adam (the Lord) and His Eve (The Bride, His Church) will rule another new heavens and Earth made from remains of the present heavens and Earth.

These regenerations of the heavens and Earth are referred to as *worlds* throughout the Bible, and in every instance, these regenerations are followed by destruction of the previous world arrangement:

"Who gave himself for our sins, that he might deliver us from this present evil world, according to the will of God and our Father:" (Galatians 1:4)

"Who shall not receive manifold more in this present time, and in the world to come life everlasting." (Luke 18:30)

"Jesus answered, My kingdom is not of this world: if my kingdom were of this world, then would my servants fight, that I should not be

delivered to the Jews: but now is my kingdom not from hence." (John 18:36)

"And Jesus said unto them, Verily I say unto you, That ye which have followed me, in the regeneration when the Son of man shall sit in the throne of his glory, ye also shall sit upon twelve thrones, judging the twelve tribes of Israel." (Matthew 19:28)

"Nevertheless we, according to his promise, look for new heavens and a new earth, wherein dwelleth righteousness." (2 Peter 3:13)

"Hath in these last days spoken unto us by [his] Son, whom he hath appointed heir of all things, by whom also he made the worlds;" (Hebrews 1:2)

"Through faith we understand that the worlds were framed by the word of God, so that things which are seen were not made of things which do appear." (Hebrews 11:3)

The Greek word in the last two verses for *worlds* is "Αιωα" (as in eon) which is an age or perpetuity of specific prevailing conditions in time upon the face of the Earth.

When you examine the Scriptures in the light of the Rule of First Mention and see the harmonious comparison of types and meanings interpreted by their Scriptural meaning, the truth comes through clearly to those who have ears to hear and eyes to see. If these things are not true, then the interpretive Rule of First Mention is invalid.

The main reason the Young Earth Creationists reject the Gap Theory interpretation is because in their zeal to defend the traditional church view of creationism, they fail to discern the differences in meaning between the Biblical words Earth and World and in so doing, fail to accept the literal wording of Genesis 1 at face value, although they claim that they do.

Let's focus sharply and review the literal and concise wording points in Genesis 1:2.

"And the earth was without form, and void; and darkness was upon the face of the deep. And the Spirit of God moved upon the face of the waters." (Genesis 1:2)

Read carefully! BEFORE God said, "Let there be light" (verse 3), there is physical matter already in existence in time and space. There is the Earth, distinguishable as a planet, along with much water. There is also darkness present, which can be defined as either a physical or spiritual entity. (See Ephesians 6:12, 1 Thessalonians 5:5, and 1 John 1:5.) The Hebrew word for darkness at Genesis 1:2 speaks of darkness in a plural sense (more than one kind of darkness).

This truth comes through clearly in some other languages. Look at Genesis 1:2 in a language that, unlike English, can accommodate a plural rendering of darkness. That language is Spanish:

"Y la tierra estaba desordenada y vaca, y las tinieblas estaban sobre la haz del abismo, y el Espritu de Dios se mova sobre la haz de las aguas." (Gen. 1:2 RV 1909)

In that language, translated from the very same Hebrew manuscript line, the translators rendered darkness *tinieblas* as a plural entity, indicating there was more than one type of darkness present. Both physical darkness and spiritual darkness were present at Genesis 1:2.

The presence of darkness tells us that an evil influence had already infected the cosmos, which resulted in all things being without form and void (chaotic state). This condition is at variance with Isaiah 45:18, where the Lord says in the Scriptures that He made the Earth (Genesis 1:1) to be inhabited. *"For thus saith the LORD that created the heavens; God himself that formed the earth and made it; he hath established it, he created it not in vain, he formed it to be inhabited: I [am] the LORD; and [there is] none else."* (Isaiah 45:18)

The English term *in vain* in Isaiah 45:18 and the English term *without form* in Genesis 1:2 are from the same Hebrew word (*tohuw*)[תֹהוּ]. In other words, God didn't first create some void and formless glob of earth in the dark and then proceed to make everything else in the six days for the very first time. He never made the Earth in vain or without form; Isaiah 45:18 clearly says that. The KJV Bible and the original Hebrew falsify the entire doctrine of Young Earth Creationism.

So, what had happened to the Earth and the previous inhabitants of this plant called Earth and why? Who or what were they? The geologic evidence clearly shows that a great variety of life forms have inhabited this planet over a great expanse of time. Their fossil remains all have one thing in common...they ALL DIED. We must conclude that death, which comes by sin, initially came from the action of someone or something that lived (and sinned) in a previous world on the face of the Earth long before Adam was created, otherwise the fossil record makes no sense if it was not produced by Noah's flood (and it was not).

Those who believe that the original Earth and all it contains were made for the first time in those six famous days about six thousand years ago are quick to point out that death came upon this world when Adam sinned:

"Wherefore, as by one man sin entered into the world, and death by sin; and so death passed upon all men, for that all have sinned:" (Romans 5:12)

That verse is absolutely true, in context. Death entered this world (our world) when Adam sinned, about 6000 years ago, and Adam was the first man who sinned. But if you don't understand the

Biblical differences between the words *world* and *earth,* you cannot grasp the truth of the following points of logic and common sense:

1. *The Scriptures say that the serpent tempted Eve and caused her and Adam to sin.*

2. *If the serpent tempted the man and woman to sin against God, the serpent was disobedient and evil <u>before</u> Adam and Eve.*

3. *And if the serpent was evil before Adam fell, the spirit of the serpent would have had to have sinned against God at some point in time before Adam sinned. Got that?*

4. *Therefore, if death comes by sin (Romans 6:23; James 1:15 [an eternal rule]), and the serpent was a sinner before Adam, then death already existed in a world before Adam and Eve sinned. It was Adam's disobedience that allowed death to enter the newly-formed pristine world. It was Lucifer's disobedience and rebellion that allowed death to enter the original, ancient world. That is what the Bible says. If you don't get this point clear in your mind, it is not possible to understand the full Scriptural picture.*

Common Sense Conclusions:

1. *Adam may have been the first man to sin, but he was NOT the first living creature to sin.*

2. *Death entered into the world when Adam sinned, but death already existed at a point in time before Adam sinned, in a world on the face of the Earth before Adam.*

Therefore, the exact English wording of the KJV translation of the Scriptures and the Ruin-Reconstruction (Gap Theory) interpretation do not contradict the validity of the fossil evidence of death's ancient presence and past workings on this planet, nor do they contradict the doctrine of Romans 5:12. Because the period of time between when the serpent sinned in his world and when Adam sinned in the present world is not defined in the Bible. That length of time could range across hundreds of millions of years of time, exactly as the geological data suggest.

Since Adam was the first man created (made in God's image), there could not have been a previous race of men in the ancient world. There were however, races of life forms, which were manlike in physical structure and appearance that Adam was commissioned to replace. *"And God blessed them, and God said unto them, Be fruitful, and multiply, and replenish the earth, and subdue it: and have dominion over the fish of the sea, and over the fowl of the air, and over every living thing that moveth upon the earth."* (Genesis 1:28)

That would account for the remains of humanoid creatures such as the so-called Neanderthal man and other very old manlike remains that are undeniable artifacts of the fossil record but incorrectly interpreted by Evolutionists as early evidence of our ancestors. They were not our ancestors, but whatever they were, they existed in Earth's past and had physical forms similar to the humans of this present world. Their disembodied spirits could be the devils that Jesus cast out of people while He was on the Earth. (See Matthew 8:16 and other verses.)

These conclusions do not contradict the statement of Scriptural fact in Romans 5:12 regarding man and the issue of sin. Adam first lived about 6000 years ago, and Adam was the first true man, created in the Image of God as a unique new creature. He was, as Romans 5:12 states, the first man to sin. Death entered, repeat ENTERED (read the verse) this world from somewhere else. (Try the deep, as in Luke 8:31.) How it first came into being is revealed elsewhere in the Scriptures (again closely review Ezekiel 28 and Isaiah 14 for details) by rightly dividing the word of truth.

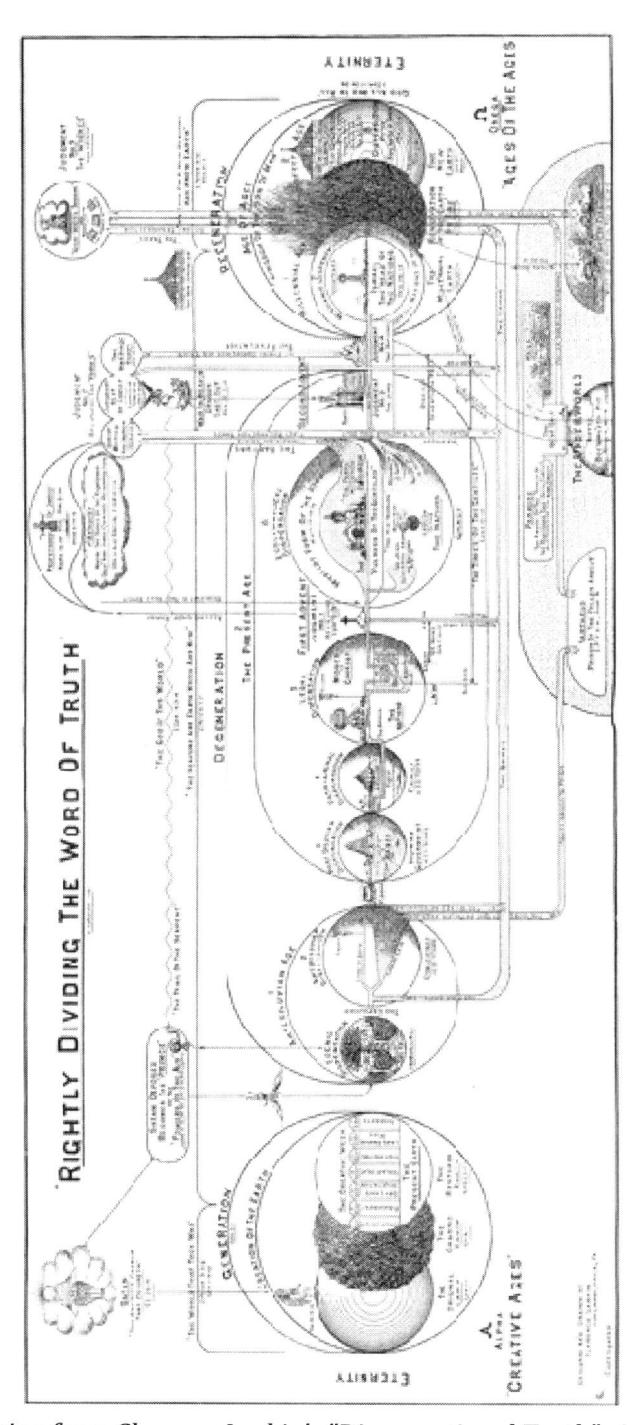

Illustration from Clarence Larkin's "Dispensational Truth" circa 1918.

Chapter 19
Geology and Prophecy: The Dead Sea Rift

In Revelation chapters 1, 2, and 3, the Lord addresses seven churches "...which are in Asia." That specific geographical area is the western coast of modern-day Turkey, located north of Israel and Lebanon. The Middle East is the focal point of End Time prophecy.

In the Gospels, the Lord Jesus Christ mentions earthquakes three times in His prophecy of the End Times.

"For nation shall rise against nation, and kingdom against kingdom: and there shall be famines, and pestilences, and earthquakes, in divers places." (Matthew 24:7)

"For nation shall rise against nation, and kingdom against kingdom: and there shall be earthquakes in divers places, and there shall be famines and troubles: these are the beginnings of sorrows." (Mark 13:8)

"And great earthquakes shall be in divers places, and famines, and pestilences; and fearful sights and great signs shall there be from heaven." (Luke 21:11)

We have all heard these verses preached over and over again, and with every TV news report of another earthquake, a preacher somewhere is inspired to use it as a sure sign that the end is near. The problem is that earthquakes happen all across the Earth every day, and the yearly averages of quake activity have remained fairly constant for many decades.

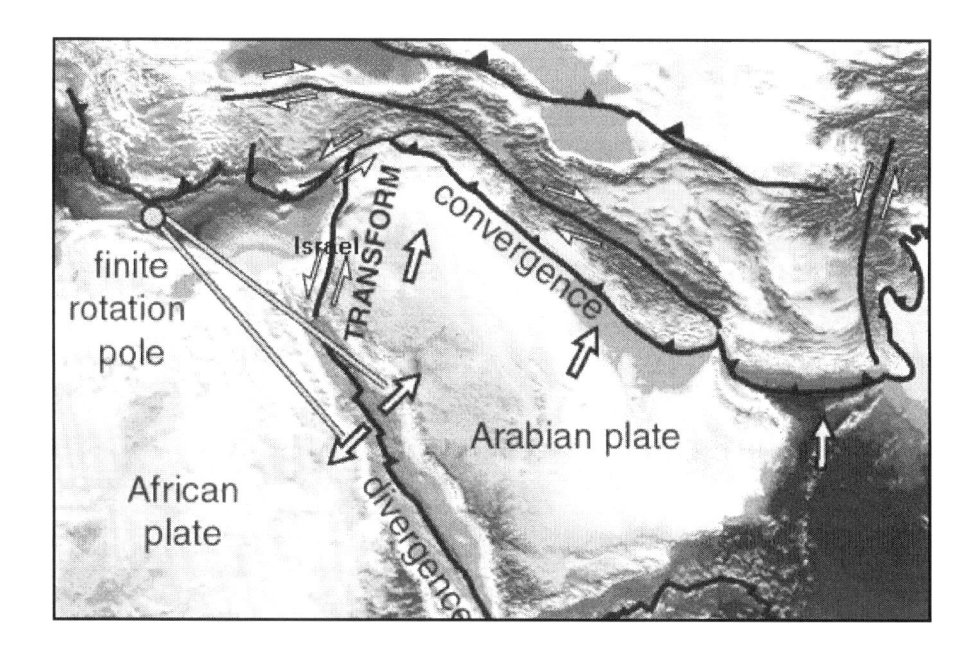

The Earth's crust is divided into about 12 major plates that are constantly shifting, producing earthquakes and volcanic activity on every continent.

The Middle East and the countries on the eastern rim of the Mediterranean basin are situated at a geologic crossroads of tectonic plate boundaries. Several major fault lines, which produce earthquake activity, crisscross the region. The arrows on the chart indicate the direction the respective plates are moving in relation to adjoining plates.

Both Turkey and Greece have experienced major quakes in recent times. In fact, geologists have recently noted that the floor of the Mediterranean Sea is fracturing like a sheet of glass. This means that the focal point of tectonic forces is shifting in the region, and an increase in activity is approaching.

Much of the intensified major future activity for this region is prophesied to occur along the Dead Sea Transform fault, a continuation of the Red Sea and East African Rift system. This fault runs directly under the Dead Sea, up through the Jordan River valley, the Sea of Galilee, and northward through Lebanon.

The destruction of Sodom and Gomorrah in Abraham's day was in the area south of what is presently the Dead Sea. The Bible's mention of a rain of fire and brimstone from heaven on those wicked cities (Genesis 19:24 - 29) indicates that the Divine judgment came from sudden volcanic/tectonic activity in a plain area which is now the submerged floor of the Dead Sea. There is evidence that the Age of the Dead Sea is only about as old as the time of Abraham. In the days of the Garden of Eden, there was no Dead Sea in that spot, but a river flowed through the rift zone southward toward the area that is presently the Red Sea (more on that in the next chapter).

Historically speaking, the Dead Sea Transform fault has displayed catastrophic tectonic activity in the recent historic past and should be expected to do so again in the near future.

It should be assumed that in addition to increased tectonic activity along the Dead Sea Transform, there would also be increased tectonic and volcanic activity across the globe during those times. But for the sake of this study, we will focus on the Holy Land.

The Dead Sea fault boundary passes about 25 miles east of Jerusalem, which according to the Bible, will be the epicenter for at least two great future earthquakes, the last of which will be the strongest quake to shake the world since man was created.

"And the same hour was there a great earthquake, and the tenth part of the city fell, and in the earthquake were slain of men seven thousand: and the remnant were affrighted, and gave glory to the God of heaven." (Revelation 11:13)

"And there were voices, and thunders, and lightnings; and there was a great earthquake, such as was not since men were upon the earth, so mighty an earthquake, and so great." (Revelation 16:18)

The area to be struck by the above-prophesied quakes will be very near Jerusalem. It is likely that in the years preceding the great quakes of the Tribulation, there will be increased earthquake activity and intensity throughout the Middle East and across the world.

Earthquakes, however, will not be the only geologic activity to occur in Israel between now and the Second Coming of the Lord Jesus Christ. According to the prophet Isaiah, there will also be volcanic activity in the regions south of Jerusalem and west of the Dead Sea.

"The sword of the LORD is filled with blood, it is made fat with fatness, and with the blood of lambs and goats, with the fat of the kidneys of rams: for the LORD hath a sacrifice in Bozrah, and a great slaughter in

the land of Idumea. And the unicorns shall come down with them, and the bullocks with the bulls; and their land shall be soaked with blood, and their dust made fat with fatness. For it is the day of the LORD'S vengeance, and the year of recompences for the controversy of Zion. And the streams thereof shall be turned into pitch, and the dust thereof into brimstone, and the land thereof shall become burning pitch." (Isaiah 34:6-9)

This Idumea is a region that in Greco-Roman times was bordered on the east by the Dead Sea and also encompassed Hebron and Beersheba, a large area south of Jerusalem. The word translated *pitch* is a Hebrew word which means *to liquefy* as spoken of asphalt, which liquefies when heated by the sun or any heat source. The reference to brimstone indicates volcanic activity and is no doubt connected with activity along the Dead Sea fault.

If taken literally, this passage says that the burning asphalt will flow like streams. Is there asphalt in the land of Idumea? You bet there is! It is a documented geological reality, just as the Bible says:

1. Footnote*: At the end of 1985, OEIL (later called INOC, Israel National Oil Company-a government owned entity) suspended all drilling operations in order to carry out a comprehensive basin analysis study over all of Israel. Only limited exploration work continued by private operators, including the drilling of two Jurassic wells in the northwestern part of the Negev, which yielded oil shows but no discoveries. INOC recommended exploration around the Dead Sea area where a large amount of **asphalt oil** shows encouraged continued exploration without resulting in any commercial discoveries. (Source: "History of Oil Exploration in Israel" -http://www.givot.co.il/)*

Can a volcano spew asphalt instead of lava? Given the right conditions, it can happen! Volcanic activity outside of the immediate Middle-East region could also factor into End-Time Geology and Prophecy. In Revelation 9:2 we find this verse:

"And he opened the bottomless pit; and there arose a smoke out of the pit, as the smoke of a great furnace; and the sun and the air were darkened by reason of the smoke of the pit." (Revelation 9:2)

Could what the prophet described here be the eruption of one of the Earth's supervolcanoes during the Great Tribulation period?

Certainly. As the above verse says, under the scenario of a supervolcano eruption, the sun and the air would be darkened globally by the smoke and ash from such a mega volcanic event. Global temperatures would fall, crops would fail, and famines would be triggered. Air traffic would come to a standstill because jets could not fly through the gritty ash plumes ejected high into the sky. Satellite communications would fail in many regions as the atmospheric-borne ash blocked out or severely disrupted Ku band communications.

Collectively, these events would precipitate a meltdown of the global economy, and the world would be plunged into utter chaos. Population centers downwind of the supervolcano eruption would be buried under meters of volcanic ash. It would certainly be a Hell on Earth that modern mankind had never experienced and would be helpless to prevent and sore pressed to deal with on a global scale.

Nevertheless, let's return our focus to the immediate Middle-East and examine another prophecy. The prophecy of a mountain in Israel being split at the very moment of the Lord's return:

"Then shall the LORD go forth, and fight against those nations, as when he fought in the day of battle. And his feet shall stand in that day upon the mount of Olives, which is before Jerusalem on the east, and the mount of Olives shall cleave in the midst thereof toward the east and toward the west, and there shall be a very great valley; and half of the mountain shall remove toward the north, and half of it toward the south. And ye shall flee to the valley of the mountains; for the valley of

the mountains shall reach unto Azal: yea, ye shall flee, like as ye fled from before the earthquake in the days of Uzziah king of Judah: and the LORD my God shall come, and all the saints with thee." (Zechariah 14:3-5)

This passage indicates that when the Lord returns, the Mount of Olives east of Jerusalem will split and form a valley through which the Jews will escape at the height of the Battle of Armageddon. The world will be so devastated at the time of the Lord's return that the prophet Jeremiah compared it to the condition of the Earth before it was restored in the seven days of Genesis:

"I beheld the earth, and, lo, it was without form, and void; and the heavens, and they had no light. I beheld the mountains, and, lo, they trembled, and all the hills moved lightly. I beheld, and, lo, there was no man, and all the birds of the heavens were fled. I beheld, and, lo, the fruitful place was a wilderness, and all the cities thereof were broken down at the presence of the LORD, and by his fierce anger. For thus hath the LORD said, The whole land shall be desolate; yet will I not make a full end. For this shall the earth mourn, and the heavens above be black: because I have spoken it, I have purposed it, and will not repent, neither will I turn back from it." (Jeremiah 4:23-28)

It should be pointed out that the above passage has been mistakenly cited by many as a proof passage for the Gap Theory because the phrase "was without form, and void" exactly matches the words to describe the Earth's condition in Genesis 1:2 before the start of the seven days. That is an error. The passage above is a reference to the second coming of the Lord Jesus Christ "...the PRESENCE of the LORD, and by his fierce anger ..." because the Lord is both present and angry, which clearly shows this is a coming future event. There are also cities in ruin during this time, and we know there were no cities built on the Earth until after Adam was created. So the time context here is most certainly future, not past. The specific wording "was without form and void" is instructive for understanding the Gap theory however, because it establishes the first use rule of that specific phrase.

At the end of the Great Tribulation period, the condition of the Earth and heavens is one of total devastation, resulting from the effects of global warfare, geologic upheaval, the great plagues, and the great wrath of God poured out on an unbelieving world. By the time the Lord Jesus Christ returns, the world will require complete regeneration.

"And Jesus said unto them, Verily I say unto you, That ye which have followed me, in the regeneration when the Son of man shall sit in the throne of his glory, ye also shall sit upon twelve thrones, judging the twelve tribes of Israel." (Matthew 19:28)

This regeneration is spoken of in Isaiah Chapter 65:

"For, behold, I create new heavens and a new earth: and the former shall not be remembered, nor come into mind. But be ye glad and rejoice for ever in that which I create: for, behold, I create Jerusalem a rejoicing, and her people a joy. And I will rejoice in Jerusalem, and joy in my people: and the voice of weeping shall be no more heard in her, nor the voice of crying. There shall be no more thence an infant of days, nor an old man that hath not filled his days: for the child shall die an hundred years old; but the sinner being an hundred years old shall be accursed. And they shall build houses, and inhabit them; and they shall plant vineyards, and eat the fruit of them. They shall not build, and another inhabit; they shall not plant, and another eat: for as the days of a tree are the days of my people, and mine elect shall long enjoy the work of their hands." (Isaiah 65:17-22)

This New heavens and a new Earth which the Lord will create in the coming future are on the face of a regenerated Earth; an Earth that was left without form and void following the Great Tribulation. The events of this passage correlate to the time of Revelation 20:1, at the beginning of the 1,000-year Kingdom of Heaven on the Earth. This creation of a new heavens and Earth is not to be confused with the new heaven and Earth of Revelation 21:1, as that is a separate creative event which happens at the end of the one thousand years. Proof of this distinction is found within the above passage where it states that "the child shall die," which shows that this is a time when death still has a grip on the new world. Death is not finally defeated until the end of the one thousand years (Revelation 21:14).

It should also be noted that in the 1,000-year coming Kingdom, with the Lord Jesus Christ ruling the Earth from His throne at Jerusalem, the newly-created heavens and Earth have been restored to conditions similar to those which existed on the Earth from Adam to Noah. That is, those born during that time will live long lives like antediluvian man. We know this because the life spans are described as "the days of a tree," and most trees live a few hundred years. (The child is 100 years old, in the above passage.)

The main point to keep in mind with respect to the Gap Theory is that the "new heavens and a new earth" of Isaiah 65:17 are regenerated on the face of the old planet Earth on which we currently live. The geology under the ground (which is here now) will still be under the ground then. Because the Earth is described as being without form and void before this new creation, it tells us that the world which the Lord created in seven days in Genesis chapter one was also a regeneration of the old heavens and Earth which were here before the days of Adam. Turn to Genesis 1:2 and read: "And the earth WAS without form and void...". The fossils and the Earth's geology from the ancient world were still under the ground when the Lord made the present world of man on the face of the old planet. Notice the consistency of Scriptural terminology in Genesis 2:4: "These are the GENERATIONS (plural) of the heavens and the earth..." The rule of first use for the meaning of the world was without form and void in Jeremiah 4:23 thus defines the phrase's first use meaning in Genesis 1:2, just as the use of the phrase "replenish the earth" in Genesis 9:1 defines the first use context of the phrase in Genesis 1:28. This is using Scripture to interpret Scripture and is an example of rightly dividing the Word of truth.

But now, back to the future again. At the end of the 1,000-year Kingdom of Heaven on the Earth, the entire universe will be completely destroyed, including the present Earth, the stars, and all physical things. Death will be once and for all done away with and the unsaved consigned to eternal torment. Then God will make a new heaven and Earth (Revelation 21:1) and will make all things new. The story will have come full circle. That is the future. Today we must deal with this present evil world and be prepared to meet God. Great geologic upheavals, astronomical events, and worse are coming in the near future according to the Bible.

"And I will shew wonders in the heavens and in the earth, blood, and fire, and pillars of smoke. The sun shall be turned into darkness, and the moon into blood, before the great and the terrible day of the LORD come. And it shall come to pass, that whosoever shall call on the name of the LORD shall be delivered: for in mount Zion and in Jerusalem shall be deliverance, as the LORD hath said, and in the remnant whom the LORD shall call." (Joel 2:30-32)

"That day is a day of wrath, a day of trouble and distress, a day of wasteness and desolation, a day of darkness and gloominess, a day of clouds and thick darkness, A day of the trumpet and alarm against the fenced cities, and against the high towers. And I will bring distress upon men, that they shall walk like blind men, because they have sinned against the LORD: and their blood shall be poured out as dust, and their flesh as the dung." (Zephaniah 1:15-17)

The day of the Lord is close at hand. Are YOU prepared?

Chapter 20

Lost Rivers of Eden

The quest for pinpointing the exact location of the Biblical Garden of Eden and the four rivers almost rivals the quest for the location of fabled Atlantis. The theories that abound are almost as numerous as the interpretations of the seven days of Genesis. Before tackling this question, let's review what is written in Genesis about the four rivers: *"And a river went out of Eden to water the garden; and from thence it was parted, and became into four heads. The name of the first is Pison: that is it which compasseth the whole land of Havilah, where there is gold; And the gold of that land is good: there is bdellium and the onyx stone. And the name of the second river is Gihon: the same is it that compasseth the whole land of*

Ethiopia. And the name of the third river is Hiddekel: that is it which goeth toward the east of Assyria. And the fourth river is Euphrates." (Genesis 2:10-14)

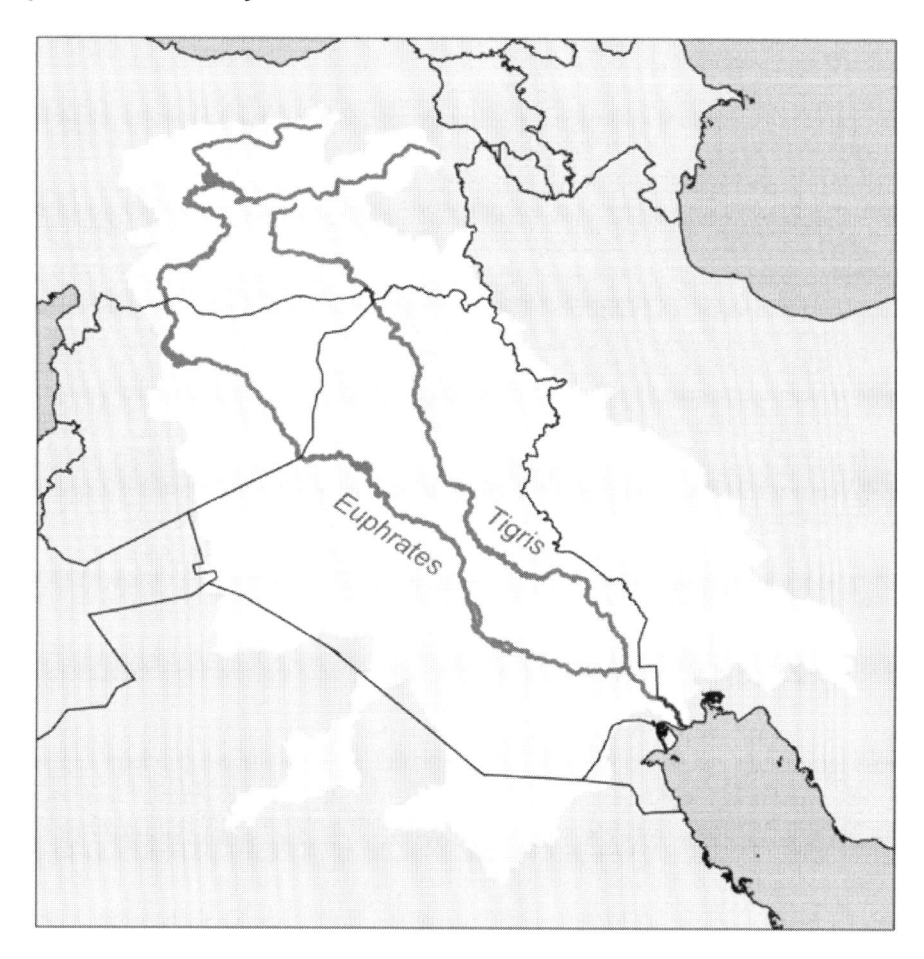

The Bible says that a single river flowed out of Eden and did something that most rivers do not do. It split downstream into four separate rivers which all fed from a common single river source. Almost all rivers start from a single source or are fed by multiple sources (tributaries). For example, the Ohio River actually begins where two rivers (the Monongahela and Allegheny) flow together at Pittsburg, Pennsylvania. The Ohio River terminates when it flows into the Mississippi River as one of that river's many tributaries. The names of rivers are arbitrary, usually denoting only a portion of a greater complex stream system, with one stream flowing into another which, in turn, may flow into yet another. This pattern of rivers as observed in nature is just the opposite of what the Bible describes about the river of Eden.

For that reason, nobody has been able to look at modern maps of the regions mentioned in Genesis and figure out exactly where the Garden of Eden was, at least by the present topography of the lands of the Middle East. Only one river of the four, the Euphrates, is known by the same name in modern times. It presently originates in the mountains of Turkey and terminates when it flows together with the Tigris River near the Iraq/Kuwait border region. Many have speculated that the Tigris is the river Hiddekel.

This has led to speculation that the Garden of Eden was located somewhere in Turkey because the present headwaters of the Euphrates River originate in Turkey, as do the headwaters of the Tigris.

You will notice that the present-day headwaters of both the Tigris and Euphrates rivers originate very close to each other in mountainous terrain. One would logically assume that if two of the rivers started there, the other two must have done so as well if Turkey was the location of Eden. Neither the Pison nor Gihon rivers are ever mentioned again in the Bible. However, the Hiddekel River is: *"And in the four and twentieth day of the first month, as I was by the side of the great river, which is Hiddekel;"* (Daniel 10:4)

This reference by the prophet Daniel comes from a vision he had while with the children of Israel during the Babylonian Captivity. This would put him somewhere in the area of present-day Iraq and would make the present-day Tigris River a fairly good candidate for the Hiddekel river spoken of by the prophet, as it is the only other great river known in that region today. But the Bible says that this river ("*...that is it which goeth toward the east of Assyria*") and a historical map of the location of Assyria, show that the Tigris actually flows southeastward.

We should keep in mind that the geographical area known as Assyria is not so easy to pin down. Although the Assyrian Empire was centered near Nineveh, the actual empire also extended into present-day Syria and Palestine. However, lacking a better candidate, and knowing that the prophet Daniel was in that geographical area at the time of his visions, the Tigris appears to be the best possible modern-day candidate for the Hiddekel River.

We now must search out the probable locations of the other two rivers. It is here that the theory that the Garden of Eden was either in Turkey or Kuwait starts to lose credibility.

First, let's identify the geographical region of the Pison River. The Bible says, "*Pison: that is it which compasseth the whole land of Havilah, where there is gold*" and gives us two good clues. There is a recently discovered fossil river that runs from the western mountains of Saudi Arabia toward Kuwait. This long-since-dry riverbed was detected by satellite imaging. Many have speculated that this may be the ancient Pison, as it has been dry since approximately 3,500 to 2,000 BC. Below is a website with references to this ancient river's path:

http://www.creationism.org/caesar/eden.htm

Although Saudi Arabia could marginally qualify for the land of Havilah, the fossil riverbed that flows across it had its origins in the mountains bordering the eastern side of the present-day Red Sea south of Israel.

It should be pointed out that those mountains are mirrored by another range of mountains on the western side of the Red Sea. The Red Sea is a tectonic spreading zone and part of the Great Rift system that runs from northward in Turkey, down through the Dead Sea and southward deep into the African continent. Obviously, when that mountain range was split by the Rift, the source waters of the proposed Pison River dried up.

This proposed river path may be somewhat of a red-herring because it does not seem to naturally fit the overall pattern. An even better fit may be that the river flowed down what today is the Gulf of Aden south of present-day Yemen (southern tip of Arabia). Yemen has both gold and onyx, and the eastward trending fault branch from the Afar triangle would have been a natural riverbed in the days prior to Noah's flood (when sea levels were lower than today). We'll keep an open mind on this one.

If this was indeed the Pison River, one of four that flowed out of the main one rising in the Garden of Eden, it does not correspond with the present-day headwater source of the Euphrates or Tigris up in Turkey. What's more, the geography of the last remaining river, the Gihon, further complicates the problem.

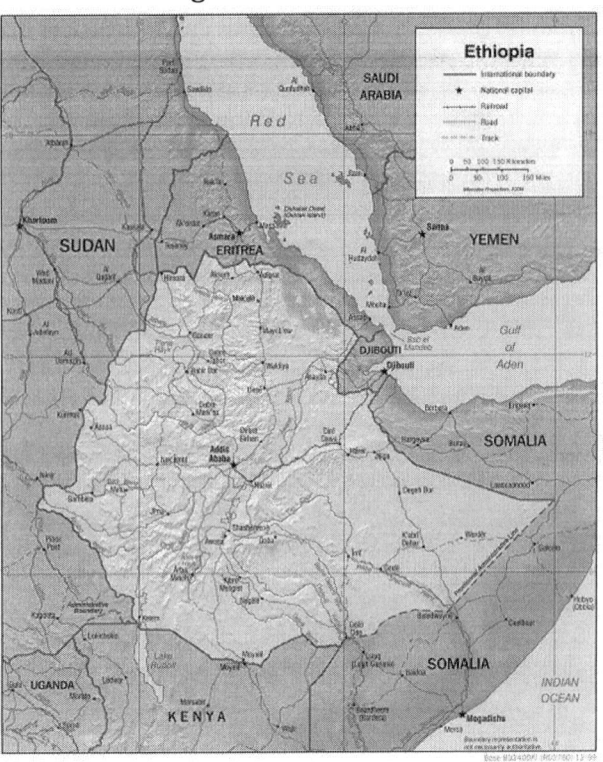

The Gihon is spoken of as *"Gihon: the same is it that compasseth the whole land of Ethiopia,"* which is the African land area west of the Red Sea and southward. Of course, the political boundaries of what we call Ethiopia today were certainly different in Biblical times, but the general area is correct. And if a river formerly flowed down what is now the Red Sea basin and southward into Africa at the Afar Triangle, it would certainly fit the description of a river that *"compasseth the whole land of Ethiopia."* (Genesis 2:13)

If we have correctly identified all four rivers, we now have two rivers (Euphrates and Tigris) originating today out of Turkey and another running down what was is now the Red Sea south of Israel and deep into Africa, following the path of the present-day Great Rift system. For the moment, we will also include the previously-discussed fossil river running through Saudi Arabia. Superimposing these on a map, we see the following trend-line across the region:

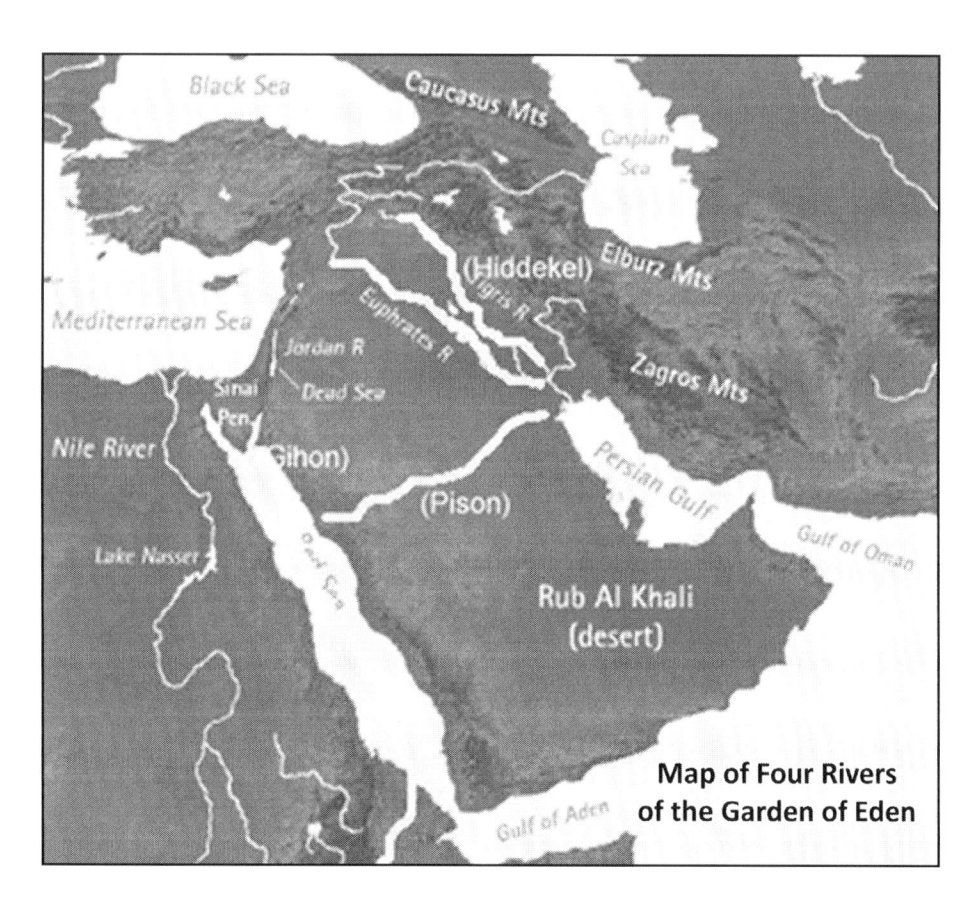

Map of Four Rivers of the Garden of Eden

The thicker white lines on the *Map of Four Rivers of the Garden of Eden* show the paths of the four rivers, as we have proposed. You should note that we did not trace over the Euphrates and Tigris rivers to their present-day sources but terminated them close to the Great Rift fault zone line. You will also note that we have not continued the proposed path of the Gihon beyond the top of the Red Sea and have terminated the proposed Pison at the Great Rift fault zone line.

All four of these rivers have one thing in common. All are connected to the Great Rift system, and that is the key to the mystery. Two rivers presently originate out of Turkey to the north, and two other fossil rivers flowed south of Israel. The geographical center of these four points of flow is neither Turkey nor Kuwait; the center is somewhere near present-day Israel and Jordan.

The Bible itself lends further credence to Israel (or someplace nearby) as the location of the Garden of Eden. If you run the name Eden through a search of the Bible, the following references provide some insightful clues:

The Bible says in this passage that the Assyrian was in Lebanon. Spiritually speaking, the trees in this passage refer to men and leaders. Cedar trees are mentioned elsewhere in the Bible as references to Lebanon (Judges 9:15, Psalms 29:5 & 104:16, Song of Solomon 5:15, Isaiah 2:13, Jeremiah 22:23 and more).

*"Behold, **the Assyrian** was **a cedar in Lebanon** with fair branches, and with a shadowing shroud, and of an high stature; and his top was among the thick boughs. The waters made him great, the deep set him up on high with her rivers running round about his plants, and sent out her little rivers unto all the trees of the field. Therefore his height was exalted above all the trees of the field, and his boughs were multiplied, and his branches became long because of the multitude of waters, when he shot forth. All the fowls of heaven made their nests in his*

*boughs, and under his branches did all the beasts of the field bring forth their young, and under his shadow dwelt all great nations. Thus was he fair in his greatness, in the length of his branches: for his root was by great waters. The **cedars in the garden of God** could not hide him: the fir trees were not like his boughs, and the chesnut trees were not like his branches; **nor any tree in the garden of God** was like unto him in his beauty. I have made him fair by the multitude of his branches: so that **all the trees of Eden, that were in the garden of God**, envied him."* (Ezekiel 31:3-9; emphasis added)

Notice also in the last of the passage that the Spirit associates the trees with "Eden that were in the Garden of God." Lebanon, although not a part of modern political Israel, was a part of the Biblical lands ruled by the Kings of Israel in times past. From this we can infer that the Garden and the source of the rivers of the Garden were somewhere close to the land of Lebanon.

Assuming this postulation is correct, that the source of the four rivers was somewhere near Lebanon, the interconnection of the river systems would need to be somewhat like the next version of the same map.

If all four rivers are connected to the Great Rift fault system, what appears is a complex river network emerging from a common point of origin that flows both north and south, with each north and south extension splitting into two separate streams, for a total of four rivers. That adds up to four separate heads.

Of course, to propose such a reconstruction, one would have to assume that the present-day headwaters of the Tigris and Euphrates were not the main headwaters in ancient times. It is possible that there could have been older main tributaries previously flowing from Lebanon, which were the main headwaters of those two rivers at that time.

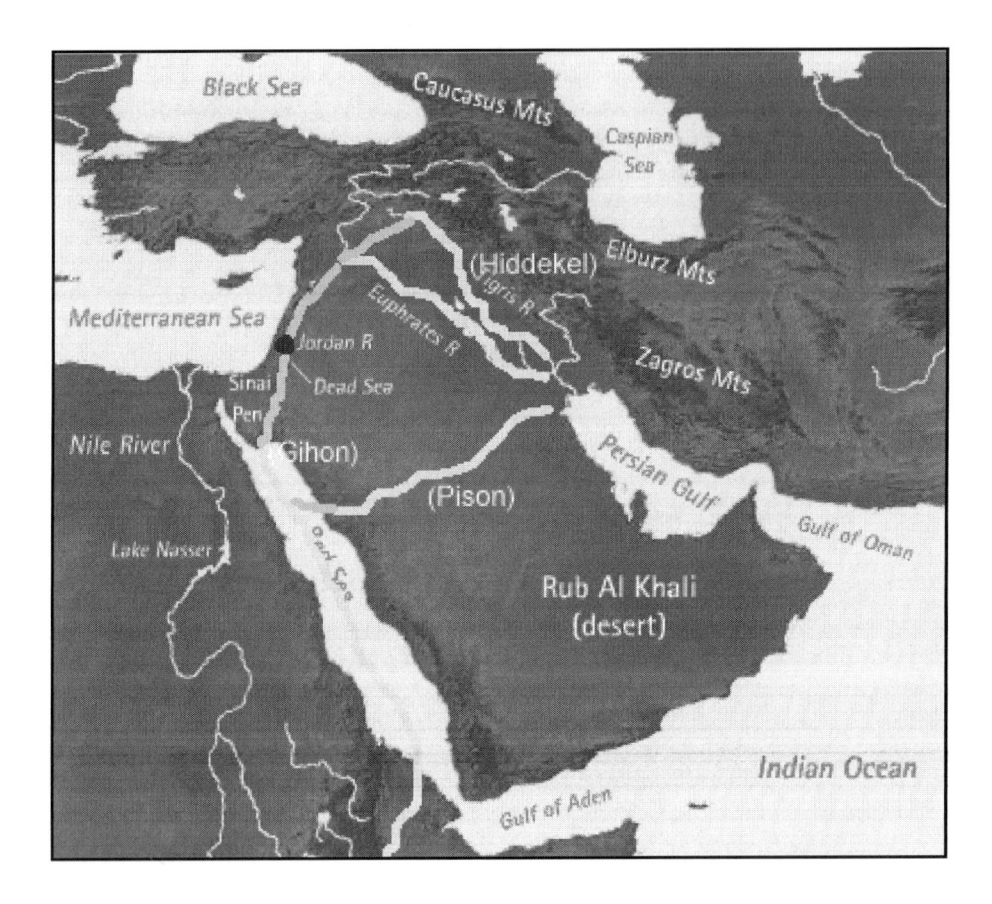

Keep in mind that the course of rivers around and through the vicinity of the Great Rift fault system may have changed or dried up because of block faulting all along the Rift zone.

Certainly, Horst and Graben faulting along the Rift could, and would, change the surface topography. Horst and Graben faulting is defined as elongate fault blocks of the Earth's crust that have been raised and lowered, respectively, relative to their surrounding areas as a direct effect of faulting. Horsts and Grabens may range in size from blocks a few centimeters wide to tens of kilometers wide; the vertical movement may be up to several thousand feet.

When did this happen? The most likely time frame would be in the years immediately following Noah's Flood. Keep in mind that the Bible says there was a significant geologic event that happened 101 years after Noah's Flood The Earth was divided. (See chapter titled *Days of Peleg and Sea Level Changes.*) The Bible also describes what was probably tectonic and volcanic activity in Abraham's days (the destruction of Sodom and Gomorrah, Genesis 19:28).

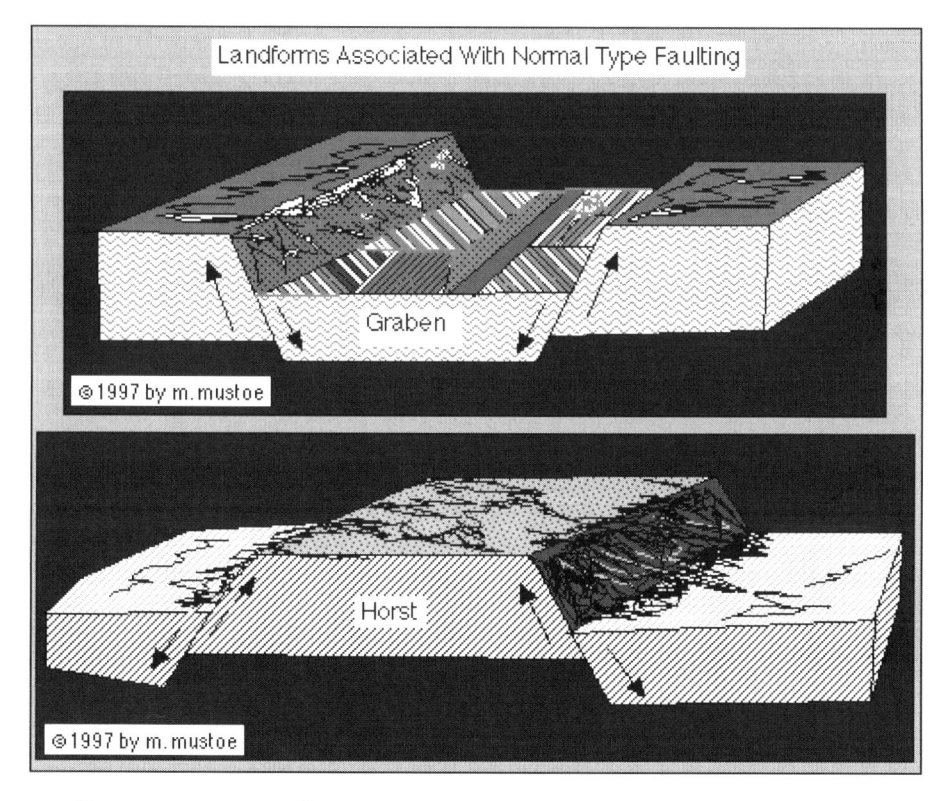

Image courtesy of Dr. M. Mustoe - www.tinynet.com/Graben.html

Imaging of the Dead Sea indicates that at one time, the river bed of what is now the Jordan River once flowed across the land surface that is now at the bottom of the Dead Sea.

This suggests that there was Horst and Graben faulting at the southern end of the present Dead Sea, which abruptly terminated the former flow of that river southward. That stream was probably the feeder channel to the ancient Gihan River, which ran down the floor of what is now the Red Sea into Ethiopia and through the Rift basin south from the Afar Triangle. Supporting coincidental evidence for this is the fact that fish species in the African Rift Valley river and lake systems are very similar to those found in the Jordan River system:

Note: The aquatic life of the African lakes and rivers belongs to the so-called Ethiopian zoogeographical region. According to Annandale, "the explanation of the Ethiopian affinity of the fish fauna of the Jordan is that the Jordan formed at one time merely part of a river system that ran down the Great Rift Valley. The Jordan was one branch of this huge river system, the chain of lakes in East Africa represents the other; and together they opened into the Indian Ocean."

See R. Washbourn, *The Percy Sladen Expedition to Lake Huleh, 1935, Palestine, Exploration Fund, Quarterly Statements, (1936)*, p. 209. (Source website: *http://www.varchive.org/itb/rift.htm*)

Considerable similar block faulting is also observed in the regions north of Israel. At *www.kjvbible.org*, we have a link to a full-color and relief detailed fault map of that region. As you will observe on that map, had waters once flowed out of this area, they would naturally have flowed northward into the Euphrates Fault system river basin. At the time of the Garden of Eden, the main headwaters of the Euphrates could have come from that direction. If the water flow at that time had continued northward along the path of the Great Rift, it would have also intersected the present-day Tigris river basin.

The prominent bodies of water along the Rift zone shown in this satellite photo are the Dead Sea (bottom) and Sea of Galilee (top). They are connected by the Jordan River, which flows south. Before the Earth was divided by the Rift, the mountainous land on both the

Israeli and Jordanian sides were joined. You are looking at ground zero of what was once the Garden of Eden.

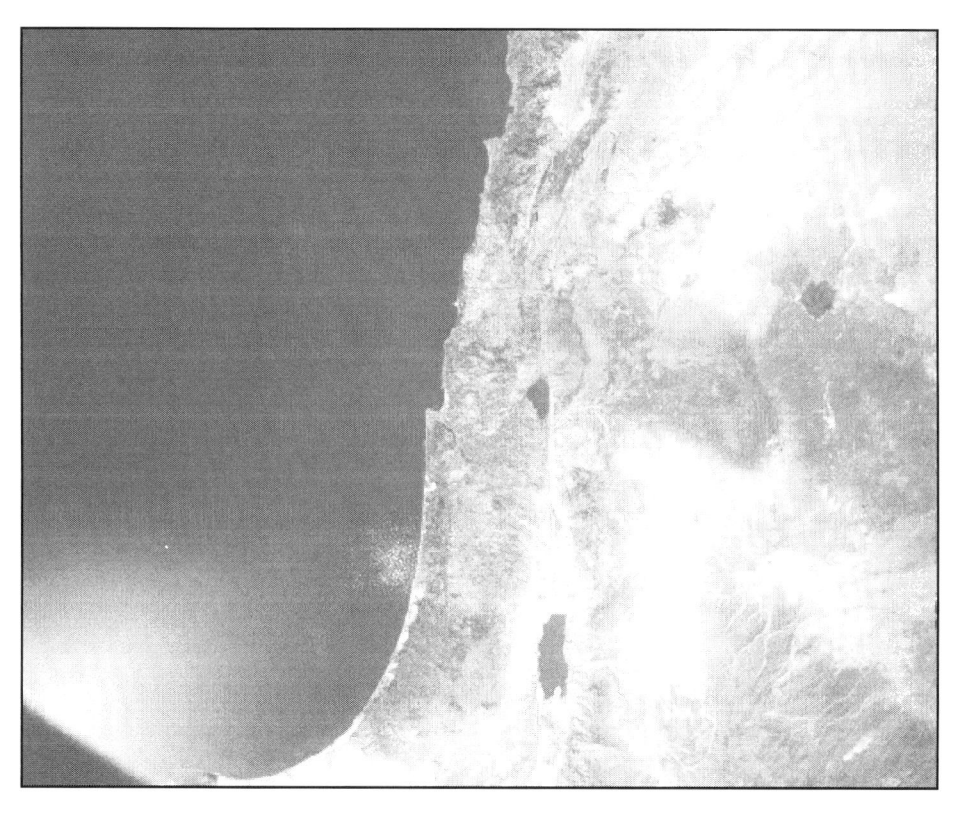

STS41G-120-0056 Dead Sea Rift Valley, Israel and Jordan October 1984 Seen from an altitude of 190 nautical miles (350 kilometers)

Here is another important point to remember. The Bible says that the river flowed out of Eden, but nowhere does the Bible give a geographical size for what constituted the area of Eden. Therefore, the actual source of the waters could have been south of Lebanon. More specifically, those waters could have originated near Jerusalem in present-day Israel.

The Israel/Lebanon region as the location of Eden and the lost river finds considerable support in the Bible. Support for this line of reasoning in found in the fact that God considers the land of Israel to be His Holy land. It was upon one of the mountains in the land of Moriah (Genesis 22:2) where Abraham was told to sacrifice his son (a type of the Lord's sacrifice of Jesus). Solomon was told to build the Temple at Jerusalem in mount Moriah (2 Chronicles 3:1), and Jerusalem was where the Lord Jesus was actually crucified. By extension, we can assume that when God sacrificed an animal to cover Adam and Eve with its skin (Genesis 3:21), that animal was a Lamb (Roman 13:8). Therefore, we can be certain from the typology that Adam and Eve, and the center of the Garden of God, were somewhere at or very near geographical Jerusalem.

What exactly do those spiritual realities have to do with the location of the river of Eden? In the future, when the Lord Jesus Christ establishes His Kingdom and Righteous Temple in Jerusalem, the Bible speaks of a river flowing from below the Temple. The prophet Ezekiel spoke of seeing this in a vision. "*Afterward he brought me again unto the door of the house; and, behold, waters issued out from under the threshold of the house eastward: for the forefront of the house stood toward the east, and the waters came down from under from the right side of the house, at the south side of the altar. Then brought he me out of the way of the gate northward, and led me about the way without unto the utter gate by the way that looketh eastward; and, behold, there ran out waters on the right side. And when the man that had the line in his hand went forth eastward, he measured a thousand cubits, and he brought me through the waters; the waters were to the ankles. Again he measured a thousand, and brought me through the waters; the waters were to the knees. Again he measured a thousand, and brought me through; the waters were to the loins. Afterward he measured a thousand; and it was a river that I could not pass over: for the waters were risen, waters to swim in, a river that could not be passed over. And he said unto me, Son of man, hast thou seen this? Then he brought me, and caused me to return to the brink of the river. Now when I had returned, behold, at the bank of the river were very many trees on the one side and on the other. Then said he unto me, These waters issue out toward the east country, and go down into the desert, and go into the sea: which being brought forth into the sea, the waters shall be healed. And it shall come to pass, that every thing that liveth, which moveth, whithersoever the rivers shall come, shall live: and there shall be a very great multitude of fish, because these waters shall come thither: for they shall be healed; and every thing shall live whither the river cometh. And it shall come to pass, that the fishers shall stand upon it from Engedi even unto Eneglaim; they shall be a place to spread forth nets; their fish shall be according to their kinds, as the fish of the great sea, exceeding many. But the miry places thereof and the marishes thereof shall not be healed; they shall be given to salt. And by the river upon the bank thereof, on this side and on that side, shall grow all trees for meat, whose leaf shall not fade, neither shall the fruit thereof be consumed: it shall bring forth new fruit according to his months, because their waters they issued out of the sanctuary: and the fruit thereof shall be for meat, and the leaf thereof for medicine."* (Ezekiel 47:1-12)

And this corresponds with what John said about the New Jerusalem.

"And he shewed me a pure river of water of life, clear as crystal, proceeding out of the throne of God and of the Lamb. In the midst of the street of it, and on either side of the river, was there the tree of life, which bare twelve manner of fruits, and yielded her fruit every month: and the leaves of the tree were for the healing of the nations." (Revelation 22:1-2)

Since the original Tree of Life was in the Garden of Eden, does it not make sense that, when the Lord makes all things new, that the future Tree of Life would be restored to its proper place? And that place is in Israel. The same place, upon the mountains of Moriah (Jerusalem), where Abraham was told to sacrifice Isaac (Genesis 22:2); where Solomon was told to build the house of the Lord (2 Chronicles 3:1); and where the Lord Jesus Christ was crucified, is where the Lamb was slain from the foundation of the world (Revelation 13:8; Genesis 3:21). All these things fit, in Scriptural type.

The Bible tends to indicate that the river from the Garden of Eden originated in Judea and from there became four heads. A forensic study of the region's geology tends to support the theory over the alternatively-proposed locations of Turkey or Kuwait. What we have not shown is the geologic model for the source of these waters originating from the area of Jerusalem.

We can only assume that the block faulting along the Great Rift zone, which has changed the courses of rivers and created the Dead Sea basin and its present southern aquaclude, has also disrupted the main aquifer(s) that once were the underground source for the fabled river of Eden. Only a remnant of this water system remains today. There is a spring of Gihon near the old temple mount and there are historical accounts of past springs and pools in and near Jerusalem in the Scriptures.

Keep in mind that Jerusalem sits just west of the Great Rift Valley. It is quite possible that legendary river of Eden originated from a massive artesian aquifer, the source of which has long since been disrupted by block faulting along the Rift. We know for a scientific fact that there is a considerable amount of *fossil* water under the Middle East in the deep-rock sandstone aquifers of the region, such as the Nubian sandstone aquifers and equivalent formations.

Keep in mind that in the days of Adam and Eve, a mist went up and watered the face of the Earth within the Garden (Genesis 2:6). Fountains of waters (underground waters under pressure gushing upward) would certainly be a logical source for the generation of such a mist and would be a logical feed-source for such a river. Certainly, we cannot exclude this possibility.

In summary, although the modern-day geology and topography of the Middle East do not readily reveal the exact location of the Garden of Eden and the four rivers source, guidance by faith from the Holy Bible and a forensic study of the region's geology reveal the matter. The available data appear to suggest that present-day Israel was the central location of the Garden of Eden.

Chapter 21
The Book of Daniel is Unsealing

People today are of the mindset that the events of the Old and New Testaments all happened back in the Biblical days of human history. They fail to grasp the awesome truth that today we are still living in the Biblical days. They never ended. What will yet happen on the face of this Earth in the years to come has already been prophesied and penned. There remain things written in both the New an Old Testaments that are yet to come to pass.

The Bible deals with the history of man's world from the beginning, across historical time, into our present time, and forward until the very end of time as we understand it. You are living in Biblical days right now. The great I AM of Exodus 3:14, who spoke to Moses from the burning bush, STILL IS and still speaks to us today through His written Holy Word and the Holy Spirit. And today, the malignant spirit of Satan is also still whispering in the ears of modern man, "*Yea hath God said?*" (Genesis 3:1)

Although the prophets and disciples have long since passed from our world, what they wrote lives on and is just as relevant today as it was in the day it was written. If you really trust the Bible, it can and will tell you where we are today and what is about to come to pass in the very near future, not just in the sweet bye and bye. We will now shift gears from *In the beginning* to *The beginning of the end.*

There is a second gap in the Old Testament in addition to the one found in Genesis. That gap is the Church Age, the roughly 2000-year period of time between the first and second advents of the Lord Jesus Christ. That gap is hidden within the prophecies of the Old Testament, but it can be seen through what is revealed in the New Testament.

Clarence Larkin probably put it best when he explained that the prophets in Old Testament days were able to see the mountain peaks of prophetic events (e.g., the crucifixion, the Day of the Lord, and the final judgment) but could not see the Church Age in the valley between the mountains. Here is the chart from Larkin's book, *Dispensational Truth,* which visually illustrates this principal (seen on the next page):

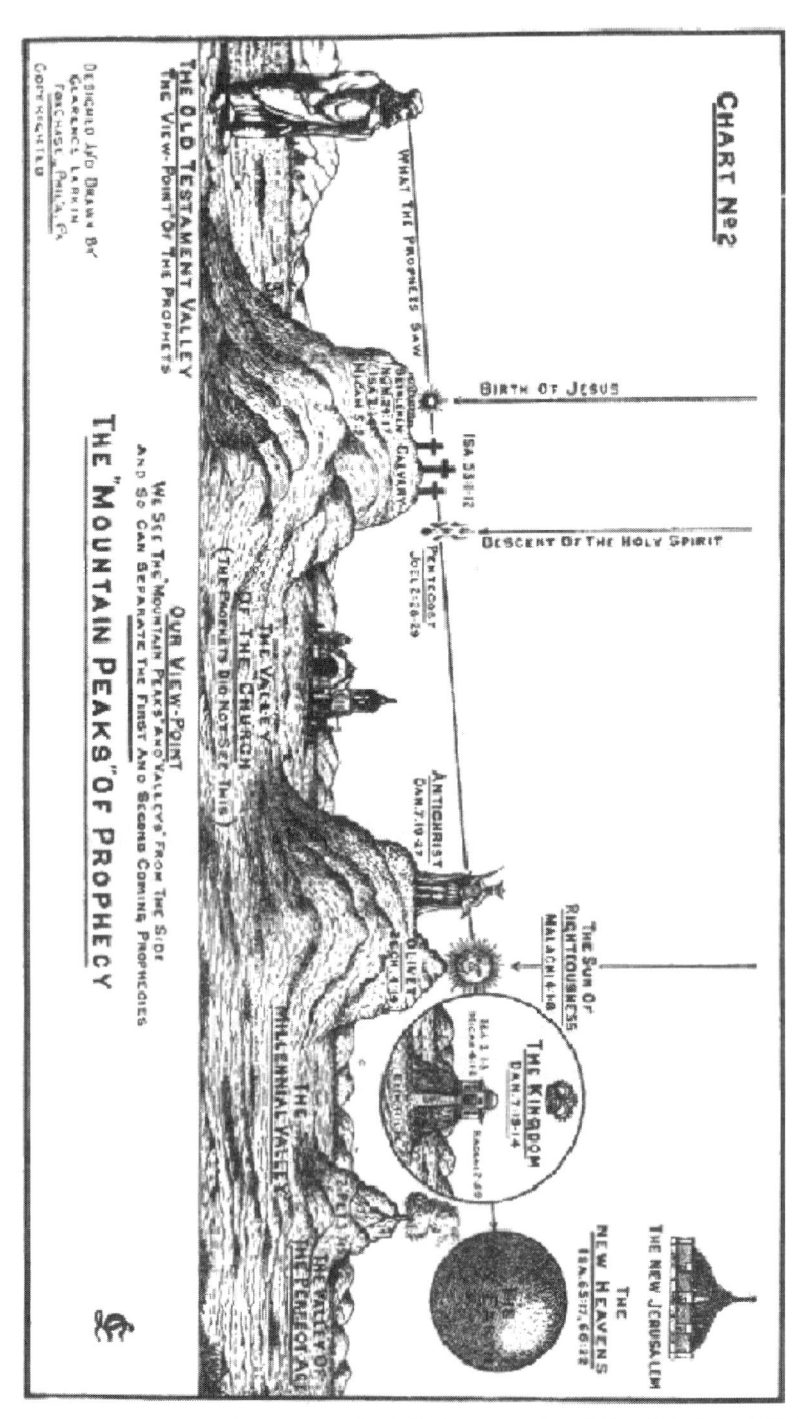

Illustration from Clarence Larkin's "Dispensational Truth" circa 1918.

Prophetically speaking, we are living today on the far side of the valley (time wise) and quickly moving up the mountain slope toward the coming of the Antichrist and the great Day of the Lord - the end times of God's dealing with the Jews, His chosen people.

Although 1948, the year when Israel became a state, would seem a natural benchmark for the start of the latter times of Biblical days, I believe a much better benchmark emerged in 1979, when the Iranian Revolution catapulted the land of ancient Persia back onto the global political stage.

The Iranian Revolution inspired an exponential rise of Islamic fundamentalist sentiment against the west, an angry wind that began to blow with increasing velocity across the Middle East and the larger Islamic world. When the Islamic world saw that Iran could blatantly snub its nose at the powerful west and get away with it, others quickly followed. The subsequent Iran/Iraq war, the rise of Al Qaeda and Osama Bin Laden, the attack on New York on September 11, 2001, the Gulf Wars, and the wars in Afghanistan and Pakistan all directly or indirectly precipitated from this seminal event. Iran is Persia, and in retrospect, we can now see that the emergence of Iran as a world power and modern-day growing global threat is prophesized in the book of Daniel. The prophetic seal on the book of Daniel is unsealing right before our very eyes. The Church Age is rapidly drawing to a close.

The Old Persian Empire encompassed the areas of present-day Iraq, Iran, Syria, Kuwait, Afghanistan, and Pakistan. In approximately 500 BC, the Empire also occupied present-day Turkey, Palestine, northern Egypt, and Libya.

The Persian Empire figured most prominently in the captivity of Israel in Biblical history, and as we shall point out, Persia also figures prominently in future prophecy and the beginning of the latter days. (Daniel 10:14.)

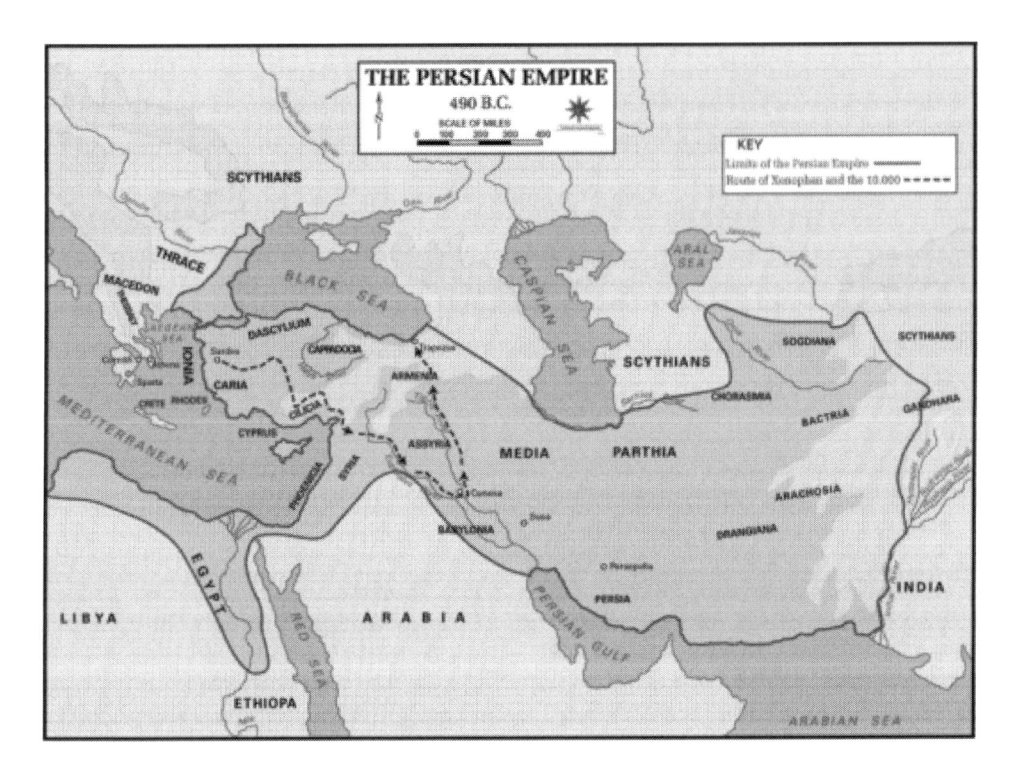

It is no coincidence that the Middle East is a powder keg awaiting only the proper spark to explode; it is no coincidence that radical Islam has become the global terror threat; it is no coincidence that Iran is threatening to wipe the nation of Israel off the map; and it is no coincidence that Israel exists as a nation, once again back in most of the very same Biblical lands that God promised Abraham thousands of years ago. None of this is coincidence; it is fulfilling and unfolding God's Words and setting the stage for the fulfillment of the coming events written about in the book of Revelation.

When Israel was in captivity during the days of the Old Persian Empire, the prophet Daniel received many visions concerning his people and Jerusalem, as well as what would happen to Israel in the times before the end. God told Daniel that those things would be sealed until this time of the end. It is written:

"But thou, O Daniel, shut up the words, and seal the book, even to the time of the end: many shall run to and fro, and knowledge shall be increased," (Daniel 12:4).

"And he said, Go thy way, Daniel: for the words are closed up and sealed till the time of the end," (Daniel 12:9).

To begin to comprehend the context of Persia (present day Iran) in the prophecies of Daniel, we need to start with the vision of the ram at the river:

"And I saw in a vision; and it came to pass, when I saw, that I was at Shushan in the palace, which is in the province of Elam; and I saw in a vision, and I was by the river of Ulai," (Daniel 8:2).

(When he had this vision, Daniel was in what today is southwestern Iran. Persia is the context and focus of this vision.)

"Then I lifted up mine eyes, and saw, and, behold, there stood before the river a ram which had two horns: and the two horns were high; but one was higher than the other, and the higher came up last. I saw the ram pushing westward, and northward, and southward; so that no beasts might stand before him, neither was there any that could deliver out of his hand; but he did according to his will, and became great. And as I was considering, behold, an he goat came from the west on the face of the whole earth, and touched not the ground: and the goat had a notable horn between his eyes. And he came to the ram that had two horns, which I had seen standing before the river, and ran unto him in the fury of his power. And I saw him come close unto the ram, and he was moved with choler against him, and smote the ram, and brake his two horns: and there was no power in the ram to stand before him, but he cast him down to the ground, and stamped upon him: and there was none that could deliver the ram out of his hand," (Daniel 8:3-7).

The Bible goes on to define the identities of this ram and the he goat spoken of in this prophecy:

"And he said, Behold, I will make thee know what shall be in the last end of the indignation: for at the time appointed the end shall be. The ram which thou sawest having two horns are the kings of Media and Persia. And the rough goat is the king of Grecia: and the great horn that is between his eyes is the first king," (Daniel 8:19-21).

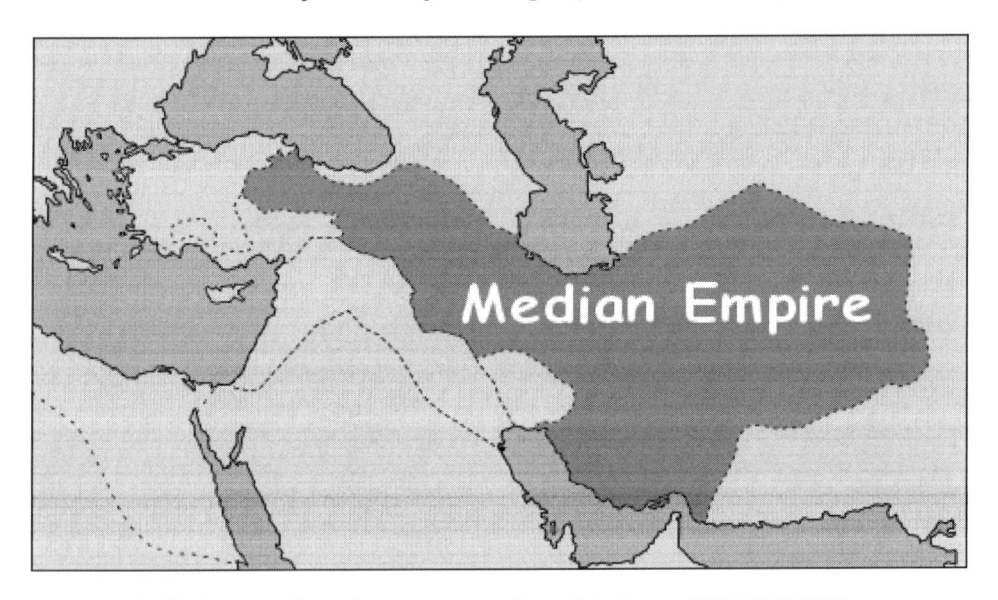

First of all, the Lord God reiterates that this is an END TIMES prophecy, a yet future event. The Lord God then identifies the two horns of the ram as the kings of Media and Persia, roughly corresponding to the lands from eastern Turkey and Iraq to Iran. (This area also may encompass portions of Syria and Afghanistan.) Exactly who these kings are is ambiguous, as the lands of ancient Media and Persia are not clearly defined by today's political map of declared states. However, we can be very certain that present-day Iran is at the core of this resurgence.

Politically speaking, Syria is currently siding with the Iranians against Israel. Turkey, which used to be an ally of Israel, is now seen as sliding toward the Iranian camp. Iraq is unstable and will probably be either drawn into the Iranian sphere of influence or occupied by Iran after the departure of US forces. Then there is the Kurdish problem, which affects corners of northern Iraq, western Iran, eastern Turkey, and part of Syria. In short, this entire area is unstable. Expect to see the unexpected in this region in the coming years.

The king of Grecia is a reference to the peoples immediately west of present-day Turkey, specifically the regions around Greece and Macedonia. It could also be a general reference to Europe and the western world. The prophecy then says that the he goat will attack the ram and crush the empire. In effect, we have a prophecy of modern-day western powers attacking and bringing down this resurgent eastern empire that is yet to rise in its full power.

Such an interpretation is contrary to the one that interprets the book of Daniel as events that have already occurred in human history. Proponents of the historical interpretation school (Amillennialists) claim that this vision was fulfilled when Alexander the Great conquered Persia. But does the Bible really support that interpretation? Notice in the prophecy that the he goat came from the West. Ok, so did Alexander the Great, but Alexander's army touched the ground every step of the way there. The prophecy says he "touched not the ground," and that part of the ancient prophecy could not be literally fulfilled (or comprehended) until the invention of the airplane. What the prophecy seems to be describing is a massive airborne attack launched from the west, the modern method of warfare (i.e., fighter jets, bombers, troop transports, and air and sea launched cruise missiles). The feet of attacking troops will not need to touch the ground until they parachute in or make marine landings.

We are certainly living in the days before this prophecy will be fulfilled, but we are also living in the times when the prophecy is actually unsealing right before our eyes, so that we can understand what is happening in this world and where all this is leading. The ram is rising; it is becoming great, but the larger of its two horns is yet to rise. Specifically, the lands of Iraq, Syria, and Turkey are yet to fully join with the Iranians. It should also be pointed out that Iran and Turkey, although both Islamic nations, are not Arab nations. These are different peoples from the descendents of the Ishmaelite.

Speaking of Turkey, it is part of the land of Asia Minor where the seven churches of Revelation are located. Are you starting to see the connection?

All of the seven churches of Revelation chapters 1-3 are situated along the western edge of Turkey. The Aegean Sea between Greece and Turkey is a geopolitical dividing line between the so called lands of Christianity to the west and the lands of Islam to the east. The Apostle John was on an island named Patmos (currently a Greek controlled island), situated in the Aegean Sea just west of the Asia Minor mainland, when he saw his vision.

Daniel's visions are a complement to the visions of John. The Middle East region is the future literal focus of the events in the book of Revelation.

Also note that all this must happen before any of the 10 kings or horns of Revelation actually come upon the scene. In fact, notice the wording of the last sentence in that prophecy:

"And the rough goat is the king of Grecia: and the great horn that is between his eyes is the first king," (Daniel 8:21).

That is, the king that leads the attack against the ram (the kings of the lands of ancient Medes and Persians), will occupy and break up this resurgent empire, and establish himself as the next ruler in the region. He will be the first of the 10 kings of Revelation (Daniel 7:24; Revelation 17:13). The rest of the kings are nations in the Middle East region, not Europe.

All of this is just background to the key focus of end-times prophecy, the nation of Israel, and the time of Jacob's troubles (Jeremiah 30). Jerusalem will be the ultimate ground zero of all geopolitical focus, and the Temple Mount will be the detonator. All present conflicts in this area of the world are but a precursor to the main events that are yet to come to pass on the Earth before the Second Coming of the Lord Jesus Christ. But, before the Lord Jesus Christ returns, the Antichrist must appear on the prophetic stage.

When this person actually first appears on the prophetic scene is not clear. In the book of Revelation, John says that one of the seven churches, located at Pergamos, is in a city where "...Satan's seat is" (Revelation 2:12-17). Since the Antichrist is Satan incarnate, Pergamos may be where this man of sin first emerges or establishes his power base. But the Bible is very clear in telling us that when he is finally revealed to the Jews and the world for what he really is, it will be in Jerusalem and in a Third Temple yet to be built in Jerusalem.

"Let no man deceive you by any means: for [that day shall not come], except there come a falling away first, and that man of sin be revealed, the son of perdition; Who opposeth and exalteth himself above all that is called God, or that is worshipped; so that he as God sitteth in the temple of God, shewing himself that he is God," (2 Thessalonians 2:3-4).

The Bible believer knows that however all this comes about, the still unbelieving nation of Israel will build a Temple on the Mount in Jerusalem and re-institute Temple worship. This temple must be built before the Antichrist is revealed and before the Lord Jesus Christ returns and destroys him and his armies.

Considering the decades of bloodshed and violence between Israel and the Arabs, and the entrenched respective positions of both the Jews and the Arabs concerning the Temple Mount and final status of Jerusalem, one can only imagine the magnitude of any sequence of geopolitical events that would bring this prophecy to pass. It WILL come to pass sometime in the near future; a literal Temple will be built and it is a prophecy you can 100% bank on coming to pass before the Second Coming of the Lord Jesus Christ. How this will happen is unclear.

Israel claims Jerusalem as its eternal Capitol. The Arab world wants Jerusalem for itself. Is there a compromise on the horizon? One key to how this could come about may also be found in the writings of the prophet Daniel. In future times, after that Temple is built in Jerusalem, there is a prophecy about a Holy Covenant already being in place for some time prior. Here are the references:

"And he shall confirm the covenant with many for one week: and in the midst of the week he shall cause the sacrifice and the oblation to cease,

and for the overspreading of abominations he shall make [it] desolate, even until the consummation, and that determined shall be poured upon the desolate," (Daniel 9:27).

"Then shall he return into his land with great riches; and his heart [shall be] against the holy covenant; and he shall do [exploits], and return to his own land," (Daniel 11:28).

"For the ships of Chittim shall come against him: therefore he shall be grieved, and return, and have indignation against the holy covenant: so shall he do; he shall even return, and have intelligence with them that forsake the holy covenant," (Daniel 11:30).

"And such as do wickedly against the covenant shall he corrupt by flatteries: but the people that do know their God shall be strong, and do [exploits]," (Daniel 11:32).

These passages of prophecy seem to indicate that there will be some form of treaty or covenant between Israel and the Arab world. It could be over the question of Jerusalem and the Temple Mount. It could be a covenant between both sides to share the Mount. The Jews build their Temple and are free to worship there, while the Arabs are free to worship beside them at the Al-Aqsa and Dome of the Rock mosques, with both sides respecting each other's religious claim to the Mount. A far-fetched idea? Not really! Look at what is said in the book of Revelation about the Temple and the Mount during the Great Tribulation:

"And there was given me a reed like unto a rod: and the angel stood, saying, Rise, and measure the temple of God, and the altar, and them that worship therein. But the court which is without the temple leave out, and measure it not; for it is given unto the Gentiles: and the holy city shall they tread under foot forty [and] two months," (Revelation 11:1-2).

Keep in mind that both Israel and the Arabs are blood cousins, the common descendants of Abraham through his sons Isaac and Ishmael respectively. Both people's faiths are rooted in the same Old Testament traditions, and they are both from common genetic stock, although the Messianic line is through the bloodline of Isaac and Jacob (the Hebrews). Politically, both of these people have something else in common - both consider Iran a threat.

On the basis of Biblical doctrine, both the Jews and Arabs have one more thing in common. Both of their religions deny that Jesus Christ is the Son of God and that God came in the flesh in the person of the Lord Jesus.

"And every spirit that confesseth not that Jesus Christ is come in the flesh is not of God: and this is that [spirit] of antichrist, whereof ye have heard that it should come; and even now already is it in the world," (1 John 4:3).

"For many deceivers are entered into the world, who confess not that Jesus Christ is come in the flesh. This is a deceiver and an antichrist," (2 John 1:7).

Based on the authority of the Scriptures, both the mainline Jewish and Islamic faiths of today (to say nothing of other world religions and apostate "Christian" cults and sects who deny the physical resurrection of Jesus) are under that spirit of antichrist. It is not inconceivable that both the Jews and Arabs, indeed the whole unsaved world, could find a common basis for religious unity under that spirit (i.e., religions of works and ritual, not faith in the shed blood of Jesus for justification before God).

Jerusalem is considered a holy city by three faiths: Judaism, Christianity and Islam. What the Bible does tell us about the Jerusalem of that future time (before the second coming) is revealed in the book of Revelation, and what is revealed gives us an unbelievable glance into the conditions at Jerusalem at that future time.

In that day, Jerusalem will be a great city in this present evil world and a global center of religious worship, commerce, and political power. It will be a corrupt place where religious authorities (much like the Pharisees and Sanhedrin of ancient times) rule over and suppress the poor and persecute the truly righteous. The sins of Jerusalem and the world will once again cause the Lord God to rise up and send prophets to Jerusalem to preach repentance and that the Kingdom of Heaven is at hand, the very same message of John the Baptist and Elijah (Matthew 17:10-11 & Mark 9:11-12). Two of those prophets are killed by the rulers of the city:

"And their dead bodies shall lie in the street of the great city, which spiritually is called Sodom and Egypt, where also our Lord was crucified," (Revelation 11:8).

In this present world system, the Jerusalem of the future is likened unto Sodom and Egypt, which tells you the level of depravity and hardship being endured in the great city at that time.

In Old Testament prophecy, cities like Jerusalem are spoken of as women, and usually in less-than -flattering terms when the Lord God is angry with them:

"Zion spreadeth forth her hands, and there is none to comfort her: the LORD hath commanded concerning Jacob, that his adversaries should be round about him: Jerusalem is as a menstruous woman among them," (Lamentations 1:17).

It is a popular belief in the fundamental protestant school of prophecy that Papal Rome and the Catholic Church system somehow come to power in the end times, and that Rome is the identity of the woman spoken of in Revelation as riding the beast:

"And the angel said unto me, Wherefore didst thou marvel? I will tell thee the mystery of the woman, and of the beast that carrieth her, which hath the seven heads and ten horns. The beast that thou sawest was, and is not; and shall ascend out of the bottomless pit, and go into perdition: and they that dwell on the earth shall wonder, whose names were not written in the book of life from the foundation of the world, when they behold the beast that was, and is not, and yet is. And here is the mind which hath wisdom. The seven heads are seven mountains, on which the woman sitteth," (Revelation 17:7-9).

Since the city of Rome is situated on seven hills (a phrase commonly associated with the city of Rome), they interpret this passage to mean the Roman Catholic Church. Therefore, they believe that Rome is "BABYLON THE GREAT, THE MOTHER OF HARLOTS" (Revelation 17:5. They further justify this identification based on this verse:

"And he saith unto me, The waters which thou sawest, where the whore sitteth, are peoples, and multitudes, and nations, and tongues," (Revelation 17:15)

Reasoning that since the Catholic Church has over a billion members in all countries across the world, and since the Catholic Church claims to be the True Church of the Apostles, this could be none other than Rome the Bible is speaking of in Revelation. They cite this verse as further justification...

"And the woman which thou sawest is that great city, which reigneth over the kings of the earth," (Revelation 17:18).

...claiming that the Catholic Church rules the politics of many countries on the Earth. The point is then made that the Vatican is a sovereign State apart from Italy and that the Holy See has its own embassies and diplomatic status around the world. All of these things are true, except that this identification of Rome as the woman riding the beast of Revelation does not exactly pass the rightly-divided Biblical smell test. And here is why.

Yes, Rome is a city that sits on seven hills, but so do the cities of Istanbul, Turkey (formerly Constantinople) and Jerusalem. Jerusalem is specifically referred to as the great city in the book of Revelation, not Rome...

"And their dead bodies shall lie in the street of the great city, which spiritually is called Sodom and Egypt, where also our Lord was crucified," (Revelation 11:8).

...and is proclaimed by the Scriptures to be the true whore of Babylon:

"And the great city was divided into three parts, and the cities of the nations fell: and great Babylon came in remembrance before God, to give unto her the cup of the wine of the fierceness of his wrath," (Revelation 16:19).

"And upon her forehead was a name written, MYSTERY, BABYLON THE GREAT, THE MOTHER OF HARLOTS AND ABOMINATIONS OF THE EARTH," (Revelation 17:5).

The Bible tells us that Jerusalem, not Rome, is the true whore of Revelation. In the future Jerusalem, the City of Peace will be the city of a great false peace. It will be a center of power much like ancient Babylon and will once again go a whoring as she did so many times in Old Testament days. At this future time, Israel will have abandoned its current democratic form of government and will once again be a theocratic monarchy, ruled by kings and ruling with the kings of the Earth. I know that you may find this to be shocking and hard to believe. After all, we all think of Jerusalem as the heart of the holy land and the place where the Lord Jesus Christ will someday reign (and He will), but not before He avenges Himself on the city that rejected the Lamb of God and nailed Him to a tree outside the city walls.

How do we know for sure that Jerusalem is the woman spoken of? Consider this undeniable truth: God says in the Bible that Babylon, the mother of harlots, is responsible for shedding specific holy blood:

"And in her was found the blood of prophets, and of saints, and of all that were slain upon the earth," (Revelation 18:24).

According to the Bible, the city of Jerusalem is the only city on the face of the Earth that meets those criteria.

"Nevertheless I must walk to day, and to morrow, and the day following: **for it cannot be that a prophet perish out of Jerusalem**," (Luke 13:33; emphasis mine).

That is the verse of Scripture that nails the woman's identity. Jesus Himself said this, and Jesus, who was also a prophet, was slain at Jerusalem. When you search your Bible, you will find that every true prophet of the Lord God who perished did so at Jerusalem.

"O Jerusalem, Jerusalem, which killest the prophets, and stonest them that are sent unto thee; how often would I have gathered thy children together, as a hen doth gather her brood under her wings, and ye would not!" (Luke 13:34)

I know that some of you will find this revelation troubling. That is understandable, since we know that God has not finished dealing with or completely forsaken the children of Israel. Paul testified to this truth.

"For I would not, brethren, that ye should be ignorant of this mystery, lest ye should be wise in your own conceits; that blindness in part is happened to Israel, until the fulness of the Gentiles be come in. And so all Israel shall be saved: as it is written, There shall come out of Sion

the Deliverer, and shall turn away ungodliness from Jacob: For this is my covenant unto them, when I shall take away their sins. As concerning the gospel, they are enemies for your sakes: but as touching the election, they are beloved for the fathers' sakes. For the gifts and calling of God are without repentance," (Romans 11:25-29).

Before God saves the Jewish remnant, they must be brought to repentance, and their eyes must be opened. What happens at Jerusalem in the future is how He brings that about (Romans 2:4; Hosea 3:5).

There is another cornerstone prophecy in the book of Daniel that you should study:

"Seventy weeks are determined upon thy people and upon thy holy city, to finish the transgression, and to make an end of sins, and to make reconciliation for iniquity, and to bring in everlasting righteousness, and to seal up the vision and prophecy, and to anoint the most Holy. Know therefore and understand, [that] from the going forth of the commandment to restore and to build Jerusalem unto the Messiah the Prince [shall be] seven weeks, and threescore and two weeks: the street shall be built again, and the wall, even in troublous times. And after threescore and two weeks shall Messiah be cut off, but not for himself: and the people of the prince that shall come shall destroy the city and the sanctuary; and the end thereof [shall be] with a flood, and unto the end of the war desolations are determined. And he shall confirm the covenant with many for one week: and in the midst of the week he shall cause the sacrifice and the oblation to cease, and for the overspreading of abominations he shall make [it] desolate, even until the consummation, and that determined shall be poured upon the desolate,." (Daniel 9:24-27).

There are two princes spoken of in this passage. There is Messiah the Prince (a reference to Jesus - note that the "P" in prince is capitalized in your KJV). Then there is the prince of the people that shall come.

This is not Jesus, but another prince (the Antichrist), and the passage is speaking of Jerusalem in the future. (Notice the "p" of this latter prince is not capitalized in the KJV.) Also notice the mention of the holy covenant, which could be a peace deal between the Jews and the Arabs that we mentioned previously.

The seventy weeks are seventy times seven years, or 490 years. This is the sum total of time God has determined for dealing with Jerusalem. This includes the time from history past (after the Babylonian captivity) until the future day of the second coming of the Lord Jesus Christ and His anointing as the King of Kings. As you can see right off the bat, it has been over 2400 years since these seventy weeks of prophecy started, and they are not yet completed. This is where the gap of the Church Age enters the picture. The prophetic clock was stopped for the duration of the Church Age.

"Know therefore and understand, [that] from the going forth of the commandment to restore and to build Jerusalem unto the Messiah the Prince [shall be] seven weeks, and threescore and two weeks:"(Daniel 9:25)

In researching this particular prophecy, I discovered that the interpretations of who gave this commandment to restore and to build Jerusalem and exactly when it was given are not fully settled historical or theological issues. It is outside the scope of this book to comment on the matter in depth, but I will share one of my own observations.

I found a wee bit of a complication in computing this time. In the above verse, it says there will be 69 weeks of years until Messiah the Prince (Jesus). Seven weeks and threescore and two weeks = 69 weeks, one week short of 70. But in a following passage it says that that after threescore and two weeks (62 weeks) shall Messiah be cut off, but not for himself This latter clause is understood to be when

Jesus was crucified for the sins of the world. So what happened to the seven weeks mentioned before?

In other words, the passages are saying two different things. In one it says that a total of 69 weeks until Messiah the Prince and the other says 62 weeks up to the point where Messiah will be cut off (the crucifixion). This tells me that these events are not the same. There remain another seven weeks (49) years that must come after the crucifixion in addition to the one week (7 years) of the future Great Tribulation period.

One could argue that these 49 years cover the transition periods at the beginning and end of the Church Age. A better suggestion is that the time of the coming of Messiah the Prince (which happens after seven weeks and threescore and two weeks) could be speaking of the return of Jesus to gather his Bride at the Rapture of the Church. That would coincide exactly with the start of the last week (seven years) of the Tribulation. That would make sense because until the King is actually crowned ("and to anoint the most Holy"), He is still technically a Prince.

Could it be that these 49 years have something to do with the vision of the ram and the first of the 10 kings? Could it be that the 49 years begin when the Jews start to rebuild the Temple?

"But of that day and that hour knoweth no man, no, not the angels which are in heaven, neither the Son, but the Father. Take ye heed, watch and pray: for ye know not when the time is. For the Son of man is as a man taking a far journey, who left his house, and gave authority to his servants, and to every man his work, and commanded the porter to watch," (Mark 13:32-34).

The fullness of the Gentiles has just about come in, and the Lord God will once again turn His mercy to unbelieving Israel and save them. But in order to do that, a great time of testing and punishment is still ahead for His chosen people. He will bring them to repentance at Jerusalem; ground zero for the Great Tribulation. Our Bible tells us that the resurgence of the Persian Empire is only the beginning of the end. The ram will soon begin pushing its influence northward, southward, and westward; there will be more wars and conflict in the Middle East region before the end.

The daily news is filled with ever-increasing concern about Iran's nuclear ambitions. Will Iran build a nuclear bomb? Will they use it? Will the Israelis preemptively attack in an attempt to stop them? The major western powers (the U.S. and Europe) are currently working to pressure Iran to cease nuclear fuel production through economic sanctions. Russia and China, who derive wealth and commerce resources from doing business with Iran, are resisting such economic sanctions. Meanwhile, the rulers of the Iranian government, a hard line Islamic regime that has publically declared it is Hell-bent on destroying the nation of Israel, will not stop their march toward development of nuclear weapons. Diplomatic efforts will eventually fail. There is a nuclear showdown approaching between Middle Eastern and Western civilizations.

In closing, consider this: In the book of Revelation, just after John is caught up to heaven (a prophetic event that has been equated by many to be a type reference to the future Rapture of the Church (Revelation 4:1), we read this passage:

"And I saw when the Lamb opened one of the seals, and I heard, as it were the noise of thunder, one of the four beasts saying, Come and see," (Revelation 6:1 KJV)

John describes hearing something that sounded similar to thunder just before the opening events of the Great Tribulation begin to unfold on the Earth. Could it be that what John heard was a Nuclear Explosion?

The Book of Daniel is unsealing. Read it!

It is my prayer that you will search the Scriptures and rightly divide them to see what things are true and honest. TRUST YOUR BIBLE!

Printed in Great Britain
by Amazon.co.uk, Ltd.,
Marston Gate.